BLACK BELT®
B · O · O · K · S

The Complete
Ninja Collection
by Stephen K. Hayes

The Complete
Ninja Collection

by Stephen K. Hayes

Edited by Vicki Baker and Jeannine Santiago

Graphic Design by John Bodine

Photography and Graphics by Black Belt Staff/Doug Churchill/
Rick Hustead/Gregory Manchess

Additional Photos Courtesy of Stephen K. Hayes

©2013 Black Belt Communications LLC

All Rights Reserved

Printed in the United States of America

Library of Congress Control Number: 2013943300

ISBN-10: 0-89750-206-X

ISBN-13: 978-0-89750-206-1

Second Printing 2014

BLACK BELT BOOKS

A Division of **OHARA** ▥ **PUBLICATIONS, INC.**

World Leader in Martial Arts Publications

ABOUT THE AUTHOR

An-shu Stephen K. Hayes began his martial arts career in Ohio as a teenager in the 1960s, and he has spent his entire adult life in the pursuit of perfection through the study of the Asian martial arts and spiritual traditions. *Black Belt* describes Hayes as "a legend" and "one of the 10 most influential living martial artists in the world."

He was born in Wilmington, Delaware, in 1949, grew up in Dayton, Ohio, and has lived and traveled throughout North America, Japan, Europe, the Arctic, China, Tibet, Nepal and India. A 1971 graduate of Miami University in Oxford, Ohio, Hayes majored in theater. During the years he lived in Japan, he used his professional acting skills in a variety of Japanese TV and film projects. Most notable to American audiences was his role alongside Richard Chamberlain and Toshiro Mifune in the NBC samurai epic *Shogun*.

In 1985, Hayes was inducted into the prestigious *Black Belt* Hall of Fame for his years of pioneering work in introducing the legendary Japanese ninja martial arts to the Western world. He was awarded the extremely rare rank of *judan* (10th-degree black belt) by grandmaster Masaaki Hatsumi of Chiba-ken, Japan. In 1997, 30 years after beginning his martial arts training, Hayes and his wife, Rumiko, founded the martial art *To-Shin Do*, a mind and body self-protection system based on ancient ninja martial arts principles updated for application to modern threats and pressures.

Hayes is the author of 20 books that translate the timeless knowledge of the East into pragmatic lessons for contemporary Western life. His books have sold more than 1 million copies, and many have been published in different languages around the world.

Hayes has taught and demonstrated effective self-protection skills to military and law-enforcement groups, including the U.S. Air Force, the FBI and members of Britain's elite Special Air Service. He has also worked on special projects under contract with the U.S. Defense Intelligence Agency. In the 1990s, Hayes regularly served as a personal-protection escort and security adviser for the Dalai Lama.

In 1991, Hayes underwent formal ordination to become a teacher in the esoteric Buddhist meditation tradition. As headmaster of the Kasumi-An Dojo, he continues to advance his study with senior masters of Japanese and Tibetan spiritual traditions.

Promoting the benefits of Life Mastery Through Martial Arts, Hayes travels the world as teacher, seminar leader and lecturer. His presentations inspire others by translating his extensive background in martial arts and meditation into practical lessons for handling the pressures, uncertainties and stresses of life. Students have reported that his teachings bring them deep encouragement and empowerment, and inspire them to achieve new levels of success in their personal and professional lives.

AUTHOR'S INTRODUCTION

While studying a form of Korean karate in my university days in the 1960s, I read a series of articles in *Black Belt* about Japan's ninja phantom warriors. In high school, I had first read about the ninja in a James Bond novel but had figured those incredible secret agents were strictly fictional. Reading those *Black Belt* reports of ninja training in Japan was eye-opening and inspiring. Such an incredible art did indeed exist, and James Bond author Ian Fleming had *revealed it*, not made it up. It was painful to know that such an art was taught in Japan but was impossible for me to learn in America.

The 1970s saw the popular growth of knockdown full-contact karate as a forerunner of kickboxing in the 1980s, tough-man contests in the 1990s and mixed-martial arts prize fights in the 2000s. I was in my early 20s, wondered just how good a fighter I was, all belt ranks aside, and for a while I got swept away in the martial arts fad of the era. Ultimately, I could not shake the realization that I had not originally been attracted to martial arts as a sportsman, and I was not really motivated by the idea of being a competition winner. At heart, I was still moved by childhood aspirations of training to be a protector, a promoter of peace through strength. I could not let go of the image of the ninja.

When I first traveled to Japan in the mid-1970s in search of a ninja-warrior-arts teacher, I knew I was going in a direction completely at odds with what seemed to be the future of martial arts in America. My kickboxer/karate buddies teased me about going to Japan to be a spy or an assassin, but despite all the ribbing, I had to go. It was an insane gamble, but I had to do it. I had to try to find the legendary ninja art in Japan, even if it meant pursuing a martial art that was likely of little or no interest to any other person.

I wrote letters to the names in the *Black Belt* ninja articles but got no reply. I was desperately determined. Something bigger or deeper than desire forced me to make my move. I had to go and find the ninja. Knowing no one in Japan, having no idea of how I would even find the ninja *dojo,* let alone be accepted as a student, I bought an airline ticket and flew to Japan anyway.

On a hot steamy July day in 1975, I stepped off a jetliner in Tokyo with the thinnest of hopes that I could find the ninja dojo I had read about in *Black Belt.* In a series of what could only be described as miracles, I did eventually find them and they agreed to accept me as a student in the grandmaster's home dojo.

Why Was This So Important as to Dominate the Martial Arts Consciousness of the 1980s?

As the 1980s unfolded, I was surprised to find my first ninja books, based upon my training in Japan and describing the Togakure Ryu ninja martial arts, rocketing to a popularity way beyond anything I might have dreamed when I first left for Japan. What was it about the image of the ninja-lone-warrior intelligence gatherer moving in the night that so captured the attention and interest of martial artists around the world?

Perhaps people were fascinated by the comprehensiveness of the ninja's martial arts training? Before my return from Japan with an art that few if any in America had ever seen before, popular martial arts seemed dedicated to one particular defining discipline. Karate was the art of linear striking. Judo was grappling to takedowns. *Kendo* was samurai sword fencing. I called those "partial arts." The ninja martial art was a strange departure from the normal single focus, with defenses against strikes, kicks, throws, chokes, cuts and stabs. A few fighters attempted what was called cross-training in multiple martial arts in the 1980s, and 20 years later, there would be a boom in what would be termed mixed martial arts. America, though, had not seen a legitimate, historical, Japanese-warrior tradition that featured training to handle all contingencies in combat.

Perhaps people were curious about the unusual nature of how and when the historical ninja had decided to fight? In conventional martial arts, practitioners trained to face a single skilled opponent in a consensual match based purely on the techniques taught in their art. The ninja, as an intelligence agent, only fought as a last resort when escape was impossible. A martial art based on deflecting others rather than challenging others seemed unique when I came back to America from Japan.

Perhaps people were captivated by the deeply psychological approach of the ninja in handling an adversary in combat? Based on ancient esoteric Buddhist teachings, a schematic of five elements in nature provides codes for understanding the dynamics of universal balance reflected in the operation of mechanical physics and human emotional response. I admit that in the 1970s in the dojo in Japan, I found this five-element model in ninja training to be but a vestige of the original knowledge. It required of me extensive independent study in temples outside the dojo in order to restore and bring back to life this important knowledge. The result was a self-defense martial art that offers a full and unprecedented understanding of the impact of emotional pulls and pushes when under attack in every confrontation from inner dilemma to verbal assault to physical harm.

Ninjutsu in Historical Japan Was More Than Just Fighting Arts

When exploring the warrior discipline of historical Japanese *ninjutsu*, it is important to bear in mind that the ninja art is way more than hand-to-hand combat alone. In feudal Japan with war after war changing the loyalties and alliances of regional warlords, ninja were intelligence gatherers and psychological warfare experts. Historically, ninjutsu was the art of influencing others in ways that worked the ninja will without those others having any knowledge that they were being influenced.

It is also likely in some cases that the term "ninja" was more a description of a task to be done as opposed to a career identity. Some serving in a ninja role might be lower-level samurai sent to observe an enemy or create dissent in the enemy's ranks. The ninja's job involved gaining access to where information could be gathered, finding that information, verifying its reliability and then getting back home to report that information to a commander who could analyze it in light of what was needed to win. It is likely that some taking roles as ninja spies received little or no fight training at all.

Whether from a ninja family or taking a one-time role as a ninja agent, some intelligence gatherers might study special combat arts with an emphasis on escaping as opposed to charging into battle to defeat an enemy. Though I followed my teacher's lead in the 1980s and referred to my martial art as Togakure Ryu ninja training, in feudal Japan, the Togakure Ryu had been more a tradition of intelligence gathering than a fighting school. When it came to the basics of hand-to-hand or weapon martial arts training, ninja of the Togakure Ryu and ninja of the Momochi family of Iga relied on Koto Ryu *koppojutsu* and Gyokko Ryu *kosshijutsu* training to develop the ability to take down an attacker and escape to safety when fighting was required.

Challenges That Arose With Publication of the Original Books

The first difficulty I encountered was deciding what to put in my initial book. The ninja arts I studied in Japan in the 1970s included a wide collection of bodies of knowledge that ranged from combat defense to hostile environment survival to operating a network of intelligence-gathering operatives. A group of skilled editors at Ohara Publications/ Black Belt Books decided the best way to cover so much knowledge was a series of volumes balanced in their contents, as opposed to trying to squeeze all that information into a single book.

The next difficulty was how much of the iconic ninja lore that informed public perception in Japan I dared to challenge. Popular ideas of what a ninja was and how he looked and what his weapons appeared to be conflicted with the authentic art I studied in Japan. Real ninja training defied a lot of the stereotypes. In Japan, we did not train in movie ninja suits with heads wrapped in masking. Our martial art practice focused on very real ways to stop fights and escape capture, and most of our weapon work was practiced with standard samurai-type swords. Movies and novels, on the other hand, portrayed the ninja as conscienceless masked mercenaries loaded with smoke-bomb grenades and oddly straight-bladed swords, who fiercely relished maniacally aggressive combat.

Another challenge was how to present in a book the authentic and correct way to perform the comparatively unusual physical dynamics of the ninja fighting arts. Unlike the karate or judo popular in 1970s America, ninja *taijutsu* martial arts did not rely on motions performed with a locked-down base for conventional power delivered with precisely moving limbs. We used continuous subtle movement to generate power from momentum, and we almost always took the adversary's balance before applying throws or takedowns instead of using throws to unbalance the enemy. In an age before video technology, this was hard for readers to grasp with the action depicted in simple two-dimensional photos with each position frozen in time and space. Looking at the photos, people just assumed our techniques were performed with karate point-to-point explosiveness or judo rough struggle, which of course they were not.

Adding to that difficulty, I had only a few beginner students studying with me in America when the first books in the series came out. Therefore, for many of the action illustrations, the production team recruited local martial artists and even a few *Black Belt* employees to take the role of the *uke,* or "the one who simulates the attack in training and receives the counter-technique." True ninja taijutsu martial arts captures or evades the assailant's attack and uses the resulting unbalance to permit the space in time and place for the ninja's counter-techniques. People unused to such unconventional movement have a hard time dealing with, let alone skillfully imitating, the real-world results of such tactics. Many of the early photos ended up looking staged, with the attacker standing there in a normal balanced posture as he receives the counter from me. It would not look like that in a real fight in which the attacker is really advancing with strength and intention and then has to struggle to regain his balance once he finds himself off-track.

With all the media attention accorded the ninja and their legendary art, it was inevitable that imitators posing as ninja teachers would pop up. When asked about the legitimacy of such "other ninja," I did my polite best to state that from my perspective, wishing did not make you a ninja. No matter how sincerely a person wanted to train like a ninja, without actually learning the authentic art with teachers schooled in Japan, a person should not call his or her tribute or imitation or adaptation actual ninja martial arts.

Ninjutsu is not a mere variation of the sports that commonly constitute martial arts today. You cannot just take your karate strikes and throw in some judo grappling and kendo sword practice with a little Zen meditation and proclaim that it is your ninja style. Donning a black suit and announcing you are a ninjutsu instructor is no substitute for an apprenticeship in the art under guidance of an initiated instructor. In the volumes in this series, I cautioned readers wishing to follow these training methods to be very thorough when investigating any local "ninja school." I do not wish to see people inspired by my writings to be taken advantage of or abused by less than scrupulous individuals falsely claiming to be masters of the knowledge described in these volumes.

The Inspiring Promise of the Art Lives On

Each of the individual volumes in the original series began with my expression of thanks to my ninja teacher, Masaaki Hatsumi. Without his generous invitation to remain in Japan and study the art his teacher, Toshitsugu Takamatsu, had shared with him, I never would have lived the life I did. Hatsumi sensei could have said no to my request, but he said yes. My appreciation continues to this day.

Enshrouded in the antiquity of history, the true story of Japan's fabled ninja is an inspiration for us all in contemporary society. In today's crowded world, where computerized tracking scrutinizes our personal lives and impersonal institutions, corporations, governments and popular media seem to assume more and more responsibility for dictating our daily lifestyles, it is an exciting reassurance to encounter the fresh timelessness of the ninja way of life. From the knowledge of the ninja, we can derive our own concepts of personal power and direction over the quality of our lives. We can rise above feelings of helplessness or futility. We can discover techniques for opening our consciousness and attuning our actions to the truth in our hearts. We can reacquaint ourselves with the harmony inherent in the way all things unfold. We can become enlightened to the reality that happiness, joy and personal fulfillment are the birthrights of every individual.

NINJA

CONTENTS ✸

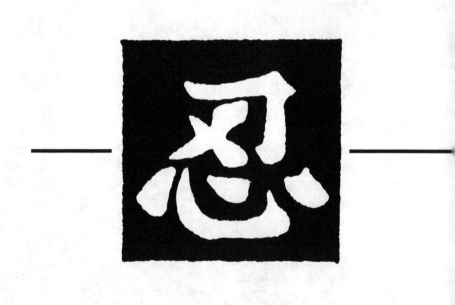

PART 1

Spirit of the Shadow Warrior

CHAPTER 1

This is one way to be invisible.
To simply become a small part of the night
moving with the winds and shadows,
doing what must be done,
completely void of emotions,
so that no one's mind can feel you,
no one's heart can hear you.

HISTORICAL PERSPECTIVES

The art of ninjutsu

Japanese martial arts have enjoyed a popularity boom in the Western world since the end of World War II. Though the fighting sports of Japan are thought to be closely tied to the traditional culture of the island nation, it is interesting to note that judo, karate and *aikido* were all introduced to the Japanese only within the past century. The lesser-known art of *ninjutsu*, however, traces its roots back over a thousand years. The mysterious art of invisibility remains only as a legend in the minds of many Japanese today, and the teachings of this esoteric system are guarded by the few remaining masters qualified to pass on the heritage of the ninja warrior wizards.

The art of ninjutsu was developed as a military specialization in the Iga and Koga regions of Japan. Totally developed physical bodies, calm enlightened minds and free-working spiritual powers, which we would call psychic abilities today, were combined in the ninja espionage agent or guerrilla fighter. The art was made up of techniques for the prevention of danger, and it included methods of physical combat, intelligence gathering and psychological warfare, and the development of occult powers.

As the centuries of Japanese history continued to unfold, the ninja families became more and more involved in their reputations as military specialists. The increased demand for ninja agents, resulting from the increased activity of the Japanese warlords, required a training system that could produce espionage or combat specialists in the shortest amount of time. Physical tricks came to replace the developed natural abilities of the original ninja warriors. Systems of combat skills based on the deception of the senses became the ninja's stock in trade, and the invisible warriors, once motivated by love for their families, came to be feared for the ruthlessness of their determination.

As a profession, ninjutsu drew on two primary bodies of knowledge as a basis for its teachings: *hei-ho* or "combat strategy" to the greater degree and *bu-jutsu* or "warrior arts" to the lesser degree.

From the 13th through 17th centuries in Japan, countless ninja families operated out of a wide range of motivations and levels of sophistication. Each family or clan had its own specific requirements for status as a ninja agent. Some groups stressed physical skills. Some stressed mental alertness. Other systems stressed political contacts. The list is long and extensive. There are, however, eight fundamental areas in which all true ninja seemed to be proficient, regardless of family affiliation:

Ki-ai: Personal harmony with the total scheme of things

The ninja had himself under control, and he had the balanced personality of an aware individual. He was aware of his own strengths and weaknesses, and he knew how to harmonize them with the personality of his adversary in order to accomplish the desired results. He knew the most opportune moments to act and when to lie low.

Taijutsu: Body skills

The ninja was trained in the techniques of unarmed fighting, including strikes, throws, locks and escapes. His fighting system was a utilitarian one based on natural movements and knowledge of the human body's weak points. Body skills also included leaping, tumbling, climbing and methods of silent movement.

Ken-po: Sword method

The ninja's sword was his primary weapon, and it was usually shorter in length than the customary samurai swords of the period. Consequently, a special method of close fighting developed with the short blade. In addition, the ninja sword was often used for purposes other than combat clashes.

So-jutsu: Spear or lance fighting

Medium-range fighting was carried out with the spear, a two- or three-edged blade mounted at the end of a 2- or 3-meter pole. The Japanese spear was rarely thrown, and it was most often used in straight, direct thrusts between the pieces of samurai armor.

Shurikenjutsu: Throwing blades

For long-range targets in individual combat, the ninja used small, concealed blades, which he threw at the hands or face of his adversary. The ninja's throwing blades could be straight or in a variety of multi-pointed designs, and they could be used accurately at distances of up to nine meters.

Ka-jutsu: Use of fire and explosives

Useful for creating diversions, forcing evacuations, and taking out walls and doors, fire, smoke and explosives found many uses in the arsenals of the ninja families. Many ninja were skilled at preparing their own explosives from natural elements, and several of the larger ninja organizations had their own chemists to produce large quantities of explosives for their use. In a culture such as Japan, in which wood, paper and rice straw were relied on for the construction of buildings, the threat of fire was a potent one well used by ninja agents.

Yu gei: Traditional cultural arts

The ninja was familiar with the traditional entertainment arts of the time, and he was often proficient in several of the arts himself. Painting, the tea ceremony, flower arranging, playing musical instruments, telling jokes and stories, and performing Japanese dances are a few of the arts popular in the ninja's realm. Besides the personal development afforded by them, a knowledge and appreciation of the arts was often needed to fill out a character identity being assumed for espionage purposes.

Kyo mon: Practical education

During every active day of a ninja's life, he was exposed to new and unfamiliar surroundings and experiences. His learning system had to be general enough and broad enough in scope to provide him with a means of handling any situation that came along. Much of the ninja's practical knowledge of the world could be labeled as working common sense, or "awareness." This is not the type of information contained in books or covered by conventional educational systems, so the ninja families relied on word-of-mouth teaching and instructional experiences to pass on the knowledge of past generations.

Considered to be far below the elite samurai status with its rigid codes of honor and propriety, the ninja were free to apply the naturalist teachings of their mystical heritage. The philosophy of ninjutsu stressed the interrelated connection of all things in the universe. Because man is not big enough to view the entire universe, the philosophy explains, the infinite number of its parts appear to man as the "ten-thousand things," or everything that seems to exist independently. To give some perspective to the view, all these things were seen in classifications of *in* and *yo*, or negative and positive manifestations such as darkness and light, heaven and earth, male and female, firmness and softness, wetness and dryness, contraction and expansion, and endless combinations of extreme polarities.

More than merely grouping opposites under a simplistic theory, the *in* and *yo* classification scheme provided an understanding to free the ninja from the limits of viewing things as right and wrong, good and bad, or fair and unfair. Any quality inherent in a thing or situation was based merely on its relationship to other manifestations of the same quality. It is sometimes difficult for Westerners to accept or even understand this lack of rigidity in what we would call morality or principles, and indeed this concept of flexibility is in direct opposition to the theories and philosophies of many contemporary martial arts. The ninja's outlook on his purpose in life places major emphasis on the total picture. The ever-changing results are far more significant than their means of attainment alone.

The historical ninja's primary political contribution was to maintain balance and harmony in society in the most effective manner possible. If bold cavalry charges involving thousands of soldiers were considered positive aspects of warfare, secretly capturing the battle codes or the enemy commander himself was considered a negative, or gentle, balance in the war activity. What the enemy would call "deceit, cowardice and treachery," the ninja would call "strategy, cunningness and wit."

Generations ago, when the ninja families of Japan were at the height of their power, membership in the ninjutsu tradition was determined solely by birth. The highly secret and invisible structure of the organizations prevented outsiders from working their way in and left only the offspring of the ninja themselves as possible candidates for the roles of agent or officer in the family profession.

At the head of each clan or organization presided a *jonin* (director, or commander in chief). Half philosopher, half warrior, the jonin took on the responsibility for determining to whom his ninja would lend their support. In most ninja organizations, the identity of the jonin was concealed from the ordinary agents and operatives as a security precaution. The jonin could then observe the workings of history from a viewpoint free from the bias of his expectations of others and free from concerns of personal safety. This role was passed down within the immediate family of the original founder, generation after generation. As children of the jonin grew, they were exposed to those teachings and experiences that would develop their abilities to view the world in a philosophical manner, understand the motivations of others, and direct the operations of a widely dispersed, highly illegal and heavily guarded organization, to which one of them would succeed as leader.

Serving directly beneath the jonin heading each ninja organization was a group of *chunin* (middlemen, or executive officers). These men were responsible for interpreting and carrying out the orders of the jonin. Acting as a go-between dividing the field agents from the head of the organization, the chunin ensured the anonymity of the jonin, and they prevented double-crosses or dangerous breaches of security. The chunin possessed the skills of knowing how to get things done and a familiarity with the strengths and specialties of all the ninja field agents at his disposal. Training for the role of chunin included lessons in time and logistics management and personnel motivation, as well as contemporary and unconventional methods of warfare.

At the base of the organized hierarchy were the *genin* (operatives, or ninja field agents). Men and women possessing a wide range of espionage and combat skills, the genin were the ones responsible for getting the

actual work accomplished. Trained from birth by their ninja families, genin inherited a legacy of total service to their unknown jonin commander, the lords to whom the jonin contracted, and to the welfare of the nation's people as a whole. The children of genin agents began their training at an early age, practicing leaping, running and balancing exercises that were disguised as children's games. As they moved into their teen years, the children began the study of combat techniques and weapons, and the psychological effects of the mental process on the body and its physical performance. In the later teen years, skills of the trade of espionage were taught, preparing the young genin for a life of service as a ninja.

CHAPTER 2

Know that the heavens were created
  to descend into the five elemental manifestations.
One piece
  a small mirror of all others.
It is all the same.
All the same.
Each piece of existence
  is its own small universe.
Earth
Water
Fire
Air
And the potential of the great Emptiness
  are there in everything.

To know the order of the universe
  is to understand the ways of nature
  and the proclivities of man.

BUILDING BLOCKS OF THE UNIVERSE

The basis for the ninja's knowledge of himself and his world

One important goal in the study of ninjutsu is developing an awareness of *ki-ai*, allowing one to come into harmony with the "scheme of totality." More simply stated, the student of ninjutsu must become a totally natural being. This system of awareness is based on a mystical knowledge of the universe as taught centuries ago by Japanese *yamabushi* (warrior mountain priests) and developed for combat by *senin* and *gyoja* (warrior ascetics who wandered in the wilderness of the Ku Peninsula).

There is nothing bizarre, unreal or imaginary implied in the mystical teachings of ninjutsu. Mysticism is simply the study of methods used in order to directly experience an awareness of natural laws and universal consciousness. By observing nature with an unbiased mind, man comes to understand his world and how he relates to it, and thereby comes to understand himself.

Stemming from esoteric Buddhist lore, the doctrine of *mikkyo,* or the "secret knowledge," teaches that all physical aspects of existence originate from the same source and can be classified in one of five primary manifestations of the elements.

As a way of visualizing the creation of the universe, it is taught that *ku,* the emptiness, became charged with polarities that later transformed

> Ku—"the emptiness" or the source of subatomic energy; the "nothing" from which all "things" take their form
>
> Fu—"the wind" or elements in a gaseous state
>
> Ka—"the fire" or elements in an energy-releasing state
>
> Sui—"the water" or elements in a fluid state
>
> Chi—"the earth" or elements in a solid state

themselves into different grades of electromagnetic charge. These charges formed atoms, which brought about the chemical gases of the *fu* state, which blended with each other to produce reactions at the *ka* level. Following this, the molecules became the vapor of the *sui* state and later solidified to bring about the solid matter of the *chi* level. This progression is referred to as the descending development of the elements. To study man's relation to the rest of the universe—physically, emotionally, intellectually or spiritually—the elemental manifestations are reversed and followed in ascending order, beginning with the chi solidity that is perhaps the simplest level with which to identify.

Combinations of atoms, with their nuclei and orbiting particles, have been viewed as models of the universe, with its whirling solar systems and galaxies. In the same manner, the human body can be seen as a miniature model of nature. Therefore, by studying the relationships of these elemental manifestations in nature, the ninja learns how to become a more natural and balanced being, more conscious of personal power and responsibilities in the stream of life.

In the human body, chi, the earth, corresponds to the bones, teeth, muscles and other solid body tissues. Sui, the water, represents the body fluids and those aspects of the body that provide suppleness and flexibility. Ka, the fire, is seen as the process of metabolism and is experienced as body warmth. Fu, the wind, corresponds to the breathing cycle—the movement of air into the body and then out and into the breathing cycles of others. Ku, the emptiness, manifests itself as noise, speech and the ability to communicate.

The physical elements of the body reverse their order of manifestation as they disappear during the process of death. Upon dying, the first element to go is consciousness of and ability to communicate with others. The breathing is the next function to cease. The next elemental manifestation to fade away is the fire, as the dead body loses its warmth. Eventually, the water element falls away and the body becomes stiff and dried out. Finally, even the earth element is consumed and the bones and teeth turn to dust or stone.

The five elemental manifestations that appear as physical matter around us are also paralleled in the stages of elevation of the personality within us. We all move up and down from one element of influence to another, and we refer to the effects of our changing consciousness as our "moods."

At the earth level, the basest of the elemental manifestations, we are conscious of our own solid physicalness and stability. There is a resistance to any change or movement and a desire to maintain things exactly as they are. Rocks are perhaps the most characteristic example of the earth principle, in that they are incapable of growth, movement or change without the aid of the other elements. When our personality is under the influence of the earth element of manifestation, we are concerned with keeping things in their places and we are conscious of the solid parts of the body. Chi, the earth element, has its center at the base of the spine.

At the water level of our physical personality, the next highest of the elemental manifestations, we are conscious of our own emotions and the fluid elements of the body. This level of consciousness is characterized by reactions to physical changes and a fluid adaptability to one's surroundings. Plants provide the clearest example of the water principle in action, in that plants are capable of independent movement and growth. They react to stimuli yet are incapable of controlling their environment. When our personality is under the influence of the water element of manifestation, we react to what we encounter and are oriented toward the heavier emotions. Sui, the fluid element, has its center in the lower abdomen.

At the fire level, the third highest of the elemental manifestations, we are conscious of our aggressive nature. Aggression in this sense refers to dynamic or expansive energy, and it is not intended to carry a negative or violent sense. At this level of consciousness, we experience feelings of warmth, enjoyment and direct control over our environment. Wild animals are perhaps the most characteristic example of the fire principle, in that they are capable of remembering and thinking, exerting control over their lives and seeking pleasure. When our personality is under the influence of the fire element of manifestation, we are aware of our expansiveness, dynamic power and our connection with others. Ka, the fire element, has its center at the lower tip of the breastbone.

At the wind level of our personality, the fourth developmental state from base physicalness, we are aware of our own freedom to move and change, and this influence manifests itself as feelings of wisdom and service. Human beings are the highest example of the wind principle, in that they are capable of contemplation, intellectual understanding and freedom. When our personality is under the influence of the wind element of manifestation, we experience compassion, acceptance and conscious consideration of our interactions with other individuals. Fu, the wind element, has its center in the middle of the chest.

The highest and most refined of the physical elements is ku, the "great emptiness of potential." Originally translated by Western scholars as "ethereal substance," this emptiness is today best represented by the concept of subatomic structure. Invisible bits of energy form atoms, which then combine to form the entire range of material things in existence. In the personality, the emptiness brings about the creative capability and the ability to direct the potential to become any of the four lower-elemental manifestations. Ku, the source of all elements, is centered in the throat.

Perhaps the most effective way to understand the influence of the various body centers of consciousness is to consider some examples of contemporary everyday experiences.

EXAMPLE ONE

You are at a ball game or crowded public park. Some distance from you, a group of drunks are carrying on. They are in their own world, having fun. Even though they are a bit noisy, they are not physically interfering with or harming anyone. From the different centers of influence, typical responses might be the following:

Earth	You endure. You do not even notice the drunks or you tune them out of your consciousness and ignore them. It does not affect you.
Water	You react. You find them offensive to you and confront them, call the authorities, or get up and go somewhere else. It is annoying.
Fire	You enjoy. You find them amusing. You watch the "street show" and see humor in the picture—the actions of the drunks, the reactions of the people around them. It is hilarious.
Wind	You contemplate. You feel good because they are enjoying themselves, but you are concerned that they might harm themselves or make others uncomfortable. With a smile, you wonder to yourself why some people have to get drunk before they can enjoy life with childlike abandon. It is touching.

EXAMPLE TWO

You have won the Irish Sweepstakes. Under the influence of the different elemental levels, your reactions might be the following:

Earth	You pay off all your debts and put the money in the bank. It does not affect your lifestyle.
Water	You quit your job to travel and do all the things you have always wanted to experience.
Fire	You build a dream house and turn your hobby into a business.
Wind	You set up trust funds for your family and invest the rest of the money where it will be of benefit to society.

EXAMPLE THREE

You are caught in a traffic jam on the freeway. The cars are inching along bumper-to-bumper under the summer skies. From the different centers, typical responses might be the following:

Earth	You endure. You are aware of time being wasted and you realize that there is nothing that you can do about it. You ride out the inevitable slow flow and let your mind wander or listen to the radio as a diversion.
Water	You react. You find the traffic jam angering and annoying. You formulate an alternate route plan and look for a way out. You change lanes back and forth to fill up gaps in the traffic or drive along the shoulder past sitting vehicles. You leave the freeway, if possible, and use smaller local roads to get to your destination.
Fire	You experience. You make the best of it. You try to get some sun on your face through the open roof of your car. You turn sideways so that you can see and converse with your passengers. You make up mental games for yourself, such as picking out the worst- and best-looking vehicles on the road, the most attractive man and woman in sight, etc.

Wind	You engage. You think the jam is unfortunate and you fear that perhaps someone has been injured or is in trouble. You work to keep the traffic flowing as best you can—pausing to let others into the flow, speeding up to fill gaps so others behind you will not have to brake. You think about ways to improve the situation for all and ways to avoid these jams in the future.

EXAMPLE FOUR

You are deciding which film to see. The strengths of the various centers might prompt you to select the following:

Earth	A documentary or war story
Water	An erotic film or an adventure
Fire	A comedy or musical
Wind	A love story or drama

EXAMPLE FIVE

Your primary outlook on why you work at your particular job reflects one center of influence:

Earth	You have to make a living in order to have food and shelter.
Water	It is a means to having a lot of money and all the possessions and experiences you want.
Fire	You enjoy the activity so much that you cannot imagine doing anything else, regardless of remuneration.
Wind	You believe that your role is to serve others and better your world, and your job is your contribution.

EXAMPLE SIX

You are by yourself at night, eating at a small roadside diner. A couple of obnoxious tough guys spot you and sit down across the table from you. Their talk is derisive and decidedly threatening. Though they have not yet physically interfered with you, it is obvious that they intend to rough you up. Through the influence of the various centers, your behavior might be the following:

Earth	You continue to eat in an undisturbed fashion. You do not acknowledge the threatening nature of the talk or let it bother you. You follow a normal routine in a quiet, confident manner while checking out the locations of doors and anything that could aid you when the fight begins. You finish the meal, pay the bill and walk out if you can. You use your coolness as a possible deterrent and let them make the first move if there is to be any physical encounter.
Water	You joke around with them and make laughing wisecracks as if you were one of their buddies. You ask them where you should go to find some entertainment, ask them about their cars or motorcycles. You sound naively sincere and you seem to be convinced they will not really hurt you. You laugh it off when they make direct reference to injuring you. You suddenly tell them you will be right back and take off for the restroom. When they amble in to corner you, you surprise attack with a trash can or weapons you can improvise. You disappear before they regain consciousness.
Fire	When it is obvious that they are about to make their move, you pick up the pepper shaker and deliberately remove the shaker cap while beneath the table you're positioning your heel in front of the crotch of the man across from you. With the cap off the pepper shaker, you suddenly roar with an explosive shout and fling the pepper into the second man's face and immediately shove the heel of your poised foot into the crotch of the thug across from you. You dump the table over on them both while kicking and beating them into submission. You disappear before any shocked witnesses can react or call the police.
Wind	You begin acting crazier than they are. You twitch around and make incoherent references to keeping a low profile for a while so the police will not find you. You giggle a lot and then fly into a rage over something insignificant. You go into some sort of fit or seizure and your attackers slip away to avoid the attention you are drawing.

EXAMPLE SEVEN

Your primary reason for taking up martial arts or golf or tennis is a result of one of the following centers being in prominence:

Earth	Physical fitness and health benefits
Water	Personal development
Fire	Social connection benefits
Wind	Enjoyable competition

EXAMPLE EIGHT

You find yourself involved in a discussion of personal religious concepts. The participants express all sorts of different and new ideas. From the different levels of personality consciousness, your reactions might be the following:

Earth	You hold your ground. Despite anything that is said, you do not alter your personal beliefs. You feel no need to defend your views or even consider the views of your discussion partners.
Water	You respond to the challenge. You defend your own position and use questions to weaken the solidity of conflicting viewpoints. You find yourself highly annoyed (or completely converted) at the close of the discussion.
Fire	You consider it a learning experience. You ask a lot of questions and consider your own views in light of the answers you receive. You look for weaknesses or discrepancies in your beliefs and use the discussion to become clearer on your own thoughts.
Wind	You interact to encourage others. You relate your personal experiences as answers to questions posed by your discussion partners. You leave the others with suitable questions that you think will benefit them as they determine their own answers.

EXAMPLE NINE

A close friend is going through a divorce. From the various centers of influence, your assistance could take one of the following forms:

Earth	You encourage your friend to do everything to end up with as much of the mutual property and income as possible.
Water	You back your friend in creating the public impression that the divorce was the responsibility of your friend's spouse.
Fire	You get your friend out into social activity as a single person.
Wind	You console your friend with the fact that divorce simply legally ends a marriage that has already completely fulfilled its purpose.

It should be stressed that no one element of influence is inherently better or worse than another. In fact, one of the grater reasons for studying the effects of the influence centers is to realize the impossibility of assigning arbitrary value judgment labels to our experiences. Every emotion in the wide range of moods available to the human being can be seen as more or less appropriate in any given set of circumstances.

There are, however, those times when a particular emotion may be regarded as negative or positive based on its effectiveness in the given situation. In the following example, a positive manifestation (effective approach to the situation) and a negative manifestation (ineffective approach to the situation) for each level of consciousness are illustrated. Appropriateness in the situation is not only determined by one's mood (element of influence) but also by the manner chosen to express the mood.

EXAMPLE TEN

Your mate dies. Your resultant behavior could be governed by the centers of influence in one of the following ways:

The positive manifestation of the **earth** center is **stability.**	You comfort others who loved your mate, too.
The negative manifestation of the **earth** center is **self-defeating stubbornness.**	You refuse to acknowledge the death and continue to speak and think as if your mate were still living.
The positive manifestation of the **water** center is **flexibility.**	You adopt a new lifestyle that fits your single status.
The negative manifestation of the **water** center is **distancing alienation.**	You retreat and dwell in all-consuming grief.
The positive manifestation of the **fire** center is **engaging vitality.**	You recall happily the love and warmth that you and your mate shared together.
The negative manifestation of the **fire** center is **clinging fear.**	You feel deserted and left alone, and you are terrified of the future.
The positive manifestations of the **wind** center are **wisdom** and **service.**	You know that your partner has moved on to a new adventure, just as you and everyone else will do.
The negative manifestation of the **wind** center is **insecure intellectualization.**	You work at analyzing the circumstances, trying to determine why your mate was taken from you or what has become of your deceased partner's spirit.

The voice is one reflection of the influence of the emptiness center, as it takes on the qualities of the four lower-elemental manifestations and inspires precise, though often unconscious, responses in others. With the earth center of influence, the voice is heavy, deep, commanding and authoritarian. The lower vibrations of the sound and the gut-level quality of the tone give the chi voice a solid, grounded feeling. Under the influence of the water level of consciousness, the voice is sexy, husky or emotional. The fire-level voice is warm, mirthful and enthusiastic, with a happy, engaging tone to it. Terror or hysteria also can take the voice to the ka level of manifestation. Under the wind influence, the voice is in the higher, softer registers and has a soothing tone to it.

When vocal expression does not match the body's center of influence, confusion or suspicion develops in the listener as the speaker's ulterior motives show through. Even in untrained individuals, an unconscious awareness sometimes produces an intuitive feeling that something is not right or is out of place with the words being heard. For example, words of love influenced by the water level of personality are interpreted as lust. Words of command influenced by the water level of personality are interpreted as emotional self-interest. Words of command influenced by the wind level of personality are interpreted as weakness. Thorough understanding of the relationship of the body's influence centers and the voice gives the ninja the ability to "see through" others and avoid arousing suspicion with his communications.

Examples of the ku, or source-level, influence could not be included in the preceding charts because there is no set, characteristic style of behavior associated with ku level of consciousness. Ku is the creative potential of becoming whatever is appropriate for the situation and the direction of energy from one level of awareness to another as needed.

Perhaps somewhat representative of the concept of ku consciousness reflected in personality is the physically enlightened master of one of the inwardly directed Zen arts usually associated with the Orient. This type of individual moves through life ever centered, firmly fixed in the present moment and always mildly joyous with whatever or whomever he or she encounters. This person is unencumbered by the rules and belief systems that limit the chi earth consciousness. He or she is not controlled by or susceptible to the emotional reactions that cloud the sui water conscious- ness. This individual is not driven by the ambitions or fears that dominate the ka fire level, nor is he or she swayed by the insecurity that appears from the intellect operating at the fu wind level of consciousness. The personality becomes so pure that there seems to be no personality there at all. These individuals are so in touch with their true natures that they become impossible to predict and therefore impossible to control.

CHAPTER 3

The benevolent warrior
> *understands the true scope and priorities*
> *of warfare.*

He first defends his country
> *the land that shelters and feeds him*
> *the community that houses his family.*

He next defends his family alone
> *the ones who turn to him for deliverance*
> *the people who share his love.*

He lastly defends himself.

In the giving of strength to protect
> *meaningful places*
> *and loving faces*
> *the ninja serves his own heart.*

FIGHTING

The mind and body harmoniously dealing with danger

One particular mood is likely to produce more desired results under any given set of conditions. In the same manner, an appropriate fighting method is needed to prevail in any given self-defense situation. Appropriateness in a fight is based on the combined aspects of the total situation, with all details taken into account. Our surroundings, our mood, the amount of room we have, social and moral considerations, the number and size of our attackers, and the severity of their intentions are all determining factors. Unlike a sports contest, there are no agreements, weight classifications or safety considerations.

Each fighting technique encountered in the training of Togakure Ryu ninja *taijutsu* can be classified by one of the elemental manifestations. The ninja's fighting method is taught as a total system that includes sticks, fists, blades, throws, mental outlooks and all aspects of personal combat that might be faced. As a general guideline, the following approaches to a fighting class reflect the specific elemental manifestations of consciousness influencing the response.

From the earth level, you hold your ground solidly, taking the onslaught without letting it affect you. You know that your strength will prevail. The legs and hips are the body's center of motion and consciousness, a familiar concept for judo players. Your adversary feels as if he is fighting against a rock—you are impervious to anything he does.

From the water level of consciousness, you shift and flow, using distancing and unexpected movement to defeat your adversary. You know that your flexibility and cleverness will win out. The lower abdomen is the body's center of motion and consciousness, a concept familiar to aikido practitioners. Your assailant feels as if he is fighting against the ocean waves—you recede from his advances and then crash back to knock him over.

From the fire level, you connect with your adversary with fierce resolve. The harder he fights, the more intense your blows become. You are committed to injuring him in direct proportion to the strength he uses against you. The solar plexus is the body's center of motion and consciousness, and the total body moving into the opponent is an action familiar to karate students. Your adversary feels as if he is fighting against a brush fire—you flare up hotter and brighter the more he beats and fans that "fire" in an attempt to put it out.

Under the influence of the wind level of the personality, you fight with evasive moves, protecting yourself well without forcing undue injury on your adversary. Your counterattacks intercept his moves and stun him without the necessity of blocking first. The center of the chest is the body's center of motion and consciousness, allowing for the quick lightness demonstrated by boxers as they duck, slip and roll with the punches. Your attacker feels as if he is fighting against the wind—you become ever elusive and occasionally sting his eyes with a little dust as a gentle dissuader.

Under the influence of the source level, the emptiness, you use your creative powers in thoughts, words and actions to create an environment in which you have no need to fight with anyone. Your adversary does not know how to fight you. His confusion or misperception defeats him.

In almost all instances of conflict or competition, these primary methods of relating to your opposition will manifest themselves. Whether it is a fistfight, an auto race or a verbal exchange, the body centers of consciousness or tension are identical, and there are appropriate as well as inappropriate approaches to handling the situation as it unfolds from second to second. These centers of consciousness and approaches to physical self-defense are not "concentrated on" or actively pursued. They are merely ways of classifying thought and action after they have taken place. These classifications are labels for our methods of relating to ever-changing surroundings. A successful outcome will be the result of properly balancing out all aspects of the situation. Unsuccessful results develop through a lack of sensitivity or awareness of what is needed to create balance.

Corresponding to each of the elemental manifestations as reflected in defensive styles is a specific fighting pose from which the initial fighting moves may proceed. The pose itself is assumed naturally as the body goes through the realization that defensive action is needed. In this manner, each posture, or *kamae*, is a physical reflection of the mental attitude and psychological set.

The earth level of consciousness is characterized by the natural posture, or *shizen no kamae*. Just like the name implies, the shizen pose is a natural, relaxed standing position. The feet are planted hip-width apart, each taking an equal amount of the bodyweight. The knees are flexed to a straight position, neither bent forward nor locked back. The body's stability is sensed in the thighs and lower portions of the hips. The shoulders are relaxed and the arms and hands hang naturally. The eyes gaze forward with a somewhat soft, distant focus, taking in all within the frame of vision without concentrating on any one limiting point.

The body should have a somewhat heavy feel to it, as if the force of gravity were more intense than it normally is. The muscles are relaxed, and their weight is felt on the undersides. In the natural posture, the fighter appears to be firmly holding his ground, confident and unshakeable as a tree rooted in the earth.

Maintaining the natural posture may be more difficult than it sounds because grounded stability is not easily imitated. There must be a total absence of superfluous body movements, such as darting about or lowering your eyes, clenching your hands, or shifting your weight from leg to leg. It is interesting to practice the shizen pose in normal daily activity to see how much unconscious movement we carry out without thinking.

As a reversed method of practice, it is enlightening to watch others in different situations as they assume varying degrees of confidence and grounded action. By watching the outward bodily manifestations of voice, movement and bearing, we can get a clear idea of how another person is thinking and relating to his surroundings.

**Defensive Posture
(ichimonji no kamae)**

**Offensive Posture
(jumonji no kamae)**

Natural Posture
(shizen no kamae)

Receiving Posture
(hira no kamae)

In self-protection situations, the natural posture is most often found being used in response to ambushes or surprise attacks under circumstances that were not considered to be threatening. A conversation partner who suddenly becomes argumentative, a person attempting to take your place in a theater ticket line, or an inanimate object that threatens to move and injure are examples of this type of interaction. The shizen no kamae, with its earth stability, also conveys a feeling of control over the situation and the power to prevent drastic violent action from taking place.

The water level of consciousness is characterized by the defensive posture, or *ichimonji no kamae*. The physical embodiment of a strategic approach to combat, the ichimonji pose enables surprising angular movements. The body is in a low, crouched position with the trunk turned sideways toward the adversary, and the legs and knees are deeply flexed to keep the hips low. The foot position roughly forms the letter L, with the leading foot pointing at the attacker and the rear foot pointing in the direction in which the torso has been turned. The body trunk is held upright over the rear leg, which supports about 70 percent of the weight. The body's balance and potential for movement are sensed in the lower abdomen below and behind the navel. The shoulders are turned with the body trunk to line up with the adversary, and the leading hand is extended forward in a fending manner while the rear hand is poised beside the face and neck in a protective manner. The eyes are gazing along the leading shoulder and arm, taking in the total body of the attacker.

The body should have a light, responsive feel to it, and all motion should begin at the abdomen and allow the body to follow. As the hips move, the feet and torso follow, preventing a loss of balance or slow, predictable movement. To assume the ichimonji posture from a natural stance, the hips are lowered back and to the side at a 45-degree angle to the anticipated attack force. As your seat moves back and down, the rear support foot shifts into position with a retreating action that drags the leading foot back slightly.

In self-protection situations, the ichimonji no kamae is best used to combat larger or more aggressive adversaries. The defensive pose and its footwork are practiced with angular zigzag pattern movements that retreat to the inside and outside of the attacker's striking limbs. A low posture will keep the body in balance and facilitate fast, erratic moves, even on unlevel ground or unstable surfaces. From the safety of the defensive posture, hard-hitting blocking strikes can be applied to the attacker's incoming limbs.

The fire level of consciousness is characterized by the interception posture, or *jumonji no kamae*. A charging, forward-moving body pose, the jumonji posture is used as a base from which to launch the punches, strikes and kicks of the ninja's taijutsu fighting method. The body faces the adversary with one side leading and the weight distributed evenly over the two legs. The feet are roughly hip-width apart with the toes pointing inward slightly. The knees should be flexed to give the feet a ground-gripping quality. The body's center of movement and balance is the solar plexus, the back is held straight without leaning forward or to the side, and the hips are low. The fists are held in front of the chest, and they are crossed at the wrists with the leading-side hand in front of the trailing-side hand.

The body should have a slightly tensed or potentially explosive feel to it. In the jumonji pose, the intention is to overtake or overwhelm the adversary. To move into the offensive posture from a natural stance, the leading foot shifts forward into position as the hands come up along the ribs and in front of the chest. The hips angle slightly to the side and drop as the body moves into the attacking pose, and the eyes lock on to their target. Progression forward and backward in the jumonji no kamae is carried out through short choppy steps or shuffling foot slides in a level, gliding manner that prevents the body from bobbing up and down. The feet move at the same moment as the upright body trunk, keeping the shoulders from falling into the attack, and related hand actions usually accompany the footwork.

In self-protection situations, the jumonji interception posture is best used to combat hesitant or cautious adversaries and to add the element of surprise to a confrontation in which inevitable explosive hostility is building. From this posture, initiative is taken in the fight, forcing the adversary into a defensive or retreating attitude. The intense techniques from the jumonji posture go after and take out the enemy's weapons rather than defend against them.

The wind level of consciousness is characterized by the receiving posture, or *hira no kamae*. The receiving posture couples a freely moving base and the power to harmonize the body with the intentions of an attacker. The feet are placed hip-width apart and carry the bodyweight evenly. The knees are flexed slightly more than in the natural posture, creating a feeling of balance in the hips similar to that experienced just before sitting down on a chair. The back is straight, in a natural manner, and the shoulders are relaxed. The arms extend outstretched to the sides with the hands open, and the eyes gaze forward in soft focus, taking in the whole picture without limiting the concentration to one single point.

The body should have an extremely light, almost floating feel to it. Epitomizing some concepts that are the opposite of those embodied in the shizen earth pose, the wind-level hira no kamae prepares the fighter for adapting to and going with the attacking moves of the enemy. This adaptive sensitivity is centered in the chest behind the breastbone. The evenly distributed balance facilitates quick and easy movement in any direction in response to the attacker's intentions. The outstretched arms have the potential of becoming tools to carry out punches, strikes, deflections, blocks, throws and locks, as well as acting as distractions and calming techniques.

In self-protection situations, the hira posture is used to handle attackers in a way that subdues them without injury, if possible. The pose itself is nonthreatening, and it appears to be an attempt to fend off an attack or to reassure an adversary that there is no hostile intention, as upraised open hands traditionally symbolize surrender or benediction. From the hira no kamae, footwork proceeds with circular or straight-line movements, as appropriate for the specific circumstances. The arms are used to entangle the adversary with spiraling actions or intercept the adversary with direct advances.

From the various fighting postures, the ninja's taijutsu (self-defense) techniques can be classified in three broad ranges of combat method. *Dakentaijutsu* (technique for attacking the bones) consists of strikes, punches, kicks and blocks directed toward the attacker's bone structure. *Jutaijutsu* (grappling technique) consists of throws, locks and chokes directed against the joints and muscles of the adversary. *Taihenjutsu* (not illustrated here) consists of flexible, adaptive—sometimes almost acrobatic—slipping, rolling and tumbling escapes and counters for throws, locks and strikes applied by the attacker. Unlike sports contests that limit the techniques to throwing, punching or grappling only, actual life-protecting combat will always combine aspects from the three major technique classifications as distance, energy and urgency dictate.

DAKENTAIJUTSU

Earth Response in the Striking Method

From the natural posture, the defender observes as his adversary initiates a right face punch (1). He maintains the natural posture and shifts his left side forward slightly (2), sending his left hand straight at the attacker's face. Then he slams the base of his left palm up under the attacker's nose and allows his fingertips to strike the attacker's eyes (3). The defender's left elbow

can deflect the attacker's right forearm, if necessary. Finally, he maintains his position and pulls straight down with his clawing left hand, catching the attacker by the lower lip and jaw (4). The fingernails are used to cause pain to the soft tissues of the mouth and gums and force the attacker to the ground. The entire sequence is completed in less than two seconds.

Water Response in the Striking Method

From the natural posture, the defender observes as his adversary initiates a right face-punch attack (1). He then falls back from the attacker's lunging punch (2) and strikes his punching arm with an injurious counterblow from the defensive pose (3). Immediately, he shifts forward into the offensive posture, using his body force to propel a

strike through the attacker's punching arm (4). The hand snaps open at the point of impact, concentrating power delivery in the edge of the palm. The knifehand strike smashes through the punching arm (5-6), taking it out of the way and unbalancing the attacker. The entire series of moves is performed in a two-second interval.

Fire Response
in the Striking Method

From the natural posture, the defender observes as his adversary initiates a right face-punch attack (1). He then charges forward in the offensive posture (2-3), bringing his leading arm up beneath the attacker's lunging punch, knocking his arm to the side. Immediately, he pulls his trailing leg into position for a kicking counterattack (4-5). The defender continues his forward momentum by slamming the base of his heel into the attacker's midsection, injuring him and knocking him backward (6-7).

Wind Response in the Striking Method

From the natural posture, the defender observes as his adversary initiates a right face-punch attack (1). He then pivots clockwise while assuming the receiving pose (2-4). As he moves past the attacker, the defender suddenly straightens his shoulders (5), sending an open-hand slapping strike to the attacker's solar plexus (6). As he moves into position behind the attacker, the defender uses both hands to secure a hold on the attacker's jacket and hair (7-8). If necessary, the defender can use the bottom of his foot to fold the attacker's knee in order to force him into submission (9-11).

JUTAIJUTSU

Earth Response
in the Grappling Method

From the natural posture, the defender observes as his adversary grabs him in preparation for a throw (1-2). The defender maintains the natural posture and brings his right hand up to cover the attacker's right hand (3). He then uses his curled fingers and the base of his palm to apply crushing pressure to the joints of the attacker's thumb (4). The defender's grip compacts the natural folds of the joints (5), producing intense pain. Finally, the attacker is forced to the ground as the defender straightens and lowers his controlling arm (6-8).

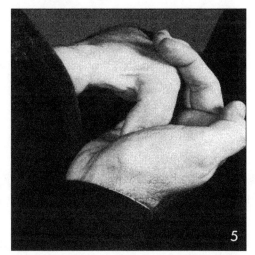

Water Response
in the Grappling Method

From the natural posture, the defender observes as his adversary grabs him in preparation for a throw (1-3). He then steps back into the defensive posture with his right foot (4-5), using his left hand to cover the attacker's right grabbing hand. He moves back farther by stepping away with his left foot (6-9), pulling the attacker to submission with an outward wrist twist.

Fire Response in the Grappling Method

From the natural posture, the defender observes as his adversary grabs him in preparation for a throw (1-2). He then charges forward, wedging the attacker's neck into a right-over-left crossed-wrist choke (3-5). As the attacker lifts and struggles to free himself (6), the defender drops into a crouch with a clockwise spin, allowing his arms to uncross naturally. The defender straightens his arms and pushes them forward while flexing his knees and rising (7-10). The attacker is thrown forward by the combined motions and is slammed onto his head or shoulders.

2

3

5

6

9

10

Wind Response in the Grappling Method

From the natural posture, the defender observes as his adversary grabs him in preparation for a throw (1-2). The attacker executes a rear hip throw, attempting to slam the defender on to his head or back (3-4). The defender goes with the throw instead of resisting (5). He then brings his legs over his head (6) with a speed faster than that used by the attacker in executing his throw. As he lands, the defender uses a finger pressure attack to the attacker's lower abdomen to force him to the ground (7-9).

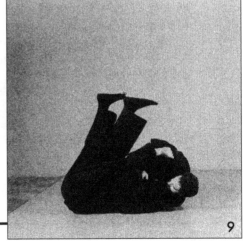

COMBAT TOOLS

Ninja training today also involves perfecting skills with several classical combat tools. Weapon training with the historical gear enhances overall coordination and provides physical models from which psychological or philosophical lessons can be taught. But most important of all, it allows the student to learn the ability to recognize and improvise self-defense tools from common articles in the environment. All ninja weapons are timeless in the sense that they are fundamental combat tools rather than unique or unusual gimmicks. Sticks, blades, pieces of rope or chain can be found readily, and the fighter who is proficient in their use need not endanger himself by having to rely on carrying a specialized weapon with him at all times.

The ninja's weapon fighting methods are identical to the ninjutsu unarmed combat in terms of body dynamics and the coordination of physical response and mental observation. The fighting poses are slightly altered to accommodate the physical dimensions of the weapons, but they do follow the general classifications of purpose relating to the five elemental manifestations, just like the taijutsu postures.

STICK FIGHTING

A natural progression from unarmed defense is the *bojutsu* stick-fighting system. Traditional weapons of the Japanese samurai culture, the wooden cane and staff are natural extensions of the arms, and they are relatively easy to master once unarmed fighting proficiency has been developed. The *roku-shaku-bo* (6-foot staff) is less than 2 meters in length, and the *han-bo* (half-staff) is a cane that is less than 1 meter in length. Contemporary students of ninjutsu find that stick techniques experienced in training are easily adaptable to real-life situations in which a walking stick, yard rake, tennis racket or even a rolled-up newspaper can easily be found in everyday surroundings and pressed into service as defensive weapons.

Earth Response With the Long Staff

From a variation of the natural posture, the defender observes as the attacker initiates a short-stick clubbing attack (1). The defender maintains the natural pose and pushes his right hand out, propelling the upper tip of his staff down and forward (2). The tip of the staff hits the attacker at the base of the throat (3), stopping his advance.

continued on next page ➤

The defender then uses his left hand to reinforce his right (4) and scrapes the tip of his staff down the breastbone in the center of his adversary's chest (5), driving him to the ground (6).

Water Response
With the Short Stick

From the natural posture, the defender observes as his adversary initiates a right grabbing attack (1). The defender falls back into the defensive posture out of the attacker's reach (2-3).

continued on next page ➤

As the attacker moves forward with a second grabbing attempt (4), the defender shifts back and to the right to avoid the attacker's left hand. Finally, the defender seizes the attacker's extended arm and holds him in place for a strike to the ribs with the cane (5-6).

BLADE WEAPONS

Ninjutsu's *ken-po* (blade) technique teaches practical skills with hand-held as well as thrown blades. The formal training is made up of fast-draw techniques for pulling the sword or knife from the scabbard and cutting in one simultaneous movement, plus fencing skills for using the hand-held blade against an attacker's weapon, and throwing skills for hitting distant targets with the released blade. Though the two-handed Japanese sword is used for some practice sessions in the training hall, today's student of ninjutsu could use a contemporary hunting knife, kitchen implement or garden tool in a true life-or-death struggle.

Water Response
With the Ninja Sword

From a defensive sword posture, the defender observes as his adversary prepares to throw a star shuriken (1). The attacker throws the shuriken at the defender's face (2). The defender ducks and deflects

the shuriken star with his sword (3). As the shuriken star flies off harmlessly (4), the defender charges into the attacker with a sword cut before he can throw the next star (5-6).

Fire Response
With the Throwing Blade

From a variation of the offensive posture, the defender observes as the attacker initiates a vertical slash with a sword (1). As the attacker moves forward (2), the defender pulls a straight shuriken (throwing blade) from its concealed sheath (3). The defender lifts the blade to a throwing position beside his head (4), gripping the shuriken by its handled end (5). The boldness of this defensive attacking action should be enough to stop the prudent adversary from continuing his advance. If it is necessary to prevent being killed by a raging attacker, the blade can be thrown by snapping the arm down and pushing the shoulder forward (6). When the arm reaches a horizontal extended position, the blade is released to sail straight across the short distance into its target (7).

75

CHAINS AND CORDS

Chain and cord weapons also follow the unarmed fighting system in their practical application. The *kusari-fundo,* a short small-linked chain with weighted ends, the *kyotetsu shogei,* a blade weapon attached to a 3-meter cord, and the *kusari-gama,* a 4-meter chain attached to a long-handled sickle, are three of the flexible ninja weapons that are practiced today for their practical application in street self-defense. Short-chain techniques practiced in the training hall can be duplicated with a belt, camera strap, dish towel or necktie when self-preservation warrants it. The long-cord methods can be used with an electrical appliance power cable, fishing tackle, water ski- or mountain-climbing rope, or a telephone receiver cord in an actual attack situation.

Fire Response With the Chain and Sickle

Holding the kusari-gama (chain and sickle) in the offensive posture, the defender observes as the attacker initiates a horizontal slash with his sword (1). The attacker charges in with the cut (2) and the defender counterattacks (3) by slinging the weighted chain around the attacker's blade as it moves forward.

The defender sidesteps and pulls the chain in the direction of the attacker's cut to direct the blade away from its target (4). The defender then steps forward, moving past the attacker's right side, and he levels the sickle portion of his weapon to hit the attacker while escaping the danger of the attacker's sword (5).

Wind Response With the Short-Chain Fighting Method

From the natural posture, the defender observes as the attacker initiates a clubbing attack with a short stick (1). Stretching the short chain between both hands, the defender slips to the side of the attacker's strike and brings the chain up from beneath the attacker's clubbing arm (2-3). Holding his hands above the attacker's arm as it is wedged in the V of the chain, the defender pivots with a clockwise motion, crossing the weighted ends of the chain over the attacker's

forearm (4). The chain naturally entraps the arm with this movement, and it is not necessary for the defender to wrap or loop the chain around the attacker's moving arm. The club slides harmlessly inside the defender's right arm. The defender continues his clockwise spinning motion, capturing and redirecting the attacker's force (5). The defender uses his left knee and the taut chain to bring the attacker into submission on the ground (6).

By continuously examining his responses to danger and conflict, the student of ninjutsu eventually can learn what is appropriate as a response to any given situation in order to bring him what he wants. He can recognize what works and what does not work, and he can develop the intuitive nature that will allow him to know the best response every time without having to think it through mechanically. The ninja warrior's approach to winning is not merely a special method of fighting. It is a total dedication to personal perfection—the achievement of harmony with the world.

CHAPTER 4

Men are helpless
  only when they see themselves as helpless,
The present is our only opportunity for power.
The passage of time controls
  and bends all things
  only when we believe in
  the passage of time.
The future lived
  is merely yet another
Now.

THE SIXTH CENTER

The brain as a tool of the spirit

Beyond the five manifestations of physicalness lies the second major realm of personal power—the mind and mental processes. This sixth center of consciousness is felt in the middle of the cranial cavity, and it is traditionally associated with the area of the brow between and slightly above the eyes.

In the mystical teachings of ninjutsu, the mind was seen as a bridge between pure consciousness and the body in which that consciousness temporarily resides. The mind is, in essence, an interpreting device, organizing or translating all that we encounter into images and impressions that are acceptable to, and understood by, our physical selves.

Everything in the universe is made up of, and manifested as, varying rates of vibrations or wavelengths. At the bottom of the spectrum, with the slowest vibratory rate, is solid physical matter. The vibrations in the atoms that make up the molecules are not readily perceivable to us. Above physical matter, at a faster rate of vibration, is sound. Faster wavelengths than sound become the sensation of heat. Beyond heat is the impression of light. The observation could be extended to include thoughts, at a wavelength or vibratory rate faster than electricity or light.

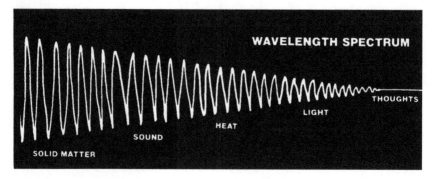

WAVELENGTH SPECTRUM

THOUGHTS

LIGHT

HEAT

SOUND

SOLID MATTER

Within each relative classification of sensations in the broad scale of vibratory rates are manifestations varying with the speed of the waves. Within the classification we call light, for instance, are slower waves that appear red and faster waves that appear blue. Within the classification we call sound are slower waves that are heard as low rumbling tones and faster waves that are heard as high shrill pitches.

The qualities of the vibratory manifestations and their resulting images are not fixed entities themselves but are relative to the sensory receptor perceiving them. It is fairly accepted knowledge today that there are sounds that cannot be heard by humans and yet are definitely audible to certain animals. There are light impressions that are imperceptible to plants and animals and yet quite real for humans. Modern communications technology provides even more dramatic examples of altering the images of a fixed set of vibrations by altering the sensing receptor. Visual images can be transformed into electronic impulses that can be further altered to become sounds, which then can prompt the generation of physical substance. (A television camera scans the surface of Mars, the data is transmitted by radio waves to Earth, and a computer rearranges the data and produces a color print of what the camera "saw.") If it were easier to affect the sensory receptors of our physical bodies, perhaps we humans could simply will ourselves to hear colors, taste sounds or feel odors for additional perspective in our daily lives or in times of special importance.

Though literal concepts of varying wavelengths and vibratory rates were unknown to the mystics of feudal Japan, their teachings nonetheless stressed the uniform structure and common source of all things. From this belief that all things are varying manifestations of the universal source (everything fits in somewhere on the vibratory rate scale), ninja developed the attitude that there are no totally independent actions or objects in the realm of existence. Seemingly unrelated phenomena actually can be linked together in interaction. As a result, a vast realm of subtle and yet direct control over our surroundings is available to all of us, if only we would acknowledge and accept that control.

The ninja of old used his mind to observe, visualize and affect his surroundings by harmonizing the vibrations of his thoughts with the varying wavelengths of the environmental aspects he wished to alter. Beginning with simple exercises that teach the effectiveness of the method, the ninja was encouraged to develop the power of the mind to clarify his intention and work his will without actions.

As an initial step, students of ninjutsu are admonished to become actively aware of the ease with which the senses become dulled over the years. Stripping away the impediments and sharpening the senses are crucial to the task of beginning to learn to perceive and interact with outside forces in a pure and direct manner.

This type of awareness approaches that of the animals, whose active consciousness is of a different order than man's. The consciousness of an animal is strongly fixed in the present moment, and the animal is relatively unaware of a past or future in the way a human being is. The animal awareness is not hindered by memories or considerations of potential outcomes, and it is exclusively locked into each existing instant as it occurs. Though the animal does not have the advantages of guidance from the past or direction for the future, it is free to pick up a whole range of subtle present environment impressions that are largely crowded out or ignored by humans. Sense impressions from infrared or ultraviolet light, cosmic rays, air pressure or magnetic fields are as real for animals as traffic signals, printed words and verbal expressions are for humans.

The first step toward personal control and the exercise of power in one's world is to merely be aware of one's body and the effects of its surroundings. A key point in the study of all aspects of ninjutsu is the development of total naturalness at any chosen level of awareness. The martial art training begins with basic physical movements and from there moves on to specialized combat skills. In relearning the naturalness of our fundamental physical nature, we are subtly forced to recognize the effects of cluttering ourselves up with unnecessary, unnatural actions in the past. Once we experience the impossible-to-avoid physical manifestations of unnatural conditioning, we then can move inward to the mind and emotions and see how we have stretched the inner self out of shape, as well.

The awareness-development exercises of ninjutsu training are complementary to the overall attitude of complete growth and realization that are inherent in the art. Various other martial arts, religions or exercise and enlightenment systems insist that the practitioner give up his humanness in order to attain the desired goals. The senses and corporeality seem to be regarded as embarrassments or evil tricks of the universe, created for the sole purpose of being overcome or transcended. Wholesome food, sexuality and emotional richness are deemed as limiting and are to be sacrificed for purity. In the more perverted systems, the human qualities are looked on as sins to be washed from the personality and apologized for.

As a comprehensive lifestyle, ninjutsu regards the body and its sense capabilities as tools for the accomplishment of life's purposes. As such, those tools are to be acknowledged for their value, well cared for and fine-tuned. Any spiritual system that denies or represses the natural physical requirements and proclivities of the body will create a grave state of imbalance that must be dealt with eventually before any true spiritual advancement can be attained. The teachings of ninjutsu advocate the development of the total entity, with all its naturally endowed balances and polarities. They reject as senseless and needlessly brutal any system, martial or religious, that demands suffering, repression, self-debasement or the abdication of joy in life for the sake of attaining transcendent consciousness or so-called salvation.

EXERCISE ONE—Earth Element

As you awaken at the beginning of the day, keep your eyes closed and allow yourself to acknowledge any fragrances or odors you notice. The smell might be overpowering like the aroma of coffee coming from the kitchen, or it might be a subtle scent like traces of mothballs in the blanket. You may not be aware of any smell at all. Allow yourself at least two minutes with your eyes closed to search around for all the variations that your nose can pick up. As you arise, affirm to yourself that you will be especially aware of your sense of smell today for the entire day.

It would be particularly effective if you could pick a day that would take you through many different environments in order to give you a wide range of stimuli. Allow yourself to notice all smells, pleasant or otherwise. Do not make value judgments about the day's odors, labeling things as good or bad. Simply be aware of the effects that the odors and fragrances have on you in all ways. You may be surprised that some odors conventionally labeled as "bad" may occasionally seem pleasant to you. Mentally assume that anything you smell today will have a pleasant odor. Close your eyes to experience subtle odors and see whether particular emotions or memories come to mind. Do not limit yourself to obvious smells like flowers or automobile exhaust fumes. Smell the television set as you sit and watch it, the pencil as you write with it and the wallpaper as you walk down the hall. Notice the effects that the smells have on you.

Throughout the day, pause periodically to consciously take a deep breath. With your spine straight, breathe in through your nose and take the air deep into your lungs. Let your stomach push out as far as it can, and hold your lungs at total expansion for a few seconds before exhaling. When you breathe out, briskly push the air out through your nose until you have forced all the breath from your lungs.

EXERCISE TWO—Water Element

As you awaken in the morning one or two days after carrying out Exercise One, keep your eyes closed and allow yourself to acknowledge any tastes you notice. Run your tongue around your teeth and gums, open your mouth slightly and taste the air as you breathe in, or run the tip of your tongue along the knuckles of your fist. Allow yourself a minute or two with your eyes closed to experience whatever affects your sense of taste. As you arise, affirm to yourself that you will be especially aware of your sense of taste today for the entire day.

It is not necessary to adjust your diet for the day; in fact, it is recommended that you eat the foods you would normally consume. The difference for the day is in the degree of attention you direct to your sense of taste. Eat all foods in a slow and deliberate manner. Close your eyes when you can to enhance your awareness of the flavors. Do not divert your attention through conversation or idle distractions, and take twice the normal time to chew each mouthful of food. Before you place something in your mouth, see whether you can imagine or create the impression of the taste you will experience. Imagine that every bite contains a new taste sensation, no matter how familiar the food may really be. Mentally assume that anything you taste today will have a pleasant and exciting flavor.

EXERCISE THREE—Fire Element

As you awaken in the morning one or two days after carrying out Exercise Two, open your eyes and allow your sight to take in whatever is directly in front of your eyes. Without moving your body at all, adjust your visual focus for a variety of distances. Look across the room at some object and its shadow. Blur your vision intentionally and see what automatically comes into focus. Shift your concentration from the blanket next to your face to something at medium range. Allow yourself at least two minutes to experiment with your sense of sight and the focusing mechanism of your eyes. As you arise, affirm to yourself that you will be especially aware of your vision today for the entire day.

Close your eyes and exert gentle pressure against your eyelids with your fingertips. Vary the angles and intensity of the pressure, and notice the changing colors and patterns that you see. As you observe the visual impressions, be aware of the fact that you are creating the sights you behold and that their reality is a product of your own mind reacting to stimuli.

Throughout the day, be especially conscious of the effects of color intensity around you. Notice how colors are used to create specific impressions or subtle emotional responses. See which colors are the most attractive to you and which colors are predominant in your clothes closet. Occasionally blur your vision slightly so that color images take precedence over the utility value or meaning of things around you. As you behold the colors, see whether any emotions or memories come to mind.

A second area of visual awareness should be "new" sights in familiar areas. Observe your normal viewing patterns to become aware of how much visual input you filter out. Close your eyes and see whether you can remember the color and pattern of a co-worker's clothing for the day. Without looking out the window, try to remember how the day's weather appears. Look around familiar areas, pretending that you were blind until now.

Consciously look at the faces around you. Do not stare with an intensity that will make others uncomfortable; simply be there in their eyes. We often develop the habit of depersonalizing our contacts with fellow human beings by avoiding close visual attention. For the entire day devoted to this exercise, concentrate on being aware of looking into the eyes of others.

EXERCISE FOUR—Wind Element

As you awaken in the morning one or two days after carrying out Exercise Three, keep your eyes closed and allow yourself to acknowledge the physical feelings you notice. Without moving at all, make a quick survey of your body, noting any impressions on your sense of touch. The feel of the cloth, the position of your limbs, and heat or contact from a sleeping partner should all be in your awareness. Allow yourself at least two minutes with your eyes closed to take in all the variations that your sense of bodily awareness can pick up. As you arise, affirm to yourself that you will be especially conscious of your sense of touch today for the entire day.

As you proceed through the day, consciously experience as many varying stimulations to your tactile sense as you can. You may be surprised that some feelings conventionally labeled as "bad" may occasionally seem pleasant to you. Mentally assume that anything you feel today will be a pleasant sensation. Be aware of cool and warm temperature variations around your body. Consciously take part in all muscular actions you perform, whether it involves running, chewing or moving objects about. Notice the sensations produced by the clothing on your body. Observe your resistance to, or compliance with, the rocking motions of vehicles you ride in.

At one point during the day, find a quiet, comfortable place in which you can lie down on your back. Relax your body, spread out and allow the concerns of the day to leave your consciousness. Close your eyes and take a full breath of air. Imagine that you are breathing the air all the way to the bottom of your body cavity, and feel your lungs expand as much as they can. Repeat this deep breathing two or three times to clear your mind and lungs. Next, begin to tighten your body, starting with the very center at your solar plexus. Feel the tenseness move through your body trunk, simultaneously working up, down and out to the sides while retaining the muscular tension in the center. Hold the tension as you move your consciousness out through your body, tensing every muscle as you go. At the final stages, curl your fingers and toes inward and exert complete tension in all the muscles of your body. At that point, you should virtually be bouncing off the surface on which you are reclining. Suddenly release the tension, relaxing all your muscles at the same time while letting go of your breath. Proceeding up one limb at a time, consciously relax each muscle until your body is totally limp, dead weight. Begin with the fingers and toes and move inward to the center of your body. Consciously feel each muscle as you let it go.

Throughout the entire tactile-sense day, be aware of any tension that you might unconsciously store in the muscles of your shoulders, face, stomach or thighs. Acknowledge that you put the tension there for some purpose and release it.

EXERCISE FIVE—Source Element

As you awaken in the morning one or two days after carrying out Exercise Four, keep your eyes closed and allow yourself to acknowledge any sounds you notice. The noise might be overpowering, like the sound of your ringing alarm clock, or it might be a subtle sound, like the traffic on the street outside. You may not be aware of any sounds at all. Allow yourself at least two minutes with your eyes closed to search around for all the tonal variations that your ears can pick up. As you arise, affirm to yourself that you will be especially aware of your sense of hearing today for the entire day.

Throughout the day, be conscious of the effects of the voice qualities displayed by people around you. See which tones, volume levels and accents affect you in positive and negative ways. Be observant of the ways others' voices affect the people around you. Use a tape recorder to record your own voice as you read sections of this book out loud. Compare what you hear from the tape recorder with your mental concept of the sound of your own voice. If that were a stranger's voice, what would be your reaction to that person based on the voice quality alone?

A second area of sound awareness should be your bodily reactions to musical notes. Allow yourself to be exposed to a variety of different types of music. Relax in a seated position with your eyes closed and your attention fully directed toward the music. Notice the reactions in different parts of your body when different musical types are experienced. Notice whether there is no physical reaction at all. See whether your mind automatically creates scenes or situations under the influence of the music. Follow the scenes out for a while and then return your consciousness to the music itself.

At some point during the day, find a place where there is no sound at all. Relax there for several minutes and allow your hearing to grow accustomed to the silence. Become aware of the steady sound behind the silence that takes the place of the constant noise that usually assaults the ears. Observe what that silence sounds like.

As a logical progression in learning to combine pure bodily awareness with the mental processes, the student of ninjutsu is taught to observe the action of the mind, in combination with regulation of the breath, to direct the body's energies in order to adapt his mood to a particular situation or set of circumstances. This selection of consciousness permits the ninja to fit in appropriately with the situation at hand or to change his perspective in order to affect the direction of the events that make up the situation.

EXERCISE SIX—Earth Level

When feeling overly excited, extremely nervous or too emotionally involved, the ninja would practice a method of controlled breathing and mental imagery to calm and ground himself and bring his feelings back "down to earth."

Direct all your attention to your breathing. Allow yourself to inhale slowly, totally filling your lungs and pushing your abdomen all the way out. It should take you approximately eight seconds to take a full breath. Do not hold the breath with the lungs and abdomen fully extended, but immediately breathe out slowly until you have forced all the air from your lungs and pulled your abdominal muscles in to their normal, relaxed position. The exhalation also should take approximately eight seconds to complete.

As you carry out this particular breathing cycle, imagine that your entire body cavity is hollow, as if it were a huge empty cave. As you breathe in, feel the air rush in along the back of your throat and down along the back of the "cave." Take the air all the way in, as if it were going to the bottom of the body cavity. You should feel the inhalation pressure in your genitals and lower abdomen. Immediately exhale, forcing the air up and out along the front of the "cave." Inhalation and exhalation should be total, and one should turn into the other without pause.

It may be helpful to visualize a symbol of the earth element while you are performing this breathing exercise. Close your eyes and picture a range of mountain peaks in the wilderness. Narrow your vision to the highest of the peaks. Picture yourself seated on top of the peak, with one leg hanging over each side as if you were riding a camel. Imagine the feel of the mountain along the inside of your thighs and calves as if the mountain were gripping you, and allow your lower body to feel as if it were becoming a part of the mountain's roots and the very earth itself.

Use the visual image along with the specific breathing method to calm yourself and increase your feelings of stability in times of stress.

EXERCISE SEVEN—Water Level

When feeling unresponsive, too rigid or enmeshed in the reasoning process, the ninja would practice a method of controlled breathing and mental imagery to increase his adaptability and flexibility, and to allow his feelings to "go with the flow."

Direct your attention to your breathing. Allow yourself to inhale slowly, totally filling your lungs and pushing your abdomen all the way out. It should take you approximately eight seconds to take a full breath. With the lungs and abdomen fully extended, hold the breath for approximately three seconds. You should feel the pressure of the breath pushing out against your abdomen, just below your navel. Breathe out by totally relaxing the lungs and muscles of the ribs while simultaneously reversing the pressure on your lower abdomen. The tightening of these muscles should force the air out of your lungs with a brisk rush. Maintain the inward abdominal pressure for three seconds before breathing in again.

It may be helpful to visualize a symbol of the water element while you are performing this breathing exercise. Close your eyes and picture a rocky coastline along the ocean. Narrow your vision to a small stretch of boulders, around which the waves are breaking. Picture yourself sitting in an inflated seat, up to your hips in the deep water. Imagine the feel of the wave currents as they shift you about from one direction to another. Mentally relax and become a part of the natural rhythm and flow.

Use the visual image along with the specific breathing method to become more sensitive and come closer to your inner feelings in times when emotional flexibility is needed.

EXERCISE EIGHT—Fire Level

When feeling low on energy, indecisive or manipulated by others, the ninja would practice a method of controlled breathing and mental imagery to recharge himself, gain command of his own direction and "fire up" for the activity at hand.

Direct all your attention to your breathing. Relax your lungs and the muscles of your ribs, and take in a quick breath by pushing out on the abdominal muscles covering your stomach. The breath should come in with a rush, and you should feel the pressure behind your solar plexus. Do not hold the breath with your ribs expanded, but immediately breathe out briskly by inwardly tightening the muscles beneath the solar plexus. Maintain a relaxed feeling in your ribs and shoulders throughout the repetitive inhalation/exhalation cycles, and use the muscles below the tip of the sternum and above the stomach to move the air in and out of your body rapidly.

It may be helpful to visualize a symbol of the fire element while you are performing this breathing exercise. Close your eyes and picture an old hearthstone fireplace in the center of the open area, and see the red-hot coals used for heating iron to the point at which it can be shaped and molded. Picture yourself in front of the coals, with your lungs taking the role of the wind bellows. Imagine the feel of the flames as they leap up with every exhalation and the intense heat that radiates through your solar plexus with every inhalation.

Use the visual image along with the specific breathing method to generate psychic energy and to increase your feelings of personal control of the situation in times when purposeful action is needed.

EXERCISE NINE—Wind Level

When feeling intellectually pressed, emotionally controlled, lacking in compassion or too self-oriented, the ninja would practice a method of controlled breathing and mental imagery to increase his feelings of being in touch with others and transcendent of his baser powers.

Direct your attention to your breathing. Relax your lungs and the muscles of your ribs, and take a quick breath by pushing out on the abdominal muscles covering the stomach. The breath should come in with a rush, pushing your stomach out and filling your lungs. Hold the breath for approximately three seconds, being aware of the pressure in the center of your chest. Slowly release the breath in a steady, controlled stream by gently tightening the muscles around your ribs and pulling up and in on the muscles of your abdomen. You should feel a tightening in the center of your chest, and the exhalation should take approximately 10 seconds to complete.

It may be helpful to visualize a symbol of the wind element while you are performing this breathing exercise. Close your eyes and picture a vast forest of tall trees. Narrow your vision to a portion of the forest along a high ridge exposed to the wind. Picture yourself standing among the trees; feel the wind moving around you. Imagine the feel of the wind as it moves on, slipping around and by anything that gets in its way. Feel the wind that your breath creates as you share the air with everything around you.

Use the visual image along with the specific breathing method to increase your consciousness of your benevolent nature and to strengthen your intellectual grasp of any situation.

Certain electromagnetic channels of the body are said to be the most sensitive in the feet and hands. Ninjutsu's *kuji-in* (nine-syllable hand seals) and their variations make up an attitude-control system based on direction of energy through the hands. The thumb represents the ku source element, with each of the fingers representing one of the four elemental manifestations.

Water (sui)

To encourage more of a sui (water) adapt-ability and power, the ring finger is folded to form a ring with the thumb, which is interlocked with the ring finger and thumb of the other hand.

Fire (ka)

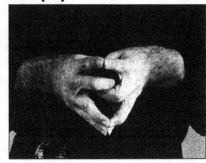

To encourage more of a ka (fire) aggres-siveness and energy, the middle finger is folded to form a ring with the thumb, which is interlocked with the middle finger and thumb of the other hand.

Earth (chi)

To encourage more of a chi (earth) stabil-ity and strength, the little finger is folded to form a ring with the thumb, which is interlocked with the little finger and thumb of the other hand.

Wind (fu)

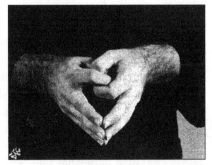

To encourage more of a fu (wind) sensitivity and harmonious action, the pointer finger is folded to form a ring with the thumb, which is interlocked with the pointer finger and thumb of the other hand.

The suggested visualizations that accompany the breathing methods in this chapter are by no means the only possible mental aids. The images have been presented as a guide or format for consideration. Some ninja would visualize different animals that represented the four qualities, such as the bear for the earth or the dragon for the wind. Some would imagine the feeling of the body's life force flowing from one or two body centers to the deficient center. Others would find it more helpful to hold their concentration on a single word while affecting their breathing, such as "strategy" or "flexibility" for the water element or "intensity" or "drive" for the fire element. Any one of the visualizations is a mere trick, at any rate, for the purpose of locking the mind's activity onto the endeavor at hand—the adjustment of the body's metabolism and direction of the personality's approach to the ever-changing demands of present-moment reality.

The physical breathing techniques themselves, on the other hand, represent a more concrete aspect of bodily control. By consciously regulating the organs that control the rates at which the air enters and leaves the bloodstream, and by applying pressure to those areas of the body in which the endocrine glands function, the body can be made to alter its pace and adapt to new situations as they arise.

Additional perspective can be given to the validity of the breathing methods by observing natural responsive breath patterns in different life situations. Notice the way your body adjusts the breathing rate and depth to naturally handle conditions of stress, emotion, concentration or fatigue. External environmental factors, whether real or imagined, trigger specific psychophysical responses that stimulate or restrict the activity of the endocrine glands and cause the adjusted metabolic rate to alter the breathing cycle. As a result of this stepped procedure, the body is enabled to handle a wide range of daily encounters. By reversing the process and adjusting the breathing rate, then mentally suggesting a specific quality of mind, the body responses associated with the breathing rate and state of mind can be artificially induced to allow the desired approach to the situation at hand.

It is a futile exercise to attempt to control your surroundings without first learning to control your own perceptions of and reactions to the surroundings. Power begins in the center of our beings and awakening to that reality is a natural development of training in ninjutsu.

CHAPTER 5

The mind directs
the energy of the physical entity
into harmony with the state of the universe.
When all about you is frantic chaos,
do not be absorbed by the crashing of gongs,
the screams of the hysterical,
or the wailing of the grievous.
Become one with the rocks that never feel the need
to weep.
Become a part of the plains that never feel the need
to shift about at the whim of minor happenings.
Your roots are buried deep.
Like those of the mountains.

ACTIVE MEDITATION

The mind-sharpening methods of the ninja

For the student of ninjutsu, understanding the mind and its workings is crucial to development as a competent fighter. The brain is a valuable self-defense tool often overlooked in many martial arts. Physical conditioning and technique memorization can take the practitioner only so far, and the advanced fighter must go on to develop the qualities of awareness and detachment.

This detachment is an ability to figuratively back off from activity in which you are engaged and observe the total picture of you and your adversary. Instead of concentrating on what you are going to do, you simply observe the attacker's actions from a defensive pose and react appropriately to his moves. Instead of concentrating on beating your adversary, you allow him to make the mistakes that will bring about his downfall.

One aspect of effective self-protection or effective martial arts training is total involvement in the activity from moment to moment. The minute your attention or awareness begins to slide forward or backward from the present instant, you are no longer "there." Mentally verbalized thoughts such as "Here's what I'll do if . . ." or "Why did I let . . ." are hindering to present-moment, spontaneous response because you are thinking of yourself as isolated from the action, both physically and in terms of time frame.

Take a few minutes to recall your most frustrating moments in the training hall or in actual self-defense. Perhaps you were sparring with a training partner who was giving you a difficult time (so you tried harder to beat him, filling the air with all your thoughts of what you should do or should have done, making it even easier for him to pick up your intentions and control you). Perhaps it was in an actual combat encounter (and your thoughts of the harm or injury he could possibly do to you hindered your natural skills and forced you to take a defensive attitude resulting in a tough time handling the situation). Perhaps you were learning a new and difficult technique (and you kept your mind on all that you were doing wrong, and you worked so hard at "trying" to do the technique that you actually felt you were getting worse at it instead of better).

Successful activity and exciting living depends on 100 percent involvement in whatever you are doing at any given moment. When the mind begins to wander, drifting to other times or conjuring up all sorts of pointless nonexistent situations (worries and regrets), the quality of your body's activities decreases and the total potential of the moment is robbed. Become totally involved, however, and the very intensity of what you are doing and thinking will capture the moment entirely.

In terms of self-defense fighting, a student must first go through intensive physical training so that he will know what actions are appropriate for various attacks and attackers. In the physical level of training, you must trust your teachers and accept what they teach you from their experience. This physical training period is a time for coming to know what works best for each personal body build. The actions of the muscles and bones, breath regulation, and your body's dynamic force are aspects of this first major practice level.

Beyond fundamental physical training is the control of the mind's activity, which is more difficult than you might think. Physical weaknesses or shortcomings are easily observed by others, and they can be remedied by suggestions from an observing teacher. Darting eyes and fidgeting hands betray nervousness. Locked knees will prevent swift, balanced movement. Drawing a fist or shoulder back will warn the adversary that a punch is coming. However, only you can know what is going on in your mind. No one can reach in there to see what you are doing or help coach you.

Zen-style meditation is a good way to practice this mental discipline and awareness. The Zen concept is very misunderstood in the West, however, and many erroneously believe meditation to be a means of "zoning out," fading from reality or entering a dream world of artificial perceptions. The meditative state is actually a state of intensified awareness, not sluggish drowsiness. Meditation practice is a means to total effectiveness in a physical endeavor.

EXERCISE ONE
Simple Meditation

Find a reasonably quiet place where you will not be disturbed. Do not seek total silence; a few natural noises will actually help. If you wish, you can place a mat on the floor or ground for comfort, and you should have a small, firm pillow nearby. Sit in the middle of the mat with your legs outstretched. Draw the left foot toward you, and place the heel in the crotch with the sole resting against the right thigh. Insert the outer edge of the right foot between the calf and thigh of the left leg. Lean forward and pull the pillow in under your seat so that it is in a comfortable position. Raise and straighten your body trunk, with the back slightly arched so that the stomach and chest are pushed forward. Rest the right hand palm up in the left hand, with the thumb tips touching. Your hands should be tucked into your lap tightly, with your elbows close to your body trunk.

The traditional meditation pose has nothing inherently magical about it. Sitting in a Western ladder-backed chair with the hips as far back as possible and the feet firmly planted on the ground can produce similarly satisfactory conditions for successful meditation. The Eastern meditation pose is recommended when possible, however, in that the supported back in a chair can permit too much bodily relaxation and lead to drowsiness and sleep. The traditional pose also provides the benefit of teaching consciousness of the proper healthful posture.

Stretch your spine to the ceiling and then settle it. Let your shoulders fall naturally. Rock back and forth and from side to side several times to get the feel of the vertical centerline. Look straight ahead and then lower your chin until your eyes come to rest on the floor about two meters in front of you. Pull your chin in as far as you can. Lower your eyelids to shade your eyes, but do not close your eyes. Close your mouth and breathe through the nose. This seated posture is the basic position for meditation practice. Your folded legs help to keep tension on the lower spine, which will keep your back straight. Remember to keep your chin tucked in and your back anatomically straight.

From this seated posture, you can begin to learn how to observe from within. In essence, you are seeking your "self."

Feel yourself breathe. Allow yourself to concentrate totally on feeling the breathing action. Something can feel your breath going in and out, and the stomach rise and fall. Something is aware of the sound of your breathing.

Repeat the word "ninja" to yourself. Somewhere in your head, something can hear the word. Try to watch the something that can hear your thoughts.

Clench your hands into fists and then return them to the meditation position. Something watches the hands move. Something quite apart from the hands observes the action. Try to watch the observing something as it considers the hands.

We might at first think of this observer in ourselves as simply being our mind at work watching our bodies. But there is more complexity than that. For if we think the word "ninja" to ourselves, the observer can watch the mind itself at work.

What is this thing that watches everything as if it were apart from us? We will call it "The Observer." It is a point of awareness that is really outside consciousness, thinking of thoughts and even emotions. It is the thing that you probably refer to when you say "I." The Observer is your awareness, and when The Observer is not present, you are in a distracted state or daydreaming as things go on around you.

Practice calling up The Observer and using it to look at things. If you are breathing, The Observer watches the breathing. If you are nervous, The Observer can watch the nervousness; that's how you know you are nervous. Experiment with the observations so that you come to know and understand how The Observer works.

EXERCISE TWO
Training The Observer

Once you recognize The Observer in you, you may begin to train The Observer to do what you want it to do. In normal people, The Observer tends to run the consciousness. This results in scattered thoughts, lack of awareness or mind wandering as The Observer skips around picking up anything that comes along. This freshness of The Observer is called "wonder" and is desirable and good. However, there are times when we need to control The Observer to prevent our emotions or outside happenings from taking us over.

This second exercise is known as "breath counting," and it is somewhat misleading in that it has very little to do with how to breathe. Counting breaths is a simple and straightforward means of using The Observer and limiting its scope to a particular duty.

Assume the seated posture described in the first exercise. Allow yourself to get settled and adjusted to your surroundings. Begin to concentrate your attention on your breathing. Take natural breaths, letting your stomach move in and out. Do not try to consciously control or regulate the breath. Just let it happen.

Begin to count the breaths with The Observer. Each time you breathe out, increase the number by one. When you reach nine, begin again at one. Your body is taking care of itself, holding itself upright, breathing naturally, blinking and swallowing occasionally. Concentrate exclusively on The Observer's counting. Do not become upset if stray thoughts creep into the mind and you find The Observer involved with them. Simply be aware that The Observer has strayed and redirected the consciousness to the job of counting again. If you become too relaxed, the mind will be at rest with The Observer. You will find yourself counting "14, 15, 16 . . ." Alert yourself, and pay attention again.

The exercise seems extremely easy at first reading. It is not, however. The simplicity is designed to make it easy to tell whether you are doing the exercise effectively. It is not difficult to notice when the exercise is not being done properly. The object of this exercise is to be aware of what you are observing and to not allow other things to interrupt the observation. This is harder work than it might seem.

Begin with short periods of observing meditation. It is less discouraging to begin with five minutes of meditation and gradually increase with each sitting. By the end of the two weeks, you should be meditating ("observing") for 20-minute periods.

Distractions will occur, of course. Noises, visual objects or thoughts will suddenly grab your attention. Do not be upset with the distractions. Simply notice them and return to your concentration. Physical discomfort may get to you, also. If it interrupts your concentration, stay seated, "watch" the discomfort for a moment and then return to the counting. If you are concentrating on the mental activity exclusively, you are not likely to notice the minor discomforts at all.

Bear in mind that the results of this exercise will be applied to the ninja fighting method in later exercises. You are not counting for the sake of counting; you are counting for the sake of disciplining your concentration. To be successful at this breath-counting exercise, you must want to be successful. Keep doing it just like you did when you were learning to punch or shoot properly. If you are not mentally ready for this, the exercise will be more difficult than the most complex physical techniques.

EXERCISE THREE
Pure Observation

The first exercise dealt with proper body positioning and finding The Observer in your personality. The second exercise dealt with training The Observer to limit its scope and to concentrate its awareness. The next exercise trains The Observer to avoid verbalizing or conceptually structuring the observations.

Assume the meditation position. Hold some small, natural object in your hand so you can examine it. It is suggested that a man-made object not be used because it might trigger memories or thoughts related to the use of the object.

Before beginning this exercise, it is a good idea to allow yourself to come to rest. Hold the object in your hands while sitting in the meditation position and temporarily forget it. Go back to Exercise Two and begin by observing your breath. If you feel confident in your ability to concentrate on counting, drop the one-through-nine routine and just observe the rising and falling of your abdomen as you breathe. Concentrate on this alone. After a few minutes, you should notice your breath slowing and your mind becoming totally involved with what you are doing. Once this acclimation takes place, you may begin your object observation.

Examine the object (stick, rock, etc.) with your eyes. Turn the object in your hands and really look at it. Observe your mind as you scan the object, and note your thoughts. You are probably verbalizing or thinking actual words that describe the object, such as "flat, rough, flexible, dry." The object of this training is to get your mind away from such verbalizing. Try to use your eyes like you would your sense of touch. Close your eyes and run your fingers over the object. You simply feel the object and are probably not using mental words to describe it to yourself.

Use your eyes again. Run your sight over the object as if you were feeling it with your eyes. Observe and take in all the features without thinking about words. You may be tempted to think words such as "it was cut off here" or "the sand rubs off in my hand" but do not. Just like you notice a feature with your Observer, go on in your examination. Learn to cut off the distracting and time-consuming habit of mechanical thinking and simply observe without making value judgments.

Over a period of several weeks, use different objects in this exercise. Keep the point of the exercise in mind for the first few sessions. After a few sittings, the words describing the purpose should be forgotten, and you should be on your way to development.

EXERCISE FOUR
Unconscious Consciousness

The purpose of this exercise is to bring the total body into the meditation process without destroying or disturbing the meditative state.

We all have the ability to use our bodies in relaxed, unconscious movement and to do many things in everyday activity that use this ability. Usually, familiarity with a physical action brings about this unconscious ability. We enter a room at night, find that it is dark and run our hand along the wall in an upward manner, flipping the lights on. We do this automatically without going through the conscious process of discovering the dark, wondering what to do about it, searching for a light switch, and deciding whether to flip it up or down, all in a deliberate manner. We might be conversing with friends while climbing out of a swimming pool. Someone throws us a towel, and we catch it and begin drying off without interrupting our speech. We do not stop in midsentence, turn and line up with the thrower, hold our arms out protectively, and hold our breath until the towel hits us. Our catch is a graceful and natural one, and we hardly give it any notice at all.

To practice this exercise, assume a natural standing pose. Lower your eyelids slightly to shade your eyes, and begin to narrow your concentration to your breathing. Allow yourself a few minutes to become accustomed to this relaxation. When you feel you have reached the settled state of meditative awareness, slowly slide back into a defensive posture with your weight on your rear leg and your body turned sideways toward your training partner. Maintain the shaded eyes and stomach breathing. Direct your attention to your training partner, and observe him with the same nonverbalized awareness that you practiced in Exercise Three. If he slides to the side, just watch him. Adjust your position if you must to keep him in sight. Do not look for anything or anticipate any moves. Simply watch him in a receiving manner as if you were a spectator at a performance of some sort. You should feel relaxed yet aware.

From a distance of about two meters, your training partner attacks with a half-speed lunging punch at your face. Allow your body to move back and to the inside of his swing as you bring your leading arm up and outward to strike the inside of the attacker's wrist. In this exercise, the attacker should retreat after his single advance. As the interrupting fist moves away, you should return to the calmness of mind in the meditative state. Concentrate on your breathing if you need to quiet your mind.

After a few moments of settling in the defensive position, again observe your training partner in the nonverbalized manner that you developed before. Do not think about him or about not thinking about him. Simply allow your eyes to take him in.

Your training partner next attacks with a front kick to your stomach or groin. Rock your weight back onto your rear leg and raise your front foot up, turning your toes inward. Allow the shin of his kicking leg to hit the sole of your extended foot. Keep your weight low over your rear leg so that you stop his kick without knocking yourself over.

The attacker should then retreat after his kick. As he moves away, you should return to the meditative state of awareness. Strive to keep your mind empty of emotions or considerations of your successfulness. Do not be concerned if your technique did not work exactly as you wished. Do not become excited if your technique stops his attack. Retain the feeling that you are an observer and that the completed exercise no longer exists. There is only the task of maintaining calm awareness in the present moment.

From the defensive position, observe the attacker as he winds up and throws a soft rubber ball at you. As the ball approaches you, leap to the side or duck to avoid it. Again, resume the defensive pose and frame of mind in preparation for his next attack. You should feel ready for anything that happens and yet expect nothing.

Continue this practice method using any single-action strike, kick or weapon attack and its counter. Individual creativity can be used once a basic familiarity with the process has developed. The purpose of the training is to learn how to observe and detect any attacking motion as it originates and to successfully deal with it as it is carried out.

Meditation practice is beneficial in ways of gaining control of the mind's activity and control of the emotions. These improvements can be enjoyed by all. A major benefit to the ninja, or any martial artist, however, is the increased accuracy in fighting, made possible by the increased observation.

Remember that meditation training for the purpose of mind control can be more difficult than physical training at times. In effect, you are adjusting a part of your personality. Do not expect a dramatic or revolutionary change overnight.

CHAPTER 6

You are not locked in that body of yours.
Your mind can soar and join other minds.
Do not be afraid
> *to explore*
> *the dynamic potentiality of all things in the universe.*
Quest ever on.
To know
> *feel*
> *and be*
> *all that you possibly can.*
Become a part of the ethereal
> *and look down upon the earth as it plays its part in the cosmos.*
Tap the knowledge of the heavens
> *to see the scheme of impersonal totality*
> *and become a part*
> *of the mind and eyes of god.*

EXTENDED REALITIES

Knowing the unknowable, perceiving the imperceptible

What is that elusive quality beyond physical mastery of techniques that allows certain fighters the ability to prevail in all encounters? The household term is "sixth sense"—somehow knowing something that can't really be known. It is feeling that a puncher is faking a swing. It is an unconscious knowledge that something is wrong just before an unarmed assailant pulls out a knife. It is knowing that an attacker awaits you in the parking lot with a pistol in his pocket. These and other skills of detection are developed by stripping away our faulty or clouded perceptions of things and events. We teach ourselves not to trust our impressions unless they are scientifically verifiable. All too often we ignore our subjective mental impressions or discount them as useless imagination, thereby robbing ourselves of a valuable source of input.

Beyond the five levels of physical consciousness, and the consciousness of the mind and its processes, lies a third realm of reality—an awareness of the unity and all-encompassing oneness that ties the universe together. This greater reality, or cosmic consciousness, is filtered through the mind and defined in ways that are understandable and acceptable to the physical organism.

According to the mystical heritage of the ninja, all individual things in the universe began as a single entity or "thought." From this universal beginning, all existence descended and divided into the limitless infinity of all things around us. It is crucial to recognize this concept in order to understand the basis of what we might call spiritual capabilities. Though the grosser physical manifestations of all matter appear to be separate, there remains a subtle connection that links the essences of all in existence (i.e., electrons from a common source grouped to form atoms, which became molecules, which became physical objects). This is in direct opposition to theories that state all things were created from the physical form upward and are therefore unconnected (i.e., physical objects were created, and electrons and molecules were merely used to give the objects their structure).

Though there is a common tendency to classify things as being either physical or spiritual, there is actually no such dividing line. Acknowledging the body, its spiritual connection with all other things, and its mental interpreter is not a statement of reality but rather a reflection of our human way of experiencing things. There is no such thing as spirit *as opposed to* physicalness, in that anything that we would call spiritual has physical reality as its base.

It may be true, however, that we are unable to understand how certain phenomena operate or come about, and until our physical science is capable of explaining it, we dismiss its mystery as being "of the spirit." Today, even the most down-to-earth and unimaginative individuals can wholeheartedly accept the concept of radio and television broadcasts as being totally within the range of physical reality. A few generations ago, however, the ability to send and receive words and images across miles of empty space would have been considered to be as otherworldly as extrasensory perception or transmutation of matter is today. Natural laws are constantly in operation around us. Our ability to use these laws to our own benefit depends on our sensitivity to their existence and our willingness to work with less than tangible phenomena.

Awareness of seemingly hidden natural factors can give the impression of supernatural powers. Strangers to the ocean find that sometimes it is easy to find the clams and sometimes the waves make it virtually impossible to come up with anything. The man equipped with a tide table for high and low tides, however, finds it is always easy to get the clams. Those who know nothing of tide tables might see the knowledgeable one as a wizard able to command the elements, for whenever he goes to the sea, the waves are seen to fall back. Rather than learn the tide table themselves, they might find it easier to simply follow him whenever he went to the sea or find it spiritually rewarding to place him in a position of reverence to which they could never hope to ascend. It would not be surprising if after his death, later generations would worship the man with the tide table as the divine one who could cause the clams to crawl from the sea onto his dinner plate by means of his will alone.

In a fashion similar to the preceding exaggerated story, the legends of the powers of the ninja came to be distorted and enhanced over centuries of Japanese culture. Imaginative tales were told of how the ninja had descended from the *tengu* (long-nosed winged demons who were half man and half crow). Popular stories often included ninja who possessed such skills as walking on water, disappearing through walls, transforming themselves into rats or leaping and flying incredible distances. The true powers of the mystics of Iga, no matter how advanced they were in reality, paled when compared with the fantastic abilities of the glamorized ninja in the children's stories.

The historical ninja of feudal Japan were famous for their knowledge of the realm that we would call spiritual or occult today. Legitimate abilities practiced were the capability of detecting the threatening presence of others, reading the intentions of people and visualizing distant places or people. Advanced students of ninjutsu today still practice specific exercises for the development of the finer senses and awareness of the seventh level of consciousness.

This seventh plateau of consciousness is an acknowledgment of the subtle effects we feel from the electromagnetic force-field influences of others. Some students are more naturally predisposed toward developing the abilities, while others require longer training to make the exercises work for them. In either case, all people will experience "off" days now and then. We do not question the possibility of basketballs going through hoops just because we might occasionally miss a free throw. The mind exercises operate in the same manner. If we believe that the exercises are of any value to us, persistence is required.

EXERCISE ONE
Reaction Development

The first exercise is a method for developing a relaxed and open state of mind, and it reduces the tendency to anticipate the thoughts or actions of another. The practice method involves two or more training partners—a controller who will give the commands for action and one or more receivers who will carry out the commands. The exercise is designed as a means of practicing correct "last-minute" responses to definite stimuli instead of reacting too soon or reacting and hesitating too soon to the anticipated stimulus that is imagined to be on its way. On the physical level alone, the exercise is an effective means for beginning students to practice spontaneously the leaping and tumbling that are such crucial aspects of the ninja's combat system.

STEP ONE

Controller

Stand in the middle of an open area or large room where there are as few physical obstructions as possible. Assume a comfortable, natural standing pose with the weight evenly distributed on both feet. Breathe with the abdomen in a natural manner.

Receiver

Take a position in a ring around the controller, along the outer periphery of the open training area. Assume the hira no kamae receiving posture with the knees flexed and the arms outstretched. Breathe in a natural manner that will attune the body and mind with the wind (touch) level of consciousness.

STEP TWO

STEP TWO
Controller
Call out a two-word action command in a clear and unhurried voice with sufficient volume to be heard easily. The command should be chosen from the following possibilities:

Jump forward

Jump backward

Jump right

Jump left

Jump high

Jump low

Roll forward

Roll backward

Roll right

Roll left

To increase the complexity and challenge of the exercises for advanced students, occasionally reverse the word order of action and direction ("Right jump" in place of "Jump right") to take the total number of commands to 20.

Receiver
Maintain the centered hira pose while you listen for the command. Suspend your thinking process and simply take in the words of the controller. As soon as you have heard both words, immediately carry out the command. Each specific command should trigger the following precise response:

— Jump forward: Slam your hips forward, lifting your feet and keeping your shoulders over your hips.

— Jump backward: Slam your hips to the rear, lifting your feet and keeping your shoulders over your hips.

— Jump right: Slam your hips to the right, lifting your feet and keeping your shoulders over your hips.

— Jump left: Slam your hips to the left, lifting your feet and keeping your shoulders over your hips.

— Jump high: Spring upward, lifting your knees and feet as high as possible.

— Jump low: Drop to the ground, folding your body to as low a position as possible.

— Roll forward: Drop to a squatting position, fold your arms across your shins and roll forward along your spine, ending up back on your feet again.

— Roll backward: Drop to a squatting position, pull your elbows in and your hands next to your cheekbones, and roll backward along your spine, ending up back on your feet again.

— Roll right: Drop to a squatting position, fold your right arm across your shins, and roll to your right along your arm, shoulder and back, ending up on your feet again.

— Roll left: Drop to a squatting position, fold your left arm across your shins, and roll to your left along your arm, shoulder and back, ending up back on your feet again.

STEP THREE

Receiver

Rise from the ground and assume the hira no kamae once again. Forget the preceding action and prepare to receive the next command.

The controller should continue to give the two-word commands, varying the interval between commands so that the receiver does not become set in any rhythmic timing pattern.

It should be stressed that this is not a competitive exercise in which the controller tries to fool or trick the receiver. The controller is there to aid in the development of the receiver and should maintain a mental attitude of indifference, trying not to make the exercise any easier or any more difficult than it normally would be.

The exercise is an important one, in that it allows us to become familiar with the feeling of reacting unhesitatingly to our first impressions. The exercise should be experienced several times before moving on to the next exercises in this chapter.

EXERCISE TWO
Feeling Presence I

The second exercise is a beginning step for developing skill in detecting the presence of others. The practice method involves two training partners—a receiver who will experience the feeling of presence and a controller who will determine at what point the presence is felt. Because of the electromagnetic characteristics of the human body, it might be helpful to practice the exercise with a training partner of the opposite sex for the first few sessions.

STEP ONE
Receiver

Stand in the middle of an open area or large room where there are as few sensual distractions (noise, smells, breezes, etc.) as possible. Assume a comfortable, natural standing pose with the weight evenly distributed on both feet. Allow your hands to hang loosely at your sides, and let your shoulders relax into their normal position. Take your time, shake your body out if you need to and become totally relaxed.

Begin a process of slow, deep breathing, concentrating on the exhalation and using your stomach to move the air in and out of your lungs. After two or three breaths, allow your eyes to close slowly as you continue your breathing rhythm.

Begin to imagine that your body is surrounded by its own radarlike force field, extending out from the skin surface in all directions much like your natural body heat radiates out from your skin. With your eyes closed, allow yourself to become more sensitive to this imaginary extension of your sense of touch. See how far out you think it reaches, and mentally picture the boundaries of this invisible power shell that encases you.

STEP TWO
Controller

Slowly and quietly position yourself in front of the receiver while he or she is concentrating on the closed-eye breathing and force-field visualization. You should be about one meter away from the receiver. Allow a few seconds to pass and then slowly raise your right arm to a position pointing between his or her eyes. Your arm should be straight from the shoulder to the tips of your extended fingers, and your fingertips should end up about one hand-length distance from the receiver's face.

Hold your right hand palm down with the fingers and thumb straight and pressed together. Slowly lean toward the receiver, moving your fingertips forward mere fractions of inches per second. As you approach the receiver's face, imagine that your arm and fingers are like a garden hose carrying a stream of water from the center of your body to a distant target.

Imagine that you can feel and see the invisible-energy current as it flows through your spine, shoulder and arm, and out through the tips of your fingers. Allow your vision to focus on the receiver's brow, just above the nose and between the eyes. See the imaginary force as a beam of light that you are aiming at your training partner's face.

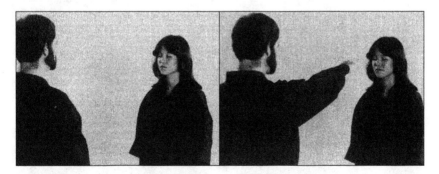

STEP THREE

Receiver

When you feel the presence of the controller's fingertips, lift your left hand to a palm-forward position just in front of your left shoulder. Maintain your relaxed standing position and keep your eyes closed as you raise your hand as a signal.

Controller

As you see the receiver's hand move into your field of vision, immediately freeze your action and maintain the distance between your fingers and the receiver's face.

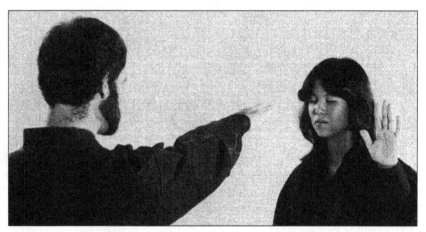

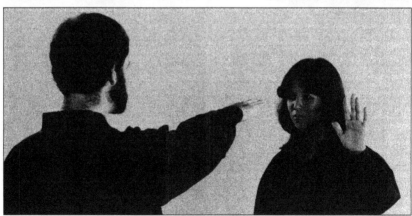

STEP FOUR
Receiver

Slowly open your eyes and check the position of the controller's hand.

All four steps of the exercise should be carried out at a leisurely pace, avoiding a sense of urgency. The controller should vary the time intervals between the beginning of the exercise and the point at which he or she aims the fingertips so as to avoid setting up a predictable cycle.

If the receiver should continue to be unable to detect the controller's fingertips, all four steps of the exercise should be carried out slowly with the receiver's eyes only partially closed. In this way, the receiver can get a better feel for the experience being sought.

After several repetitions of the exercise, the controller and receiver should switch roles.

It should be stressed that this is in no way a competitive clash between the two training partners. It is a developmental exercise in which both students take turns assisting each other in discovering their own capabilities. The controller never tries to confuse or sneak up on the receiver. The controller is constantly concentrating his or her attention on properly carrying out the exercise so that the student assuming the role of the receiver can develop skill and confidence. At the same time, the receiver is not at all concerned with winning anything or impressing the controller. The receiver is constantly concentrating his or her attention on properly carrying out the exercise in order to learn to recognize and differentiate between actual stimuli and imagination. The purpose of the exercise is to actually feel the presence, not merely guess correctly that the hand is there.

EXERCISE THREE
Feeling Presence II

This exercise is a slightly more advanced step for developing skill in detecting the presence of others. The practice method involves three or more training partners—a receiver who will experience the feeling of presence and two or more controllers who will determine at what point and from which direction the presence will be felt. The third exercise is more difficult to carry out successfully than the second because of the increased number of factors influencing the receiver. It is therefore highly important to avoid becoming entangled in "figuring out" the exercise and attempting to explain it with rational concepts. Receiver and controllers alike should simply relax and have fun with the exercise and not take it overly seriously.

STEP ONE
Receiver

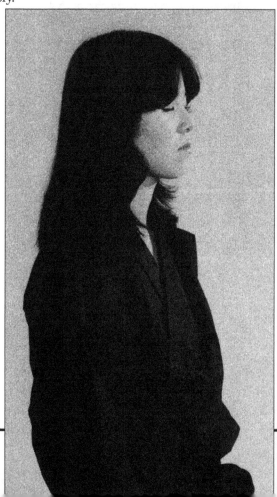

Stand in the middle of an open area or large room where there are as few sensual distractions as possible. Assume the shizen no kamae with the weight evenly distributed on both feet.   .

Just like in Exercise Two, begin a process of slow, deep breathing, concentrating on the exhalation and using your stomach to move the air in and out of your lungs. After two or three breaths, allow your eyes to close slowly as you continue your breathing rhythm.

Just like in the preceding exercise, begin to imagine that your body is surrounded by its own radarlike force field, extending out from the skin surface in all directions. With your eyes closed, allow yourself to become more sensitive to this imaginary extension of your sense of touch. Without moving, feel all around yourself and imagine the sensation of something breaching your power-shell boundary.

STEP TWO
Controllers

Slowly and quietly position yourselves in a circle around the receiver while he or she is concentrating on the closed-eye breathing and force-field visualization. You should all be about one meter away from the receiver and equally distant from each other. Allow a few seconds to pass and then use subtle facial or bodily gestures to determine which of the controllers will attempt to influence the receiver. When selected as the active controller, slowly raise your right arm to a position pointing at an imaginary band encircling the receiver's head at eye level.

Hold your right hand palm down with the fingers and thumb straight and pressed together. Slowly lean toward the receiver, moving your fingertips forward mere fractions of inches per second. Like in Exercise Two, imagine that your arm and fingertips are a hose transporting an invisible current of energy to the point at which you are aiming.

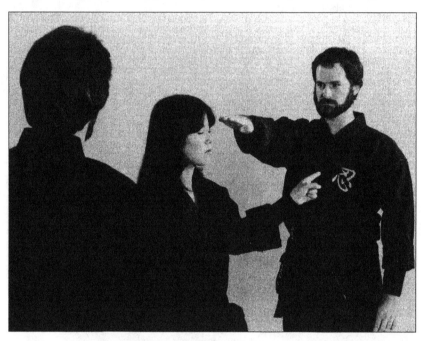

STEP THREE

Receiver

When you feel the presence of the controller's fingertips, lift your left hand into position in front of your chest. Use your thumb or first finger to point in the direction from which you perceive the presence of the controller's fingertips. Maintain your relaxed standing position, and keep your eyes closed as you raise your hand and point as a signal to the controllers.

Controller

As you see the receiver's left hand move up into a pointing position, immediately freeze your action and maintain the distance between your fingers and the receiver's head.

STEP FOUR

Receiver

Slowly open your eyes and check the position of the active controller's hand.

Like in Exercise Two, all four steps of this exercise should be performed at a leisurely pace, avoiding any undue haste or feeling that things should be sped up. The controllers should vary their timing and selection sequence in order to prevent setting up a predictable cycle. Just like the previous exercise, there is no sense of competition on the part of the controllers or receiver. The mind must be kept relaxed and open, and no sense of threat or pressures should interfere with these first steps toward confidence.

EXERCISE FOUR
Feeling Intentions

The fourth exercise is a beginning step for developing skill in detecting the intentions of others. The practice method involves two training partners—a receiver who will experience the feeling of the other's intention and a controller who will determine from which direction or which side of the body the intention is felt. Exercise Four is an important elementary technique for building up familiarity with subtle sensations of nonverbal communication.

STEP ONE
Receiver

Once again, assume a relaxed, natural stance in the middle of an open area or large room where there are as few distractions as possible. Allow your hands to hang loosely at your sides, and let your shoulders relax into their normal position. Take your time and become totally relaxed, breathing naturally by moving the air lightly in and out of the upper portions of your lungs.

Controller

Position yourself directly in front of the receiver, about one meter away. Raise both hands to a position next to your ears, above and slightly outside the boundaries of your shoulders. In this position, your head and upheld arms should resemble the letter W when you are viewed from the front or back. Allow your hands to be open and palms forward with the fingers slightly curled inward, which is their normal relaxed state. Your eyes are aimed forward, focusing on the receiver's collar area at the base of his or her neck. There should be absolutely no tension in your arms or shoulders.

STEP TWO
Receiver

Allow your vision to rest on the controller's face. Do not stare into his or her eyes or concentrate at all. Relax and observe with a soft focus that takes in the whole picture.

Controller

Without making any physical movements at all, mentally choose one side of your body with which you will step forward and seize the receiver's collar or jacket lapel. While standing perfectly still, mentally visualize yourself stepping out and grabbing the receiver with the hand you have selected. Take your time and create a strong mental impression of your intention. Imagine that you can feel an invisible energy current as it flows through the spine, shoulder and hip, and arm and leg of the side you will move forward. Do all this in your mind and nervous system, and make no moves at all with your bones and muscles.

STEP THREE
Receiver

Maintain your soft visual focus and allow the subconscious or subjective levels of your mind to pick up an impression of the controller's intentions. You may pick up a strong feeling or nothing more than a subtle hunch as to which side he or she will move. It may take only a split second for you to know which hand and foot will come at you. You will move the opposite side of your body away from the side the controller advances.

Controller

Physically carry out your visualized intention by stepping forward and grabbing the receiver's collar or lapel with the side you have chosen (right foot and hand to the receiver's left lapel; left foot and hand to the right lapel). Move with about the same speed you would use when stepping forward and gripping a door handle. Do not fly out at the receiver in surprise, and do not creep out in slow motion. Continue the mental strength of your intention while you carry out the physical moves.

STEP FOUR

Receiver

As the controller moves forward toward you, step back and to the inside of his or her grasp, pulling your body out of reach. Move your hips first, and keep your body in an upright posture as you assume the ichimonji defensive pose. Do not lean back or try to wriggle away from the grab. If the controller comes forward with the right foot and hand, you step back and to your right with your right foot. You also may need to drag your left foot back slightly to clear the controller's reach. If he or she advances with the left side, you slip back and to your left with your left side.

Do not race or jerk your body back. Your backward step should time out perfectly with the controller's forward step to keep you at a safe distance if you were successful in picking up the intentions as he or she moved.

After each performance of the exercise, the receiver and controller should exchange roles, allowing a few seconds between each exercise in which to settle the mind and focus the consciousness. The time intervals between the beginning of the exercise and the point at which the controller physically moves should be varied, as should the right and left side, so as to avoid setting up a predictable cycle.

As with the other exercises in this section, this is not to be treated as a competitive clash between the two training partners. It is a developmental training method in which both students assist each other in strengthening their own capabilities. The controller is always concentrating his or her attention on properly directing the feelings of the intentions. At the same time, the receiver is concentrating his or her attention on properly carrying out the exercise in order to learn to recognize and respond to actual stimuli from others. The purpose of the exercise is to actually pick up the intention, not merely to guess correctly which side will advance.

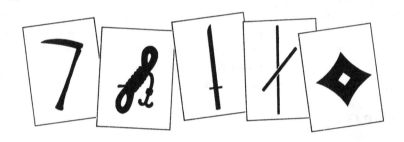

EXERCISE FIVE
Thought Projection I

The fifth exercise is a means of developing skill in projecting thoughts to others and picking up the thoughts of others. The practice method requires a set of 25 easily prepared symbol cards, and it involves two or more training partners—a receiver who will detect the thoughts and one or more controllers who will project the thoughts. The fifth exercise is easy to carry out, and it does not involve any overt physical activity. Like the other exercises in this chapter, this procedure should be enjoyed and carried out with a relaxed attitude and not worked at or analyzed. Have fun with it, and do not take it too seriously.

The symbol cards can be drawn on one sheet of paper from the patterns and then duplicated on a copier to obtain five sheets. The paper can then be glued on cardboard stock and cut into card shape, giving you five swords, five throwing stars, five fighting canes, five climbing ropes and five sickles, for a total of 25 symbol cards. The cards should show the picture symbol only, and they should have no written words or other symbols on the face.

STEP ONE
Receiver

Sit on the ground or in a chair in the middle of an open area or comfortable room in which there are as few sensual distractions as possible. You should have a pad of plain paper and a pencil or pen in front of you. Relax into a comfortable sitting position and be aware of the breath passing in and out through your nose, concentrating your attention in the upper portions of your nasal passages.

Controllers

Sit on the ground or in chairs behind the receiver, at least two arm-lengths away. You should have the shuffled deck of 25 symbol cards facedown in front of you, containing five copies of each of the five symbols. Position yourselves so that all controllers can see the symbol cards, and relax into a comfortable seated pose that will not distract your attention.

STEP TWO
Controllers

Pick up the first card on the deck and place it back on the deck faceup. Concentrate your gaze on the exposed card, limiting your consciousness to the visual sense alone. See the design and "feel" it with your eyes. Do not mentally verbalize a word for the object pictured.

Quietly say the word "card," just loud enough to be heard by the receiver, and continue to concentrate totally on the symbol.

STEP THREE
Receiver

Relax and allow your eyes to close lightly. With your eyelids lowered, look upward, as if you're viewing an imaginary black screen between your eyes. Allow the image of one of the five symbols to materialize on the black screen. The effect may take several seconds to produce or may appear instantly, and the symbol itself may appear clearly or may be nothing more than a hunch or abstract impression. There is no single proper method valid for all people. Each individual will develop his or her own special way of recognizing the subtle impression as it is received. Once you have an impression, sketch it on the paper in front of you and number it with the figure 1. Increase this number by one with each subsequent round of the exercise.

Quietly say the word "next," just loud enough to be heard by the controllers, and redirect your concentration to the feel of the breath through your upper nasal passages.

STEP FOUR
Controllers
Take the card from the top of the deck and place it faceup in the bottom position of the deck and forget about it. Pick up the new top card and place it back on the deck faceup. Concentrate your attention on the exposed card, and continue through steps two, three and four repeatedly until you have gone through all 25 cards with the receiver recording his or her impressions for each card exposed. The original card will appear faceup in the deck to indicate that the full cycle has been completed.

To score the exercise, the controllers and receiver go through the deck together, comparing each card as it appears with its sequential position in the numbered list of drawings made by the receiver. Five correct matches out of 25, or 20 percent, reflects the natural one-out-of-five odds in the system. Any number of correct matches beyond five could indicate actual skill at picking up the thought impressions of others. Multiply the number of correct impressions by four to determine the percentage, and keep a continuous record of results for each person.

EXERCISE SIX
Thought Projection II

The sixth exercise is a somewhat more advanced training experience for the purpose of developing skill in projecting thoughts to others and in picking up the thoughts of others. The exercise involves two or more training participants—a receiver who will detect and carry out mentally visualized instructions and one or more controllers who will devise and project mental commands for action. Though the sixth exercise can be carried out with a single receiver and controller, it is usually more effective and easier to produce successful results if one receiver works with a large group of controllers simultaneously visualizing the same instruction.

STEP ONE
Receiver

In a quiet room or corridor apart from the controllers, stand in a relaxed shizen no kamae natural posture, or move about with slow, undeliberate, natural movements. Keep your mind unfocused and quieted. Without concentrating or forcefully searching for thoughts, allow your consciousness to pick up any impressions that seem to appear in your mind.

Controllers

In a quiet room where there are many small movable objects, such as a normal home living room with a television, stereo, wall-hung pictures, and random articles on tables or shelves, select among yourselves an object and a simple action involving that object. It might be opening a window, turning off a light or stacking certain books. Once you have agreed on a common set of instructions, silently visualize the receiver carrying out the action. With your eyes shaded to reduce the possibility of distraction, imagine that you are watching the receiver stepping through each detail of the imagined command. Do not use words or verbalized thoughts; simply "see" the receiver carrying out the action.

After sufficient time for the group to agree on and visualize a command in detail at least three times, a previously appointed controller should step out of the room to notify the waiting receiver that the exercise has begun.

STEP TWO
Receiver

Enter the room and follow any hunches or mental impressions that have appeared in your consciousness. Move to the area of the room where you feel the controllers' instructions take you.

Controllers

Without verbalizing, continue to replay in your mind the scene of the receiver acting out your imagined instructions.

STEP THREE
Controllers

Use the sound of hand clapping to assist the receiver in carrying out your wishes. As the receiver nears that section of the room where the target object lies, use light hand clapping to indicate that he or she is following your thoughts. Use loud hand clapping when the receiver has touched the target object and loud, rapid clapping when he or she seems to discover and carry out the explicit action instructions. Stop clapping if the receiver leaves the target area or performs an action other than the target response.

Receiver

Continue to move about the room approaching objects under the guidance of your feelings and the controllers' applause.

STEP FOUR
Controllers

Verbally inform the receiver that the exercise has been completed once he or she has carried out the specific intended action.

CHAPTER 7

The ninja gains his perspective
    by expanding his perceptions
    to see that everything is change
    and reality is temporary.
Approaching falsehood
    as though it were truth
    and truth
    as though it were falsehood
    the ninja finds no surprises.
There are times when strength
    is really a weakness
    laughter is power
    in is yo
    and innocence is wisdom.

THE ART OF UNDERSTANDING

Seeing others through knowledge of the self

One of the highest goals in ninjutsu training is the cultivation of the ability to move through all moments of living guided by personal, natural "knowing." Seeing through the clouds of deception in life situations, whether imposed by self or others, is a matter of clarifying our perception by removing the cultural and emotional barriers that we have permitted to grow up as blinders around us.

A working familiarity with the concept of *in* and *yo* balancing, referred to in Chapter 1, is one direction from which we can approach the elimination of our limiting blinders. More commonly referred to as *yin* and *yang* in the popular media, this system of perception has encountered a widespread acceptance in recent decades. Unfortunately, like so many other abstract concepts that have been imported from the East and subsequently Westernized, the *in-yo* understanding has undergone substantial adjustments to allow it to fit with conventional Western beliefs. The system somehow seems to have been simplified and abridged to the point that it is a convenient analogy for explaining the supposed absolute opposites in the universe, the progression of all things and situations into something different, and the inevitability of good and bad reversing themselves. As handed down intact by generations of ninja, however, the concept has far more significance than a mere exotic label for the phenomenon of relativity.

It is taught that in the beginning, or actually before the beginning, there existed only a vast potential as a single thought or germinating cause. This concept is accepted by wide-ranging belief systems, from Hinduism to "the way" of sage Lao Tzu's Taoism to "the Word" of God in Christianity and Judaism. Though we can attempt to imagine what this original, total, all-inclusive formless existence was like, it is virtually impossible in reality for humans in our present state of evolution to conceive of such limitless vastness. We cannot overcome the fact that we are observers outside of, and looking at, the concept of the all-inclusive totality.

From this first stage of single totality, or *tai kyoku,* emerged the existence of fundamental polarities. Lao Tzu writes of the oneness of the Tao becoming the duality of yin and yang *(in* and *yo* in the Japanese language), and the Bible states that God created the heavens and the earth, or the first polarity. Regardless of the symbols used to describe the phenomenon, this polarity is nothing solid or concrete but rather the potential individualization of all things in the universe. In essence, this fundamental polarity is the sexual concept of male and female on a cosmic scale.

In is the darkness, femaleness, the quality of "going to," or negative polarity. In this sense, the word negative does not have a disparaging or condemning meaning; it is used to indicate that which draws, attracts and stores, as in a negative electrical charge or (-) magnetic pole.

Yo is the light, maleness, the quality of "going from," or positive polarity. These two qualities are said to have existed originally as potentialities alone. They became the fundamental separation of the oneness of the universe, which then permitted the further progression of pure energy into matter. The one became the two, and the two then became the essence of electrical energy charges, which eventually permitted the formation of electrons and subsequent atomic structure.

Using In and Yo as Tactics

In past generations, ninja warriors developed a working knowledge of the *in-yo* concept as a strategy for bringing about desired results. Because all things emanated from a common universal source and developed into countless infinite possible relationships with each other, it is a matter of carefully repositioning our awareness in order to create alternate arrangements of the elements in any situation. The elements continue to exist, and their relationship is merely adjusted. The ways of *ten-chi-jin* provide three different methods of approaching this altering process.

The principles of heaven, or *ten,* provide the means for the ninja to alter his relationship with his environment by causing his surroundings to change. The *in* and *yo* balance is shifted so that the ninja remains the same and the elements of the surrounding situation must change. By causing a more *yo* condition in his surroundings, the ninja increases the vulnerability of his enemy. The ninja makes his adversary want to fight even though he is unprepared. He causes the enemy to move when actually he wants to rest, and he causes the enemy to abandon advantageous positions. By causing a more *in* condition in his surroundings, the ninja decreases the threatening nature of his enemy. The ninja makes his adversaries wait when they are anxious to fight. He causes them to lose confidence in their knowledge and crowds them into narrow rooms or passages where they cannot take advantage of their superior numbers.

Combining awareness of the five levels of personality as revealed in the elemental manifestations with the conscious control of the thought processes, and the intuitive reception and acknowledgment of subtle vibrations from the surroundings, the historical ninja developed the skill of directing the personality and thoughts of others. This knowledge is one of the factual bases for the ninja's legendary ability to work his will without actions and achieve his goals without effort.

In broad terms, the direction of another's consciousness can employ either a positive or negative application, depending on the purpose at hand and the receptiveness of the individual to be influenced. Some adversaries will consistently exhibit a particular style of behavior and epitomize one of the five elemental manifestations of personality. Others may fluctuate between personality traits as they are influenced by their environment, but they do have certain characteristic modes of behavior in which they are said to be "in their element." Through extensive self-evaluation exercises, the ninja builds the heightened intuitive sensitivity necessary for reading the lifestyle and personality of the target to be swayed. The successful utilization of ninjutsu's interaction with the five character styles is a product of the ninja's ability to know his adversary's most appropriate strength or weakness, to which a corrupting influence may be applied.

In psychological confrontations, using the earth influence, the adversary's resistance and fighting spirit are weakened by supplying him with enjoyable diversions. Under the water influence, the enemy's anger is prompted to lead him into vulnerability through rash and unthinking behavior. From the fire level of influence, the ninja creates fear and hesitancy in his enemy. Under the wind influence, the adversary is weakened by appealing to his sentimentality or softheartedness. Under the influence of the "emptiness," the ambitious or vain adversary is deceived by flattery and false loyalty.

This system of influences that manipulates an adversary's thought patterns is recognized as being a mere temporary interference in the playing out of long-range objectives. Whether influencing another individual for the sake of defeating him or for the positive purpose of gaining his cooperation, the results of the behavior alteration are, at best, temporary. Just like a boxer's feint loses its shock value after too many applications, the effectiveness of the personality tricks can wear off if an adversary becomes desensitized to their impact. Even positive manipulation of another's personality will take its toll on the ninja's mental qualities if they are carried out too long. Unceasing flattery of another's distended ego, or the continued soothing of the volatile temper of an irrational individual, will begin to affect the energy balance of even the strongest of determined ninja.

The principles of earth, or chi, provide an alternate way for the ninja to alter his relationship with his environment. The *in* and *yo* balance is shifted so that the ninja changes and the elements of the surrounding situation remain the same. By assuming a more *yo* role, the ninja creates a favorable environment by increasing his leverage in a situation. When confronted by a powerful enemy, the ninja increases his own power to a level that surpasses his enemy's. When the adversary knows more, the ninja increases his knowledge in order to compensate. When outnumbered, the ninja increases his numbers. By assuming a more *in* role, the ninja creates a favorable environment by decreasing his vulnerability in a situation. When pursued by a furious enemy, the ninja drops back to a position behind his enemy. When his secret identity is uncovered, the ninja makes himself valuable to the enemy. When caught in a flood, he swims with the current.

Instead of directly affecting the personality or behavior of his enemy, the ninja can alter his own approach to any given situation. By expanding his perception in order to become aware of all the possible behavior and reaction mode choices that exist, the ninja can open up new insights into alternate outcomes for the situation being faced. In this manner, ninjutsu's chi grounding process provides a method for predicting the most likely future thoughts and actions of an adversary. By blending a working knowledge of the five personality styles, observation and recollection of personal reaction patterns, and intuitive sensing of unique case probabilities, the ninja can develop a predictable scheme of events and then fit the likely occurrences with his own plans of action as appropriate for the desired results.

Inherent in this method of dealing with survival is the need to examine objectively the situation composed by our adversary and us. We must avoid reading any values into his or our respective positions; instead, we must observe our tactical relationship. When self-preservation is involved, there is a tendency to allow fear to assign nonexistent advantages to the enemy facing us.

If our adversary awaits us in a darkened house, we may see him as having the advantage of being able to watch us without being observed, and thereby able to set up his attack. He seems to be in a fortress and we feel exposed. If an attacker confronts us with a knife, we may panic at the recognition of the fact that his weapon is an overwhelming advantage. If we are unfamiliar with knife-fighting techniques, we may unthinkingly resign ourselves to being helpless. If we face an assailant who is huge in size, we may be totally intimidated by our comparative smallness. We may figure that one punch is all it would take to put us away.

Shifting viewpoints, however, can bring a completely altered perspective. By imagining ourselves to be in the place of our adversary and then looking at all the weaknesses presented by the new outlook, we can use the tendency to see the negative to our own advantage. To see the other man's vulnerability, we put ourselves in his place.

As the killer concealed in the darkened house, we realize that we are trapped in there and that tricks could force us out of our hiding place or that we could simply be outwaited. As the knife fighter, we realize that our weapon causes our opponent to be extra-alert, that it gives him a moral license to go to any extreme to defend himself. There is also a tendency to concentrate all the attention on the weapon and forget the vulnerability or practical use of the other arm and legs. As the larger fighter, we realize how easy it is for a smaller opponent to move quickly and get inside our guard. We also can see how a small man can use his lower center of gravity to unbalance or throw us.

The principles of mankind, or *jin*, provide the means for the ninja to leave the situation exactly as it is and create the impression of alternate realities through the use of illusion and the limited vision of others. The *in* and *yo* balance is stretched into exaggerated proportions so that the true relativity of the elements is obscured beyond recognition.

The major factor separating the methods of ninjutsu from ordinary fistfighting, everyday psychology or conventional military action is the application of *kyojitsu ten kan ho,* or deception strategy. Literally translated as "the method of juxtaposing falsehood and truth," this strategy is applied to all the ninja's activities. This reliance on misrepresenting the balancing elements of *in* and *yo* makes use of the psychology of preparing an adversary to think in one manner and then approaching him in another.

The tactic can be applied from varying extremes to confuse the adversary's perception of reality. Falsehood can be presented as truth. We can create the impression of strength in areas where we are, in reality, weak, or we can create the image of weakness to conceal our strengths. In the opposite sense, reality can be presented in such a way as to create the impression of falsehood. We can exaggerate our weaknesses to the point that adversaries think they are being deceived and then they hesitate to take action against us. We also can boldly present our strengths so that our enemies think we are bluffing, so they charge into our superior capabilities without sufficient strength or preparation.

Simple examples of the deception strategy as applied in the jin logical approach can be seen in unarmed fighting. Watch yourself in a mirror to see how your body looks as you prepare for and deliver a high punch. When working with a training partner later, drop your shoulder at the moment it becomes obvious that you are punching high and punch to your opponent's ribs or stomach. The punch is not initiated, stopped and restarted at a lower level. It is merely a low punch thrown with the body dynamics usually associated with a high punch.

In a close-in clash in which fists have turned into grappling hands, grab and pull your adversary toward you. He will probably instinctively try to pull away. As you feel his pull, change your motion to a push while stepping behind his foot and throw him to the ground.

As you initiate an attacking counter-defense, wind up and start a punch at your adversary's face. When he brings his forearm up to block, open your fist and apply a bone-breaking open-hand strike to the target his forearm presents.

Examples of the confusion tactics also can be seen in blade fighting. As you slash at your attacker's head with a sword or long knife, and he attempts to block with a blade or metal bar, pull in suddenly with your arms, shortening your reach, and let the tip of your blade catch his forearm or hand.

A blade or stabbing weapon also could be concealed behind the arm by gripping the handle in an underhand manner with the blade extending up behind the back of the elbow.

In an actual self-defense confrontation against a blade-wielding assailant, you can assume a fighting position that suggests you are unskilled at self-protection with a knife. When your attacker relaxes his guard in front of the "inept victim," you can launch into him with your true capabilities.

Historically, the juxtaposing of falsehood and reality was often used by Japanese ninja in escape tactics. A ninja might throw a heavy stone into a moat or a river and then hide in nearby foliage to trick those seeking him into searching the ripples of the water. A ninja might rush up to a group of castle guards with a frenzied tale of some calamity behind him. As the guards rush off, the ninja could slip through the gate to go and "warn" other guards while making his escape instead.

The pretense of innocence, or the appearance of being off-guard or not suspecting, is also a way of using the deception strategy. Traitors within an organization might be allowed to remain, and they might be supplied with false information to confuse the enemy. The appearance of a castle or camp unprepared for war could be a trap to lure the enemy into attacking against superior numbers. Perhaps the most universal and fundamental application of this innocent deception was the anonymity of the historical ninja. The ninja had a cover occupation and family, and if he were successful, no one ever learned that he was in truth a ninja agent.

In its truest form, the way of ninjutsu is the way of *in shin tonkei,* which can be paraphrased as the contemporary "accomplishing the most with the least amount of effort," or winning and obtaining the desired results while interfering with the natural order of things in the smallest degree possible. A general characteristic of ninjutsu is the tendency to rely on *in*, or negative and dark, escapes and battle plans when dealing with adversity or opposition. Whenever presented with a choice between a battle or subterfuge, the ninja relies on the more passive deceptive strategy. When choosing between conquering an adversary's will or guiding his thinking, the ninja prefers to assist the adversary in wanting to see things the ninja's way. Unhindered by rigid codes of honor that could force other men into suicidal actions despite their own better judgment, the ninja is free to employ his common sense in order to accomplish his objectives while eliminating personal danger. For the unenlightened observer, this method often creates the impression that the ninja has given up his ideals or surrendered while his true intentions and the actual desired prize are kept well-concealed or disguised. By relying more on the *in* approach, the ninja reduces the discernability of his influence on the situation, and thereby reduces his vulnerability at the hands of those who would retaliate or hold him responsible for unforeseen occurrences. The ninja's motto of "no name and no art" works to prevent him from unknowingly making a target out of himself, and it keeps him out of the sights of those who would not wish him well.

The ninja's *in* approach to living, which followed the ways of nature, was in dramatic contrast to the bold *yo* philosophies of the samurai warrior class. The way of the samurai was said to be the way of death, and the true samurai structured his life in preparation for the moment of his death. To die in fierce combat in service to his lord was said to be the ultimate purpose or achievement of the samurai life, and an exquisite death was the desired prize. The social order, the proprieties, a strong sense of justice and moral right, complete dedication to a ruler, and the almost stylized refinement of the emotions characterized the height of the samurai nobility.

The ninja was looked down on with contempt and disgust by the samurai, and, indeed, the ninja's responsive, naturalistic in shin tonkei outlook appears to be a disordered, prideless, rowdy and perhaps even cowardly life when compared to the structured dignity of the samurai. The historical ninja was only as loyal as the moment demanded, fighting for the rulers of the day who condoned the ninja's life ideals. The ninja observed no social structure or priorities and, except for belonging to a loosely formed clan, likely possessed no family name in the community whatsoever. Guided by their mystical philosophies of the balancing *in* and *yo* interaction among the elements of nature, the ninja acknowledged no absolute concept of justice, fairness or morality, and they held in their hearts the knowledge that the vast universe would continue to unfold with the beauty of impersonal totality that knows no right or wrong.

The samurai was guided by external considerations. The method or form used to accomplish something often became more important than the final outcome itself. This philosophy dictated that the way one appears is the only reality, and that one concentrates on the details of speech and action in order to develop the heart and spirit. If one appears foolish, one is foolish. If one appears weak, then one certainly is weak. If one appears to be an immoral coward, then one is an immoral coward. This tradition of bold *yo* manliness is reflected today in the training of many of the contemporary Asian martial arts. Unlike ninjutsu, power is worshiped in these martial arts, loyalty is rewarded, discipline is expected and dynamic action is seen to be the only key to handling any crisis.

The martial art of ninjutsu does have its strong *yo* elements. However, the system also includes a wide-ranging scope of alternate *in* approaches to life's conflicts. Internal considerations shape external reality from the heart and spirit, and life becomes a reflection of our beliefs. The results outweigh the means in the final analysis. The truth is held in the heart, the personality sees with more than the eyes alone, and the external elements become our tools, or toys, for use in the fulfillment of our soul's intentions.

The world continues to spin into days and nights, winters and springs, and we can accept, understand and relish the experience or dissipate ourselves by resisting and demanding that the universe conform to the small-scale ignorance of some rigid creed or list of beliefs. This is the ultimate joyous lesson to be learned, the total freedom that formed the ninja shadow warrior's code of life, and expanded into the tenets of the philosophy of ninjutsu—the way of winning naturally through the art of understanding.

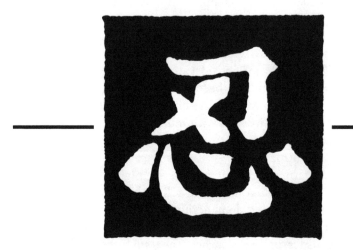

PART 2

Warrior Ways of Enlightenment

CHAPTER 8

Ninjutsu skills
*   in which we train*
*   would best be known as the art of winning.*
We will assist the sincere
*   with our ability to win with the spirit.*
Their dreams become the force of our vision
*   which becomes a vibrant intention*
*   taking shape in the mind*
*   and weaving into the fabric of reality.*

SPIRITUAL PURITY

Ninja morality in history

"**A**ttaining the core essence of the ninja art begins with the paring away of unessentials to reach a base state of personal spiritual purity and culminates in the ability to move freely without defilement between the polar realms of brightness and darkness, as necessitated by the scheme of totality."

According to the observations of Yasuyoshi Fujibayashi, this is what it means to be a ninja. In *Bansenshukai*, his 17th-century encyclopedia of *ninjutsu*, Fujibayashi noted that the ultimate purpose of the ninja's art lies not in the mere perfection of violent and destructive methods but in the cultivation of personal harmony with the surroundings and an intuitive sensitivity that permits the living mortal human to know and go along with the scheme of totality that flows through the universe.

Despite the emphasis on spiritual purity, the historical Japanese martial community has never really accepted the ninja art as one of the *do* disciplines, those Zen-like practices said to be a means of pursuing enlightenment. During the peaceful centuries that followed the Tokugawa family's unification of Japan, the once warlike samurai technique systems such as *kenjutsu* (sword combat), *jujutsu* (unarmed combat), *kyujutsu* (archery), *jojutsu* (staff fighting), *iaijutsu* (fast-draw sword) and others were systematized, stylized and refined to become cultural exercises like *kendo*, judo, *kyudo*, *jodo* and *iaido*. This ritualization of a previously personalized and spontaneous activity is fairly typical of the Japanese way of doing things. Because the ways of war were no longer required and, in fact, were not encouraged at all by the Tokugawa rulers, the physical aspects of combat that were so familiar to all were simply adjusted slightly and given a new purpose for continuation.

This ritualization process had its roots in previous centuries of Japanese cultural history when the learning of the *Gokyo* Five Classics of Chinese literature was a requirement for attaining the status of a government officer in pre-Heian Japan, just like it had been in China. Though the repeated exposure to the Chinese classics had little direct relevance to the daily activities and decisions required of the ancient Japanese ruling class, it was probably believed that the learning process itself was the purpose of the study. This attitude was later carried over to the ways of *sado* (ceremonial preparation of green tea) and *kado* (recitation of poetry, as well as the art of arranging flowers). Beyond this, the *do* concept came to include the *shudo* art of the written character and the numerous ways of the martial tradition.

The ninja's art is conspicuously absent from the list of *do* disciplines because the ninja existed as cultural opposites of the samurai who generated the *do* concept. The secrets of the ninja art were known by only a few families who were then referred to as Iga-mono and Koga-mono, depending on which of the two remote regions they inhabited. They were not usually given the samurai title of *bushi*. For this reason, the knowledge was not well-known to samurai society. The physical aspects of the ninja's art were pragmatic applications and, because of that very pragmatism and lack of formality, did not lend themselves well to the stylization necessary for the transformation to a *do* art.

According to Iga Ryu ninja Fujibayashi, as well as later authorities such as Koga Ryu ninja Seiko Fujita and Togakure Ryu ninja Shinryuken Masamitsu Toda, the art of the true ninja is much more than the mere technique system than the word "ninjutsu" would imply. Because the ninja art is not of samurai origin, thereby making *nindo* a cultural impossibility, and because the practitioner of the ninja art is expected to approach personal enlightenment *before* learning the combat techniques, the more advanced ninja of later Japanese history (following the founding of the Tokugawa shogunate in 1603) have preferred to call their art *nin-po,* or "the law of the *shinobi* (ninja) realm."

The Bansenshukai

Fujibayashi's *Bansenshukai,* literally translated as "Ten Thousand Rivers Collect in the Sea," is a collection of knowledge and commentaries on attitude from dozens of ninja family systems that thrived in the Iga and Koga regions of south central Japan. Historical authorities characterize the writings as extremely systematic and logical, both in the scope of knowledge contained and the thorough way in which the topics are itemized. Fujibayashi compiled the original work in the summer of 1676, during the reign of the fourth Tokugawa shogun. He was a member of one of the three most influential Iga ninja families, the Hattori and Momochi families being the other two in prominence at the close of the *Sengoku Jidai* (Warring States Period).

The first of the 10 hand-bound volumes contains an introduction, historical examples, an index of the contents and a question-and-answer section. The guiding philosophy of the ninja is presented, in this first volume titled *Jo,* as a discussion of successful warfare. The ninja is admonished to remember that when a leader truly guides the minds of his followers, even great numbers of adversaries can be overcome. When a leader or commander's followers are not in alignment with his thoughts, failure and loss will surely result. One spy or counteracting agent can bring the downfall of an entire army. Therefore, the ninja believes that one person can defeat thousands. The *Bansenshukai* stresses that ninjutsu is the most effective method of military strategy.

The second volume is titled *Shoshin,* and it discusses the sincerity, motivation and moral strength of intention necessary for the ninja. Because the skills of the ninja's art admittedly include methods that some individuals would call treachery, deception, theft and fraud—not to mention incredibly thorough violence—a strong statement of purpose and outlook is presented before going into techniques. In previous centuries, just like today, the majority of people seemed to believe that any thug, mercenary or terrorist dressed in a black costume and hood could be called a ninja. Some may point out that the techniques and practices seem to appear similar in nature, but the true ninja is set apart by his motivation, purpose and scope of vision. The mere terrorist or mercenary is limited by a narrow frame of reference and a restricted concept of the total picture, of which his actions, reactions and thoughts make up an influencing part. The true ninja is prompted to act through a personal realization of responsibility recognizable only through an intuitive knowledge that destiny has demanded his taking part. The first step in the ninja's education, whether the process is called ninjutsu or nin-po, is to clear up any mental or spiritual cloudiness that would interfere with the ninja's natural sense of knowing.

Even the most skilled of ninja is useless without the guidance and direction of an effective leader. The third book, *Shochi,* covers the methods of managing a ninja organization and ways of successfully using ninja. This third volume also describes considerations for preventing enemy agents from working into the ninja leader's own clandestine organization.

A working knowledge of *in* and *yo* (yin and *yang* in the Chinese language) balancing is crucial for true knowledge of the ninja art. *Yo-nin,* the fourth of the 10 volumes, deals with the *yo,* or bright side of the ninja's power. Using the dynamic and positive power of the intellect and creative thinking, the ninja can obtain the intelligence information he needs without becoming physically involved in the spying activity himself. By directly or indirectly employing others to gain his knowledge for him, the ninja knows all the necessary facts for an effective military decision. By learning the enemy's strengths and weaknesses, the ninja knows how to handle the enemy successfully while maintaining the appearance of having done nothing or of having taken no action.

The methods of knowing the enemy's intentions without taking active part in combat action include the following:

- *Tonyu hen:* for continuous observation through agents placed during peaceful times

- *Kinnyu hen:* for location of agents after war breaks out

- *Mekiki hen:* for observation of the geographical layout of the enemy's territory

- *Miwake hen:* for observation of enemy force numbers and capabilities, along with other details of enemy strength

- *Kanmi hen:* for observation of the enemy's strategy and positioning

The fifth, sixth and seventh volumes of the *Bansenshukai*, all titled *In-nin*, deal with the *in* or dark side of the ninja's power. Using stealth, deception, confusion tactics and terrifying surprise attacks, the ninja could bring the enemy under his control. Employing methods that the conventional samurai of the time considered to be dishonorable, contemptible and even cowardly, the ninja were free to rely on disguises, night fighting, sneaking in, capturing enemy leaders and cultivating key enemy personnel for betrayal in order to accomplish their aims. Volumes five, six and seven contain these unique methods of the ninja combat system, from individual clashes to group hit-and-scatter plans.

Ninjutsu techniques are most often presented in cryptic or poetic wordings to prevent the uninitiated from learning the secrets. For example, in one passage, the ninja is reminded of the effectiveness of *murasame no jutsu* (art of the rain in the village) in certain specific situations. The actual technique itself is not explained. Combat moves such as *onikudaki* (demon crusher) appear perplexing in their poetic form. The blunt rendering of the name as "inward uplifting elbow leverage to dislocate the shoulder of the attacker" was apparently thought to be too direct for the written record.

The methods of darkness listed in the *Bansenshukai* are actually coded words and jargon in catalog form to serve as reminders only for qualified members of the ninja family. The words and symbols are intentionally so obscure that only by studying with a legitimate teacher can the student come to know the true meaning of the technique descriptions.

Tenji, the eighth volume, covers the ninja's methods for interpreting and evaluating conditions in the environment. This body of knowledge includes weather forecasting, tide tables, moon phases, and the determination of direction and location by observing the stars. This volume has its basis in generations of experience with systems such as *gogyo setsu* (theory of the five elements), *in-yo do* (Taoist principles) and *ekkyo* divination (the *I Ching,* or *Book of Changes),* derived from scientific observation and folklore, as well as Indian and Chinese systems of predicting future trends and happenings.

Ninki, a description of ninja gear, begins in volume nine and continues on into the 10th volume, which is labeled the "tail volume" rather than volume No. 10. This is perhaps in keeping with ninjutsu's reliance on the No. 9 as a means of inspiration. The final volume could then be referred to as an additional text so that the *Bansenshukai* could be said to consist of nine actual volumes.

In the ninth volume, the description of *toki* covers the climbing gear of ninjutsu, and it includes a wide variety of equipment that was used to get ninja safely up and down castle walls, trees, cliffs and sides of ships. . *Suiki,* based largely on the practical advice from pirates, covers the water gear of ninjutsu. The equipment described provides numerous methods for crossing over or moving under bodies of water. The ninja's *kaiki* is a collection of tools designed for the purpose of breaking into locked or fortified buildings, castles and storage areas. Pieces of equipment for picking locks, boring through walls and moving doors are described.

In a manner similar to that used in the description of volume five, six and seven's combat techniques, the ninja equipment in volume nine is presented with physical dimensions and specifications only. No attempt is made to coach the uninitiated in the proper use of the gear. The *Bansenshukai's* wooden foot gear referred to as *mizugumo* (water spiders) in Andrew Adams' *Ninja: The Invisible Assassins,* for example, are often laughed at for being totally impractical as a means of crossing over the surface of water. What contemporary scoffers do not realize, however, is the fact that the mizugumo were not used to walk across ponds and lakes at all. The foot gear was used to move steadily with a skating action over swampy, marshy areas, flattening out grasses and distributing the ninja's bodyweight over a broad area of mud, shallow water and plants, much like snowshoes are used to cross safely over deep drifted snow.

Kaki, referred to as "fire gear," completes the final portion of the *Bansenshukai.* The formulas explained in this tail volume cover the preparation and use of explosives, smoke bombs, medicines, sleeping potions and poisons. The explicit directions are written in the regional dialect of 17th-century Iga-area Japanese, however, which makes translating a slow and difficult job even for a Japanese person who is schooled in the ancient written forms of the language. For example, local plants are referred to with nicknames of the era and area. "Bear's paw" indicates an herb and not the foot of the animal. "White horse's breath" would mean a certain blossoming plant and not the more elusive substance that the name would bring to mind.

The important underlying lessons of history are not to be recognized in the surface manifestations of techniques, strategies and weapons as described in the *Bansenshukai,* however. The real value and effectiveness of the historical weapons, battle strategies and communication networks does not lie in the perfection of skills cataloged in a 300-year-old reference book series. The lesson is the realization that effective weapons, tools and means of accomplishment are all around us in everyday articles and situations. If the goal is to be effective in today's surroundings, it will be necessary to leave the antiques in the museum and get involved in what is available today. The historical trappings are fun and remind us of our Japanese ninja heritage, but they should not be allowed to become the focus of the training.

Today, authentic Japanese Togakure Ryu ninja training is one of the most all-encompassing methods of danger prevention, self-protection and total living available for study in the world. Historical perspective and creative contemporary applications are blended in the training to provide modern practitioners with a stimulating and inspirational course of self-development that forms the basis for a progressive way of life. Students now train to master the following disciplines:

Junan taiso	Yoga-like body flexibility exercises
Taijutsu	Unarmed combat
• *Taihenjutsu*	Body movement, breakfalls, leaping
• *Dakentaijutsu*	Striking and kicking
• *Jutaijutsu*	Grappling and choking
Bojutsu	Staff fighting
Hanbojutsu	Short-stick fighting
Ninja ken-po	Fighting with the ninja sword
• *Kenjutsu*	Fencing skills
• *Iaijutsu*	Fast-drawing skills
Tantojutsu	Knife fighting
Shurikenjutsu	Blade throwing
Kusari-fundo	Weighted short-chain weapon
Kyoketsu shoge	Cord and blade weapon
Kusari-gama	Chain and sickle weapon
Teppo	Firearms
Ninki	Specialized ninja gear and tools
Fukiya	Blowguns and darts
Heiho	Combat strategy
Gotonpo	Use of natural elements for escape
In-yo do	Taoist principles
Seishin teki kyoyo	Personal clarity
• *Meso*	Meditation
• *Shinpi*	Concepts of mysticism
• *Nin-po mikkyo*	Ninja "secret knowledge" of the universe
Kuji-kiri	Projecting nine-cut power fields
Kuji-in	Nine-seal energy channeling

Contemporary practitioners of ninjutsu are by no means limited to the training aspects set forth in the foregoing list, however. Any martial art—except for a Zen-style *do* that is not at all concerned with combat applications—that insists on posting detailed lists of limitations such as "106 weapons" or "42 choking methods" is doing its students a grave disservice by conditioning their minds to think in an orderly structured manner when confronted with danger. With that kind of mechanical training background, the mind will automatically attempt to categorize any new situation by comparing it with previous training examples.

The authentic ninja art exists for the use of the practitioner, and the individual practitioner is not expected to conform to or reduce himself or herself to fit the art. For this reason, ninjutsu is not an art that is easily adapted for conventional military training. New recruits have a set period in which to learn fundamental skills that they will apply on the job. The open-ended outlook of ninjutsu, along with the art's refusal to set up limiting lists of techniques and the art's emphasis on individual second-to-second analysis of the situation as it unfolds, make it highly unsuitable for troops who will be expected to work as a unit following the commands of a remote leader. The command concept relies on unquestioning obedience; the ninja concept relies on individual intuitive sensitivity and spontaneous decision-making.

Ninjutsu has never been a soldier's art. Historically, the ninja usually found themselves opposing soldiers in combat, during which they had to use creative imagination and total commitment of intention to overcome otherwise overwhelming odds. If engaged in any military activity, the ninja's major contribution was as an adviser, a role in which he could apply his unconventional outlooks, his network of strategic contacts, his psychic sensitivities and his physical skills, if necessary, in order to balance out the limitations of conventional military thought of the time.

The historical ninja has at best been "misunderstood" by contemporary military and martial arts historians who think they are authorities on Japan's feudal era. The samurai are looked up to and praised for their unswerving, undying loyalty to the one lord they served, and their willingness to fling themselves into death unquestioningly for the sake of their lord's honor is proudly held up as some sort of example for martial artists even today. Ninja are routinely condemned with accusations of capriciously selling their loyalty to the highest bidder of the moment, and are therefore regarded with disgust as being totally devoid of honor. This type of malicious characterization is usually perpetrated by those writers and historians who wish to glorify the samurai mentality, and it does not acknowledge the over-exaggerated emphasis placed on group welfare at the expense of the individual in feudal Japanese society.

In truth, the ninja was more loyal to his own family than to any one human being. The ideal lives on while human beings change with the seasons. What had once been a benevolent and just ruler could become a cruel and greedy tyrant over the years, and the ninja, sensing the ruler's abandonment of the original ideal, would be forced thereby to give his support to other rulers who were more in alignment with the ninja family's philosophy. The samurai, on the other hand, was taught to avoid questioning the motivations of his superiors and make himself fit for combat only. This code sometimes created the situation in which the samurai knew that his lord or that lord's heir had become a madman, and yet the samurai was still morally obligated by his standards to fight to the death for any whim of the monster that his lord had become.

Certainly, history does have its tales of professional terrorists who would commit any deed for a fee while posing as a ninja. These were, however, desperate wretches who lacked the philosophical foresight and guidance of the major ninja families and are better described as thugs in black clothing than ninja. Today, contemporary terrorists, as well, sometimes enjoy claiming kinship to Japan's legendary ninja in an attempt to justify their own brutal behavior. Neither the self-righteous murderer who blows up hotel lobbies full of tourists nor the trigger-happy social misfit who hires on to train professional torturers for oppressive dictatorships come anywhere near to carrying on the ways of the ninja. Blurred by heart-twisting hatred or lust for the thrill of violence, the spiritual purity described by Fujibayashi's *Bansenshukai* becomes clouded with the personal desires that prevent people from acting in accordance with the scheme of totality.

The true ninja is moved to action through love of family and community, and a personal sense of responsibility for the positive channeling of destiny. This motivation cannot be overlooked by anyone researching or studying the art of the ninja. By willfully returning to the unencumbered state of spiritual purity that is possible only through surrendering those limiting fetters placed on the mind, dedicated practitioners of ninjutsu can come to know the truth that is enlightenment and can then venture between the brightness and darkness unscathed, protected by the universal laws realized through training in the life ways of the ninja.

CHAPTER 9

There are those misguided persons in the world
   who would see you harmed.
They will confront you with fists
   or await you in the darkness with their blades drawn.
Do not fear them
   or become angry with them.
Allow your heart to hold the emptiness of purity.
Your receptive spirit will hear the sadness and rage
   of your attackers' intentions
   and your body will flow
   with the winds of their hatred.
You will take them to the destruction they seek.

PREPARATION FOR ENCOUNTER

Ninja ways of dealing with danger

The ninja's combat art is best described as a way of successfully dealing with danger. More than mere self-defense, this ability to live with danger affects the ninja's outlook on every thing and situation he or she encounters. In most conventional martial arts that stem from samurai origins, practitioners are taught to recognize danger, confront it with training-honed skills, and either triumph over it with humility or be consumed by it with honor. The art of ninjutsu, on the other hand, offers a wider range of possibilities for dealing with potential destruction.

   First lesson: Work at setting up your life in such a manner that the enemy never thinks to appear before you. This is realized through developing the spirit.
   The most fundamental approach is to prevent danger from coming into being. Understanding yourself and then extending that understanding to others is the key to making this method work. As a life skill, this

involves cultivating the proper attitudes, foresight and sensitivity that will permit you to be consistently in the right place at the right time. The ninja method of preventing danger is not a negative or paranoid process in which you always expect the worst and constantly wait or search for it. Quite the contrary, by adopting a positive outlook based on a firm confidence in your abilities to direct your own world, you will find that you can often manipulate elements and events in your environment so far ahead of time that no one but you realizes that anything else could possibly have transpired. Vastly more far-reaching in scope than slipping over castle walls in the darkness or outfighting deadly samurai against normally overwhelming odds, the historical ninja's awesome power to guide the scheme of totality is what originally won Japan's shadow warriors their undisputed respect and fear.

Second lesson: Work at transcending your emotions so that you do not always automatically respond with a defense when a defense is not needed. This is realized through developing the mind.

When the ninja's personal power is not sufficient to prevent the dangerous situation from materializing, the second approach is to successfully endure or outlast the danger. As a life skill, this involves tempering the emotions with the intellect so that threatening situations do not necessarily produce an immediate response but are evaluated in a detached way so as to determine whether a response is really warranted.

The written Japanese character for *nin* as in ninjutsu, nin-po and ninja (the same character is also pronounced shinobi) has the literal meaning of "endurance, perseverance, or putting up with," in physical and psychological contexts. Whereas the samurai not only had to achieve his aims but also had to accomplish his goals in a more or less accepted and honorable way, the ninja was prevented from having any family house name or honor by the political structure of Japanese society and was thereby free to concentrate his energies on the attainment of his intended goal alone. For this reason, the ninja could often allow others to perceive the apparent *appearance* of the ninja's failure or humiliation, when in reality the ninja had attained exactly what he or she really wanted in the first place. By affecting the perspectives of self and others, the ninja can attain that which is needed without stirring up a desire for retribution, revenge or defensiveness in others who might provide opposition.

This willfully enduring or appearing to take no action can be more difficult than first imagined. If you are exposed to danger, there is normally a strong feeling of discomfort as long as you are in the presence of the danger. By rising up and overcoming the danger, you eliminate the threat and thereby return to a relaxed or relieved state. Conquering the danger, whatever it may have been, might not have been the most appropriate action to have taken, however, if it exposes your position and opens you up to increased danger. It is far more difficult to endure the danger without tension, to dwell impassively in the very shadow of death, taking no action that will give away your intentions, and allowing the danger to go its own way, leaving you unharmed and untouched.

Third lesson: Work at perfecting the skills for successfully handling physical violence directed against you. This is realized through developing the body.

When the ninja has not been able to guide the happenings of fate in order to prevent danger and has not been able to allow the danger to pass by without effect, actual defensive tactics will then be necessary. Physical combat methods usually come to mind first, rather than third, for many people when they think of martial arts. In actuality, however, physically coming to grips with danger is the least preferable method of returning life to harmony and naturalness, in that it involves the greatest potential risk of something going wrong.

Nonetheless, contemporary ninja training usually begins with physical lessons because a solid grounding in physical reality is a prerequisite for any valid intellectual or spiritual growth. The techniques of hand-to-hand or weapon combat can then serve as models for understanding the effects of the mind, emotions and spirit on the outcome of a conflict or confrontation.

The physical self-defense elements of ninjutsu blend a wide range of natural body weapons and combat tools into a single comprehensive total fighting art. Whether *dakentaijutsu* (striking) techniques, *bojutsu* (stick-fighting) techniques or *shurikenjutsu* (throwing-blade) techniques are being employed, the body moves with identical footwork, dynamics and energy direction. Merely replacing a fist with a short club does not alter the ninja's way of moving in the fight. Substituting a sword blade for a sweeping kick does not at all change the feeling of the ninja's technique as it unfolds.

In essence, the ninja combat method is more accurately described as a set of principles rather than a collection of techniques. Because all bodies and personalities are unique, no attempt is made to coerce the practitioners of ninjutsu into imitating or taking on one rigid standard set of movements. Instead, guidelines are provided to encourage the most effective use and application of all the natural emotional and physical reactions that occur during a conflict or confrontation.

Having its foundations in the tantric lore of northern India, *mikkyo* (secret knowledge) teaches that all physical aspects of existence originate from a common source and can be classified in one of the *go-dai* (five elemental manifestations of physical matter). *Chi,* the earth, symbolizes solid matter. *Sui,* the water, symbolizes liquids. *Ka,* the fire, is the symbol of combustion or the elements in an energy-releasing state. *Fu,* the wind, symbolizes gases. *Ku,* the void, is representative of the formless subatomic energy that is the basis for the structure of all things. This go-dai symbolism is also used to describe the emotional nature of human beings and to provide a symbolic structure for the teaching of effective physical combat principles in ninjutsu.

The go-dai five elements provide a series of symbolic codes that can be used to describe the varying ways in which we all respond to direct confrontation. The chi (earth) influence is seen in the confident stability (or stubborn narrow-mindedness) of the personality, and it is also acted out by the fighter who firmly holds his ground and overcomes attackers through unvacillating presence and strength. The sui (water) influence is seen in the strategic flexibility (or alienated distancing) of the personality, and it is also demonstrated by the fighter who uses tactical angling and footwork to overextend his attacker so he is vulnerable to an effective counterattack. The ka (fire) influence is seen in the perceptive connection (or fearful desperation) of the personality, and it is displayed by the fighter who uses direct energetic interceptions as defenses in a combat clash. Fu, the wind influence, shows up as the efficient freedom (or competitive insecurity) of the personality, and it is reflected in evasive, elusive fighting methods that slip by the attacker's movements to get to the targets. Ku, the fifth element, is the creative space (or spacey confusion) of the personality, and it shows up as absolute spontaneity and inventiveness in a fight.

The following examples help to characterize the physical, emotional, perceptual, mechanical and intellectual relationships of the five elemental manifestation code labels.

Emotional Responses

Earth	You are the junior-high-school principal confronted by a 13-year-old troublemaker who did not expect you to approach him. Your natural feeling is one of confident command that can handle all and that needs to fear nothing.
Water	You are alone on a subway at night when a huge, rough-looking thug enters your car and looks right at you with a surly leer on his face. Your natural feeling is one of tactical aloofness ready to angle away and drive back in against his vulnerable body targets.
Fire	You are confronted by the teenager who gave your young daughter such a savage beating that she was hospitalized. Your natural feeling is one of pure aggressive interception that causes you to forget any concern for yourself.
Wind	A beloved relative has had too much to drink and violently confronts you over a misunderstanding. Your natural feeling is one of compassion that provides a sufficient defense to restrain him without a retaliation counterattack.

Physical Center of Tension and Movement

Earth	Thighs and seat
Water	Lower abdomen, navel
Fire	Solar plexus
Wind	Center of chest, heart

Source of Body Dynamics

Earth	Strength
Water	Power
Fire	Energy
Wind	Resiliency

Adversary's Perception of Your Fighting Actions

Earth	Nothing affects you or hurts you. You are immoveable.
Water	You seem unreachable, and yet when reached, you are always ready with a counterattack.
Fire	You cannot be stopped. There is no chance to get anything in on you.
Wind	You are slippery, always disappearing and causing his original attack to backfire against its application.

Characteristic Body Vibration

Earth	Up and down
Water	Side to side
Fire	Forward and backward
Wind	Rotating on spinal axis

Characteristic Footwork

Earth	Feet firmly in place; immoveable
Water	Backpedaling zigzag angling away from attack
Fire	Forward-moving shuffle or run; applying pressure
Wind	Circular, sidestepping and slipping evasions

Each of the elemental manifestation codes can be seen reflected in the body postures employed in the ninja's fighting method. The postures, or *kamae*, are assumed naturally as the body goes through the realization that combative action is necessary. Each fighting posture, whether employed for unarmed defense, sword or blade fighting, stick techniques, or methods employing the chain and cord weapons, is a physical manifestation of the emotions, attitude and mental set.

For a fuller understanding of the application philosophy of ninjutsu's fighting postures, which are actually temporary bases from which to launch techniques, it is crucial to remember that the postures are never used as static poses or stances. Using the printed format of a book, it is impossible to effectively depict the vibrancy, energy and dynamism that are the very life of the ninjutsu kamae in combat. A photograph on a page gives the inaccurate impression that the posture is to be held continuously as the ninja moves about in combat. Quite the contrary, in real combat, the postures are assumed for mere seconds as they become necessary and then are just as quickly dropped when their effectiveness has passed. As a parallel, a photograph of a ninja in one of the fighting postures could be compared to a photograph of a basketball player suspended in midair as he completes a dunk. We would no more expect the basketball player to continuously hold his midair pose than we would expect the ninja to freeze into one of his combat poses. The feet continuously work to alter the ninja's distancing, angling and positioning.

EARTH ELEMENT

*Unarmed Natural Posture
(taijutsu shizen no kamae)*

*Unarmed "Immoveable" Seat
(taijutsu fudo za)*

Sword Kneeling Seat
(kenjutsu seiza)

Short Chain Looped Through
Belt Ready for Drawing
(kusari-fundo shizen no kamae)

Short Stick Natural Posture
(hanbojutsu shizen no kamae)

WATER ELEMENT

Unarmed Defensive Posture
(taijutsu ichimonji no kamae)

Unarmed "Tiger"
Defensive Posture
(taijutsu doko no kamae)

Unarmed "Crane" Defensive Posture
(taijutsu hicho no kamae)

Sword Level Defensive Posture
(kenjutsu ichi no kamae)

Staff High-Blocking Posture
(bojutsu jodan uke no kamae)

FIRE ELEMENT

Unarmed Offense Posture
(taijutsu jumonji no kamae)

Unarmed Attacking Posture
(taijutsu kosei no kamae)

Sword High-Striking Posture
(kenjutsu jodan no kamae)

Staff Middle-Striking Posture
(bojutsu chudan no kamae)

Short-Chain Striking Posture
(kusari-fundo ichi no kamae)

WIND ELEMENT

Unarmed Receiving Posture
(taijutsu hira no kamae)

Unarmed "Bear" Open Posture
(taijutsu hoko no kamae)

**Staff "Heaven and Earth" Posture
(bojutsu ten-chi no kamae)**

**Sword "Water Willow" Posture
(kenjutsu ryusui no kamae)**

**Short-Chain Receiving Posture
(kusari-fundo hira no kamae)**

CHAPTER 10

Just as the tangled grasses
take over the mountainside
and the roots of the pines
split clusters of boulders,
the ninja's inventiveness and creative outlook
easily defeat the immobilized enemy
trapped in his own morass
of ponderous narrow vision.

TAIHENJUTSU

Ninja methods of rebounding from the ground

The unarmed combat techniques of ninjutsu are referred to as *taijutsu* (skill with the body). As subclassifications within the broad category of fighting without artificial weapons, there are three major groupings of techniques. Dakentaijutsu, or striking methods, employ *koppojutsu* (bone smashes with the fist and bottom of the foot) and *koshijutsu* (organ and muscle stabs with the fingers and toes). *Jutaijutsu*, or grappling methods, employ *nage* (throws), *shime* (chokes) and *torite* (close-in reversals and locks). *Taihenjutsu*, the body-movement skills that make up the third major subclass, include *ukemi* (methods of breaking falls), *tobi* (leaps), *taisabaki* (body angling) and *shinobi iri* (silent movement).

Though rarely taught in the vast majority of martial arts schools in the Western world, the skills of hitting the ground safely and rebounding ready to continue the fight or escape swiftly are crucial for the mastery of a truly combat-oriented fighting art. Real-world self-protection goes

far beyond the rules and limitations enjoyed by participants engaged in contemporary recreational martial arts programs. To be truly combat ready, today's martial artist must be prepared and trained not only to fight the conventional standing fistfight but also to be able to fight from an automobile front seat, the floor of a broom closet, in the middle of a chair-packed diner, and on the way down a flight of fire-escape stairs. Total self-protection capabilities also would have to include successfully tumbling from a moving truck, going over a high wall to avoid an attack dog, and flattening out on a floor surface to avoid being hit by gunfire.

The ninja taihenjutsu techniques are first taught as slow-motion fundamentals from a low crouched position on a protective mat. Principles of lowering the center of gravity, exhaling with movement and relaxing the body are emphasized. Once the feel of the techniques is acquired, practice is moved to grassy outdoor stretches for increased realism. As the practitioner's skills mature, training then moves to asphalt road surfaces, staircases and other actual locations where the skills will be required in real-life defensive combat.

THE FORWARD ROLL

The forward roll is used to accommodate offensive techniques that throw or pull the defender forward onto the ground. The natural movement and energy of the attacker's technique is enhanced and carried through by curling the body so that the defender ends up on his feet again instead of on his face and chest.

Forward Roll

From an unarmed defensive posture (1), allow your body frame to form an arch that begins with the extended leading arm and shoulder (2). Tuck your head down and rock forward briskly, allowing your body-

weight to roll onto your arm (3), across your shoulder and over your hips (4). Keep your feet tucked in and continue the rolling motion (5) to come back up onto your feet (6).

THE BACKWARD ROLL

The backward roll is used to accommodate techniques in which the attacker throws or pulls the defender backward onto the ground. The natural movement and energy of the attacker's technique is enhanced and carried through by dropping the seat and tucking the legs so that the defender ends up on his feet again instead of his back.

Backward Roll

From an unarmed defensive posture, step back (1) and drop to the ground in as direct a manner as possible (2). Arch your back and bring your head

down to your upper chest while allowing your rolling momentum to continue (3). Keep your feet tucked in and roll right up onto your feet (4-5).

**Backward Roll
Practical Application**

THE FORWARD HANDSPRING

The forward handspring is one method of accommodating offensive techniques that knock or send the defender forward. The weight is flipped onto the outstretched arms, and the body flexes to send the feet forward over the head. The defender then bounces up from the ground to regain his footing.

Forward Handspring

From a standing position (1), dive out so that your body-weight sinks down onto your bending arms (2). Your elbows and shoulders should flex to accommodate your moving weight (3). Immediately push back against your lowering

weight while kicking forward (the direction of travel) with both upraised feet (4). Flex your back in an arch to snap your hips after your feet (5). Finally, follow the lead of your feet and straighten out into a standing position (6).

THE SIDEWAYS HANDSPRING

The sideways handspring accommodates an attacker's technique that knocks or sends the defender sideways. The weight is leaned sideways, and the body flips to send the feet to the side over the head. The defender then cartwheels up from the ground to regain his footing.

Sideways Handspring

From an unarmed defensive posture (1), leap out to the side while lowering your leading shoulder (2). As your extended hand hits the ground, kick off with your feet to propel your hips up and over your

shoulders (3). Extend your limbs widely so that the rolling action will cover as wide an area as possible. The sideways momentum should pull your body back up onto your feet again (4-5).

**Sideways Handspring
Practical Application**

Sideways Leap

From an unarmed receiving posture (1), slam your hips in the direction of travel, pushing off with your trailing leg and clearing your leading leg by picking it up (2). Keep the leap as level as possible, moving directly sideways without bounding up and down

with the move (3). The action should center in the legs and hips and take the upper body along. Do not throw your shoulders to get your body in motion. Then as you land on your leading leg (4), plant both feet on the ground and assume the unarmed receiving posture once again (5).

Sideways Leap
Practical Application

199

Lateral Body Drop

From an unarmed receiving posture (1), center your body-weight on one foot and swing your free leg across in front of your ground leg (2). Then lower your seat directly to the ground (3). Lift your extended leg up, which will flip your

body over onto your back (4). Continue to "reach" with your extended leg (5) until both feet are again in touch with the ground (6). Allow your rolling motion to move you into a standing position again.

**Lateral Body Drop
Practical Application**

202

CHAPTER 11

The steel from the earth
  and the wood from the forest
  are tempered by the fire
  and washed in the stream for purity
  to become the servants
  of the winds of your intention.
Use your weapons with prudence,
  employing them only when
  the scheme of totality demands it.

TRAINING FOR COMBAT REALITY

Ninjutsu methods for overcoming attackers

T he constantly evolving combat method of Togakure Ryu ninjutsu allows for changes and developments in the ways that people are likely to attack. Based on a timeless understanding of human attitudes and physiology that far transcends the rigid limits of temporally inspired techniques, all the ninja fighting methods serve as practical, reliable routes of self-protection that use the natural physical and emotional response tendencies of the human being. This practicality must be present as the core philosophy of any combat-effective fighting system.

The art of ninjutsu was not developed or practiced for the sake of the art itself, nor were there any symbolic goals such as belt rankings or sports titles involved. Ninjutsu developed as a utilitarian and dependable method for accomplishing personal intentions with the least possible amount of personal danger.

The emphasis in ninja training is not on the techniques themselves but rather on the feelings that come up during application of the techniques. Practice sessions, whether inside the *dojo* or outside in natural surroundings, freely blend the methods of unarmed combat, stick fighting, blade work and short cord techniques to produce the feeling of a total system rather than independent blocks of knowledge for each specialty. This teaching method admittedly requires more time for mastery because the personality is internalizing concepts by stripping away false or unnecessary intellectualizations rather than the intellect memorizing set numbers of compartmentalized techniques.

There are two sides to the learning process involved in developing skill in self-protection fighting: the mind and the body. The first aspect of the training is to develop an unconscious, spontaneous mind and body response to an attack. This by no means suggests rigid programmed reactions of a "strike and then think" nature but rather a natural and relaxed response that is developed through repetitive practice that removes the need for conscious logical steps. This unconscious action can be seen as you head a sports car up an incline, discover that it is becoming increasingly steep, work the clutch and accelerator with your feet, and downshift to ease the strain on the engine, all without deliberate, conscious involvement. The second aspect of training is the exposure to the experience of effective and appropriate defensive techniques. The physical techniques themselves are important, of course, because they are the entire method of practice during the training session and they will condition you for later responses during self-protection. However, the mental and spiritual conditioning is the highest goal of the training, because without the proper mental set, even the most devastating of techniques will not be recalled when they are needed.

As a guide for effective ninjutsu training, it is crucial to understand the significance of the following considerations:

1. *Be there 100 percent. Allow your consciousness to hold on to each moment as if it were all that existed. Concentrate totally on your purpose and actions.*
   Do not let your mind wander from the training activities at hand.

2. *Keep your center of gravity as low as possible while still permitting easy movement.*
   Do not concentrate your strength in your shoulders or upper body.

3. *Keep your movements relaxed and fluid, delivering the impact at the last second.*
   Do not tense up by trying to maintain power through the entire technique.

4. *Use the entire weight of the body to create power and knock your attacker back or down.*
   Do not try to outmuscle the attacker with the movements of your limbs alone.

5. *Keep your footwork fast, responsive and appropriate.*
   Do not settle into and maintain a fixed stance for the fight.

6. *Use proper rhythmic breathing to generate and restore energy. Breathe out with application movements and in with retreating or preparation movements.*
   Do not hold your breath when releasing energy through technique application or interception.

7. *Control the direction of your eyes, keeping your attacker in sight.*
   Do not concentrate so much on your technique that you do not notice a possible change in the attacker's action or position.

8. *Bear in mind the purpose of the technique.*
   Do not attempt to carry through a technique that is no longer needed. (If the attacker lets go before you can complete the wrist lock, that's fine. Your purpose was to get him off you, not execute a textbook technique.)

9. *Use every moment to increase your personal knowledge and powers.*
   Do not merely go through the motions for the sake of exercise or forced discipline.

The following examples are provided as illustrations of ninja combat-method training. The techniques are not necessarily to be memorized but rather serve as guidelines for understanding the principles. The ultimate goal is not to memorize dozens of robot-like series of movements but to strip away the attachments of the intellectual mind. If your fighting ability is based on memorized techniques, then time and human forgetfulness will decrease your fighting ability if you even temporarily discontinue active training. If, on the other hand, your fighting ability is the product of stripping away and letting go of all the mechanical thought processes that limit the mind, you will have nothing to lose through forgetfulness. You will have transcended the need for constant uninterrupted training, and you will have realized the essence of "being" rather than "becoming."

Single-Hand Choke Escape I

From a ready position (1), the attacker grabs the defender by the throat (2). The defender responds by going with the attacking pressure (3). Note: (A) shows the correct hand position for dislodging the attacker's hand. She steps back into a stable defensive

posture while dislodging the attacker's hand (4). Continuing back with her footwork (5), the defender twists out against the attacker's wrist to throw him to the ground (6). Note: (B) shows the correct hand position at this point. The defender uses her bodyweight in motion, not her arms alone, to down the attacker.

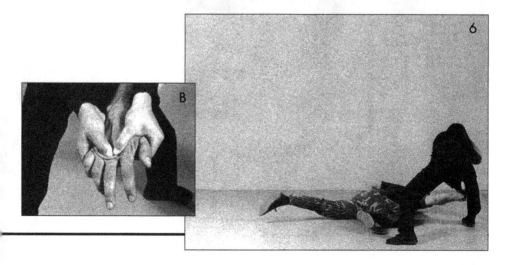

Single-Hand Choke Escape II

From a ready position (1), the attacker grabs the defender by the throat. The defender, by going with the attacker's

pressure (2-3), steps back into a defensive posture while freeing the attacker's hand (4). Continuing back with her

continued on next page ▶

footwork, the defender pulls
the attacker's wrist inward

with a twist (5-6) to throw him to the ground (7-9).

Defense Against Redirected Attack I

From a defensive posture (1), the defender observes as the attacker moves forward with a front hand punch to the face (2). In response, the defender throws his leading foot to the outside rear position (3) and counterpunches into the at-

tacker's extended punching arm (4). The attacker recoils his arm with the power of the defender's strike and allows the momentum of his body to turn him into a spinning back kick to the defender's midsection (5-6). As the kick

continued on next page ▶

rises toward him, the defender counters by kicking into the back of the attacking leg (7). As the attacker's leg is pushed to the ground again (8), he goes with the spin to execute a rear hammerfist strike to

the defender's head (9). The defender drops to avoid the strike and then steps in with a throat-crushing grip (10-11) that slams the attacker back and up (12).

Defense Against Redirected Attack II

From a defensive posture (1), the defender observes as the attacker initiates a front-hand jab (2). The defender shifts to the rear and side to avoid the jab and counters with a speed punch to the attacker's lead-

ing wrist (3). The counter is actually an attack from the defensive posture, not a block. As the attacker continues with a lunging punch to the ribs (4-5), the defender rocks forward and to the outside

continued on next page

of the punch and uses her leading hand to redirect the punch (6). The defender then rams her knee into the bone structure of the attacker's leg

(7-9) and follows up with an extended knuckle punch into the bones of the attacker's ribs or neck (10).

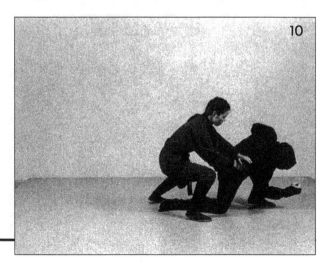

Defense Against Punching Attack

From a defensive posture (1), the defender observes as the attacker executes a hooking knockout punch to the head (2). Once the punch is committed to its path, the defender drops straight down to avoid being hit (3). The move is a body drop, not a boxer's duck.

From the grounded position, the defender springs back up toward the attacker, using her legs to generate power (4). As she rises, the defender shifts her rear leg into a forward position (5), increasing the power of her punch to the attacker's lower ribs (6). The completed

continued on next page ▶

punch uses the defender's bodyweight in motion to deliver power rather than the simple extension of her arm. The defender then shuffles forward with a rising shin kick to the groin (7-9) and a heel stamp to the knee (10-11). Because the defender's arm

muscles are not as strong as the attacker's, she must overcome his strength by avoiding his strikes and using her whole body for the counterstrike. Finally, the defender completes the maneuver with a heel stamp to the back of the attacker's leg (12).

Knife Defense Against Knife Attack I

From a receiving posture (1), the defender observes as the attacker closes in with horizontal slashing cuts to her hands and midsection (2). As the attacker slashes inward with a pulling cut, the defender allows her body to fall back momentarily and then rocks forward with an outward hacking cut to the outside edge of the attacker's weapon arm (3). As the blade wedges into its

target, the defender moves forward to use her bodyweight and position to prevent the attacker from slashing back at her (4). Continuing her momentum, the defender moves directly behind the attacker (5), leveling out her knife so that her bodyweight in motion, not the muscles in her arm alone, drives the knife into its target (6).

Knife Defense Against Knife Attack II

From a receiving posture (1), the defender observes as the attacker closes in with horizontal slashing cuts to her hands and midsection (2). As the attacker slashes outward with a pushing cut, the defender allows her body to fall back momentarily, and then without hesitation, she rocks forward while simultaneously grabbing the attacker's weapon arm and executing a downward slicing cut to the

inside of the attacker's upper arm (3). The defender continues the momentum of her blade as it passes underneath the attacker's arm (4) and then swings her blade up into position to control the attacker by holding him in a defenseless position (5). If necessary to save her life, the defender could then cut downward along the attacker's neck from behind his shoulder (6).

Defense Against Double-Punch Attack

From a defensive posture (1), the defender observes as the attacker begins a double-punch combination. The defender shifts back and to the inside of the first punch with an injurious counterstrike to the attacking arm (2). As the attacker recoils and then dives in with his second punch (3), the defender shifts her bodyweight forward into an

offensive posture and causes the attacker to slam his chest into the point of her elbow (4). The attacker's second punch misses its target because of the defender's sudden and unexpected change in movement. The defender then executes a clawing hand strike to the face (5), followed by an outside arm lock that forces the attacker to the ground (6).

Defense Against Combination Attack

From a defensive posture (1), the defender observes as the attacker executes a leg-sweeping kick (2-3). As the attacker's leg shoots out, the

defender lifts his foot to avoid the strike (4). The attacker immediately flies forward with a leading-hand punch to the defender's ribs (5).

continued on next page ➤

As a counter, the defender smashes down with his leading fist (6) and uses his coiled leg to kick forward into the attacker's midsection (7-8).

234

The defender then moves into an offensive posture (9) as he knocks the attacker back with a palm-edge strike to the side of the neck (10-11).

Defense Against Wall Pin

The attacker slams the defender up against a wall (1-3). As the attacker shoves, the defender arches his back and lowers his head forward to cushion the impact. The defender then allows his body to fall forward (4) as the attacker initiates a face punch (5). By lowering his center of gravity and moving forward, the defender jams up the attack. The defender next extends his arm over the grabbing arm of the attacker, allows his arm to swing down and around, and drops his bodyweight to trap the attacker's arm from above (6-7). By turning his body into the attack and continuing the swing of his arm, the defender exerts straining pressure on the outside of the attacker's elbow and shoulder (8), which turns the attacker's body to prevent his punch

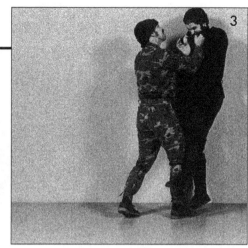

continued on next page

from connecting. The defender then simultaneously lifts up on the elbow, drops his seat and
leans back (9), which slams the attacker backward into the wall. The defender next re-grips
the attacker's body (10), lowers his seat once
again and slings the attacker forward into the
wall (11-12). Knee-slam follow-up strikes (13-14)
disable the attacker's legs and bring the fight to
a close (15-16).

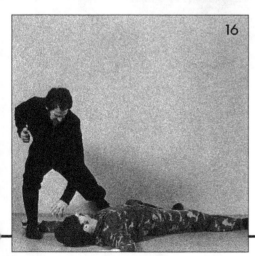

Defense to Offense Transition

From an offensive posture (1), the defender is preparing to go from defense into offense against the attacker. As the defender begins his move, the attacker flies forward with

a punch to the face (2). The defender drops to the inside of the attacker's punch and directs his fist into the underside of the attacker's extended arm (3-4). Then quickly trapping

continued on next page ▶

the attacker's foot with his own foot (5-6), the defender rams forward with a thumb-drive strike to the attacker's upper ribs (7), stunning him

and knocking him back. Finally, two-handed pressure on the attacker's knee forces him to the ground or breaks his ankle (8-10).

Metsubushi Defense Against Sword

From a receiving posture (1), the defender observes as the attacker prepares to execute a slashing cut with his sword (2). The defender retreats into

a defensive posture as the attacker raises his sword. From a concealed pocket inside her jacket (3), the defender produces a packet of metsubushi

continued on next page ▶

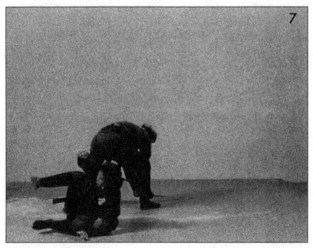

(blinding powder), which she throws into the eyes of the attacker (4). As the attacker attempts to complete his blind

cut, the defender escapes
by rolling past the attacker
unseen (5-9).

Sword Against Sword I

From a natural posture (1), the defender observes as the attacker approaches. As soon as the attacker reaches for his sword, the defender draws his sword while moving forward into an offensive posture (2). The thumb of the left hand presses the guard to free the blade from its scabbard. The defender turns his drawing action into his first cut against

the attacker's arm (3-4). Properly executed, this move is totally an attack. There is no hesitation or defensiveness about it. After the first cut, the defender continues forward with a downward slashing cut to finish off the attacker (5-6). The bodyweight in motion carries the blade into its target. The cut is not propelled by arms alone.

Sword Against Sword II

From a seated position (1), the defender observes as the attacker moves into position before him with the sword upraised. Staring into the attacker's eyes, the defender uses his left hand to subtly reverse the position of his

sword to edge-down in his sash. Then staying low, the defender bursts forward with a fast-draw upward, ripping cut as the attacker moves in with his downward cut (2-4). The defender's move is an attack with no defensive hesitation.

continued on next page ▶

The defender then continues forward, slamming his body-weight into a horizontal cut across the attacker's midsec-

tion (5-9) while moving to the side to avoid the attacker's falling sword (10).

Sword Against Sword III

From a defensive posture (1), the defender observes as the attacker lunges forward with a downward diagonal cut (2). The defender then throws his sword forward to meet the

blade of the attacker without attempting to stop his motion (3-4). As the attacker's sword continues forward, the defender allows his sword to fall away with it (5-6), firmly

continued on next page ▶

guiding (not blocking) the attacking blade from its target. After the attacker's power is no longer a threat, the defender releases his sword with his leading hand and grabs the attacker's jacket sleeve to keep

him from turning with another cut (7-8). The defender then lowers his own sword point into a position from which he can control the attacker's movement (9).

Unarmed Defense Against Knife I

From a receiving posture (1), the defender observes as the attacker moves in with a vertically plunging knife stab along the neck and behind the collarbone. Instead of

recoiling back predictably, the defender moves forward along the outside of the attacker's descending knife arm (2-4), guiding it away with his leading hand (5). Capturing

continued on next page ▶

the attacker's momentum,
the defender then extends the
attacker's knife arm and subdues him with knee smashes

to the back of the elbow (6-7)
and a heel stamp to the side
of the knee (8-9).

Unarmed Defense Against Knife II

From a receiving posture (1), the unarmed defender observes as the attacker uses a knife to hold him at bay with short slashes and lunges. The attacker charges forward with an upward stab to the lower tip of the defender's breastbone (2). The defender adapts by flowing forward and

outside of the attacker's knife arm, using his leading hand to stabilize the attacking arm (3-4). Immediately, the defender grips the attacker's knife wrist and steps forward with an extended knuckle attack to the bones in the back of the attacker's knife hand (5-7). The defender's bodyweight

continued on next page

in motion provides the power to stun the attacker's hand, and the blade will usually fly free. The defender then turns against the attacker's wrist, using his bodyweight to snap

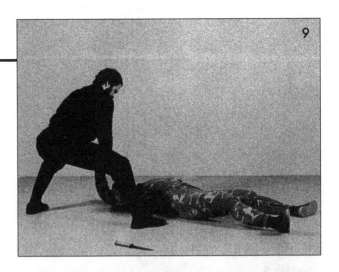

the wrist and throw the attacker to the ground on his back (8-9). The final maneuver is to twist the attacker's wrist to the right, in this instance, to keep him under control (10-11).

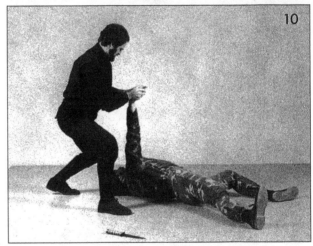

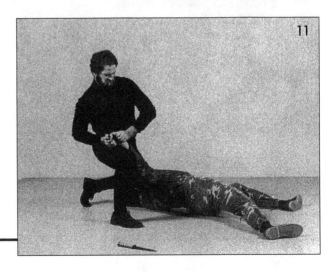

Shuriken Defense Against Sword

From a defensive posture (1), the defender observes as the attacker moves forward with a slashing attack (2). The defender throws his leading foot back with a leap

to avoid the cut (3-4). As he backpedals away from the attacker, the defender reaches into his jacket and produces a stack of nine shuriken throwing stars (5).

continued on next page ▶

As the attacker bears down on him, the defender fires off several of the blades to drive the attacker back (6-10). Note: (A), (B), (C) and (D) show the correct technique for throwing the shuriken in rapid-fire

succession. The throwing stars are fanned off the top of the stack one at a time very quickly, the hand snapping back for the next blade as soon as the first one is thrown.

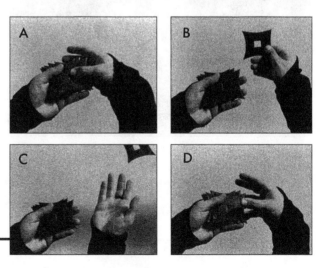

Short Chain Against Club

From a defensive posture (1), the defender, holding a chain, observes as the attacker approaches with an iron club. As the club moves into position for a downward smashing strike to the head or shoulder, the defender moves forward into an offensive posture and meets the descending club

hand with the taut chain (2). Holding the clubbing hand in place temporarily with the chain, the defender moves to the attacker's side (away from the attacker's free hand) from which the defender can tie the attacker's clubbing hand against his own neck (3-5).

continued on next page

The chain then wraps around the attacker's neck, and the defender's right thumb applies the choking pressure to

the attacker's windpipe (6-8).
Finally, the defender pulls the
attacker to the ground (9).

Knife Against Stick

From a defensive posture (1), the defender observes as the attacker approaches with short, slashing knife work (2). The defender rocks forward

into an offensive posture and sends the tip of his cane into the knife hand of the attacker (3-4). The defender continues

continued on next page ▶

his forward motion (5-7) using
his bodyweight and natural
speed to generate power as

he releases his rear gripping hand to send the cane forward into the attacker's face (8-10).

Stick Defense
Against Staff Attack

From a defensive posture (1), the defender observes as the attacker flies forward with a diagonal staff strike to the head or neck (2). In response, the defender moves in to stop the attacking motion (3) and then

uses his leading arm to control the attacker's staff (4). Lowering his bodyweight for power, the defender cracks the tip of the short stick into the attacker's temple (5), knocking him unconscious as he tumbles to the ground (6).

EAST

NORTH

SOUTH

WEST

The Taizokai Mandala

CHAPTER 12

The fingers interwoven
  to channel the determination,
  a tensing of the bones and muscles,
  passage of the breath
  and setting of the resolve
  propel the ninja
  to seize and ride the winds of fate.

ATTUNING WITH THE UNIVERSE

Thought, word and deed as a single tool of accomplishment for the ninja: Kuji-in

In his volume titled *Nin-po: Sono Hiden to Jitsurei (Secrets and Examples of the Ninja Ways)*, now no longer in print, Iga Ryu ninjutsu historian Heishichiro Okuse observes that Japan's historical ninja are characterized by their thorough and scientific approach to analyzing and solving problems, and yet they are at the same time closely associated with highly occult and spiritual practices. From Okuse's viewpoint, this is really no contradiction at all. Ninja combat training tends to stress the pragmatic physical aspects in precise and rational ways with little or no attention paid to artistic or aesthetic considerations, but the ninja of old also realized that a lot of their successes came through influences other than scientific pre-detailing of operations to be undertaken. Some people would call these subtle influences luck, coincidence or accident, but the ninja learned that a rational and logical approach had to rationally and logically include all factors that could possibly influence an outcome.

Ninjutsu's reliance on the practice of mikkyo stressed the truth of the concepts that there is no such thing as coincidence, there are no accidents, and luck is just unguided or unchanneled power playing itself out in our daily affairs. This conviction that spirituality is a legitimate and working part of reality comes from a heightened sensitivity resulting from continuously dwelling on the border edge between life and death. To a veteran ninja who has lived through countless skirmishes against overwhelming odds and has seen too many unexplainable happenings and miraculous twists of fate, there is nothing more rational than taking all possibilities into account.

From the mystic teachings of mikkyo came the ninja's insight into the workings of the universe, and from the application of this understanding came the ninja's personal power. The compendium of wisdom teachings known as mikkyo had its foundations in the esoteric tantric lore of India, Tibet and China. In the early part of the ninth century, Japan was introduced to these concepts through the research of traveling monks such as Saicho and Kukai, who traveled to China as young men in order to study with learned sages there. Mikkyo teachings of power and magic also came to Japan through the work of wandering monks, shamans and hermit priests who fled their native China after the fall of the Tang dynasty.

In later centuries, the same teachings underwent a stylization and elaboration in their native India and Tibet, and they were transformed into a religion of worship and adoration of a spectrum of gods that represented the varying levels of consciousness in the universe. In feudal Japan, however, the teachings were transmitted as a body of knowledge that stressed the power inherent in every individual person. Not merely a religion but a working set of principles or universal laws, the teachings of mikkyo were taken to heart and practiced rigorously by *yamabushi*, *sennin* and *gyoja* mountain warrior ascetics, the segment of Japanese society that would later become the forerunners of the ninja. In a series of brutal territorial wars, these people were hunted down. The need for defense of their mountain wilderness homes and families soon developed, and thus was born the incredible shadow warrior of Japan, known as the ninja.

The practice of power generation through mikkyo involves the combined use of *mantra* (sacred or "charged" words), *mandala* (schematic pictorial renderings of the structure of the universe, for the directing of concentration) and *mudra* (energy-channeling hand posturings) for the total coordination of all the energies of the personality. Bringing together thought, word and deed in harmonious alignment in which each quality complements the other is seen to be the key to working one's will in the world. This power is referred to as the *sanmitsu,* or three secrets of mikkyo spiritual power.

Japanese Word	Sanskrit Concept	English Equivalent	Symbolizes	Sanmitsu
Nenriki	mandala	concentrated intention	the will	thought
Jumon	mantra	power words	the intellect	word
Ketsu-in	mudra	hand posturings	physical action	deed

Nin-po mikkyo, the ninja's spiritual power teaching, provides two distinctive views of the structure of the universe, each view depicted in a highly symbolic diagram known as a mandala. The two mandalas represent totally opposite perspectives and are used in conjunction with each other to inspire the insight necessary to capture the significance of why the universe operates the way it does. In greatly oversimplified terms, the universal process can be viewed from the inside out, concentrating on the physical manifestations of creation and working toward an understanding of the universal laws (effect explains the cause), or the universe can be regarded from a viewpoint of total scope, concentrating on gaining a knowledge of the universal laws and working toward an understanding of the intricate interworkings of all aspects of daily life (cause explains the effect).

The essence of the material world is captured in the *taizokai* mandala, the schematic rendering of the "matrix realm." Matrix is used here in its original concept of "womb," or place in which something originates. From this approach, we come to realize that we all exist *within* the universe. Each star, planet, human, animal, thing, word, thought—indeed everything on which a label can be hung—is a part of all the parts that interact to make up what we know as the universe. All of us and all our actions are seen and acknowledged as existing within the inside of the god, just as the god is conversely seen to exist within each of us. As a means of approaching enlightenment, the taizokai mandala structure and symbols are studied for the clues necessary to bring about a realization of the universal laws that are manifested in the ways that daily worldly life unfolds. Through personal experience of our individual consciousness operating at different levels, the greater perspectives inherent in the lessons of life are brought into focus. We can come to see that the universe is vast enough and complex enough to contain all the contradiction and paradox that mankind's limited vision seems to observe.

The essence of the spiritual world is likewise captured in the *kongokai* mandala, a schematic rendering of the diamond realm. The diamond is considered to be the symbol of multifaceted clarity, brilliance and hardness and the jewel that is the highest possible refinement of form for unmanifested pure knowledge, spirit or ultimate truth. From the kongokai approach, we come to realize that all in existence is merely the form that our awareness gives to the universal laws in operation around us. What we would see as or believe to be "reality" is our subjective realization of "actuality," or that which is in action itself or that which acts in its purest form. By transcending and leaving behind the material world through the mystic's process and going directly to the experience of the universal law itself, we can attain the state of *shin-shin shin-gan*, or "the mind and eyes of god," from which we can look back into the material world with a heightened, enlightened perspective.

In the training hall, the mandala symbolic representations are hung on both sides of the open hall. From the viewpoint of the position of power in the dojo (the central point of focus opposite the entrance), the kongokai mandala is on the right and the taizokai mandala is on the left. These positions would, of course, be just the reverse for students in the dojo, who face the central point of focus rather than look out from it. The mandalas are hung vertically, although their true concept is mentally laid out on a horizontal plane, creating the effect felt when looking at a city map tacked up on a wall.

When considering one of the two mandalas in meditation, the practitioner can study each particular mandala in light of the purpose of the unique piece of artwork. When contemplating the taizokai mandala of the matrix realm, the ninja looks within himself or herself for an understanding of the material world. It is a falling-inward process of going to the center of our very being and thereby reaching the center of the

WEST

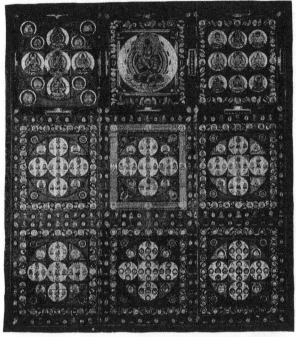

EAST

The Kongokai Mandala

universe. When contemplating the kongokai mandala of the diamond realm, the ninja transcends himself or herself for an understanding of the world of universal laws. This is a lifting-outward process of leaving the self behind to attain a cosmic vision of totality. The two practices must complement each other for balanced personal development.

Undue emphasis on either of the two realms will produce a warped personality. Those who would concentrate exclusively on the material realm will become overly mechanical and technical in their outlooks, and their ninja art will become nothing more than a mere mechanistic system of physical combat devoid of morality, spirit and life. Those who would concentrate exclusively on the realm of pure knowledge will lose touch with reality around them and their ninja art will become nothing more than an empty ideal or intellectual exercise, devoid of practicality, relevance and energy.

Words and actions are useless without the guidance of thought behind them. Direction is necessary. The power of concentrated intention is a subtle lesson picked up through determined perseverance in coming to a personal understanding of the significance of the two mandalas. This is the first step, and it is referred to as tempering the will.

The power of the will is then more firmly established through spoken vows that plant the intentions firmly in the realm of the physical by giving them the reality of vibratory presence. The ninja's thoughts are creations that become real "things" once they have been given physical sounds to carry them out into the world.

Chinese Lion Dogs

Stone Chinese lion dogs guard the temple entrance and greet initiates with a roaring "ahh-ohh-mumm-nnn" jumon vow, the mantra of the totality of the universe. The animal in the foreground represents the matrix realm, the material world, the left side of universal power, and the *in* side of the *in-yo* polarity (Taoist yin-yang in Chinese). His jaws are wide open with the "ahh" seed syllable of the taizokai mandala. The lion dog in the background represents the diamond realm, the world of pure wisdom, the right side of universal power, and the *yo* side of the *in-yo* polarity. His jaws are clamped shut with the "vmm" seed syllable characteristic of the kongokai mandala. Together, the two animals are a symbol of the indivisibility of the two realms that simultaneously occupy the identical time and space in the universe.

The Kane

In the ritual kane, the bell portion represents deep inherent wisdom, and the vajra handle represents wisdom in compassionate action. The blending of the two in one single object symbolizes the unity existing between the physical and spiritual worlds. The ceremonial bell reminds us of the truth of impermanence. The phenomenal world is like the sound that the kane bell emits; it can be perceived but cannot be kept. Like the sound of the bell, all things are transitory and exist only through the senses of the observer. Even life itself is like the peal of a bell, ever-changing, inconstant, unstable and predestined to the impermanence that is the essence of all things. For the ninja, realizing the significance of this impermanence is one key to approaching enlightenment.

The Kongo and the Taizokai

The mikkyo kongo, or diamond thunderbolt (left), is the symbol of the kongokai (diamond realm). The indestructible hardness and clarity of the diamond symbolizes the power of truth and illumination to smash through ignorance and illusion. The three points represent the ability of thought, word and deed to produce enlightenment. Meditation on the kongokai concerns itself with the question, "What is the actual ultimate truth?"

Symbolic of the finite material world, the rosary of 27 skulls (right) depicts the taizokai (matrix realm). The nine levels of power as realized through the three working methods of the physical, intellectual and spiritual make up this symbol of the left hand of the universe. Meditation on the taizokai concept concerns itself with the question, "How can ultimate truth be realized?"

The doctrine of tantra, which teaches methods of using the powers of the physical world to bring about personal enlightenment, asserts that the process of producing sound epitomizes the ever-going process of creating the universe. The first tangible manifestations of the absolute were made in the form of sounds or vibrations. The tantric teachings of nin-po mikkyo preserve the symbols of these fundamental vibratory rates in *shuji* ("seed" characters), the written form of Sanskrit used between the fourth and sixth centuries during the Gupta dynasty in India. This *siddham* script was introduced into China for the writing of tantric formulas by the Indian patriarchs teaching there and was carried to Japan by the monk Kukai in the ninth century. The writing form has since been preserved by the esoteric tradition in Japan.

The *jumon* mantras ("charged words of power") of the ninja's mikkyo are sounds or phrases used to give vibratory reality to the intentions of the ninja. In most instances, the jumon vows are uttered in the original language transmitted from the Himalayas, although some of the vows are voiced in classical Japanese. The jumon are intentionally preserved in words that have no meaning in daily routine conversation so we can express our pure determination through sound forms that cannot be lessened in intensity by reflecting daily social interaction. The sounds imply interaction on a level much higher than a conversation between two intellects. The original sounds are also thought to be purer or closer to the specific rates of vibration that will harmonize with and bear effect on the other vibrations that constitute physical reality—sights, sounds, feelings and so forth.

Because it is the actual resonant sound itself and not the literal meaning of the words that makes the jumon effective, no attempt can be made in this volume to give instruction in the use of the voiced mantras. It also could be argued that the entire esoteric formula of how to set the mind, tune the vibrations of the voice and engage the body should not appear in specific notation in a published volume such as this. Those individuals who believe it's their destiny to become a part of the ninja tradition will seek out the teacher who they need for such advanced training.

For the purposes of information only, it is possible to grasp a small experience of the nin-po mikkyo jumon through the vocalization of two primary sounds, one blending into the other. Open your mouth and throat as wide as you can, creating the sensation of a yawn. Tightening your stomach slowly, breathe out through your mouth while producing a full-throated sighing sound from deep within your body. It should sound like a breathy, resonant "ahh." Continue the sound and bring your lips together, stretching them over your parted teeth to close your mouth while maintaining your jaws in an open position. The tone should now be a buzzing, vibrant "mmm." Continue the original sound and bring your teeth together firmly, compacting your tongue against the inside surfaces of your clenched teeth. The tone should now be a level, vibrating "nnn." Allow the sound to die away slowly as you expel the last of your breath.

This series of sound groupings blended into one continuous "word" is considered to be the ultimate universal mantra. When voiced repeatedly in synchronization with a large group of other people in a cool, darkened room (to reduce sensual distractions), the "ahh-ohh-mmmnnn" mantra blends the personal breathing rhythms, voice qualities and spiritual intensities of each individual. When practiced with people who are thoroughly enjoying themselves, the resultant effect can be quite awesome.

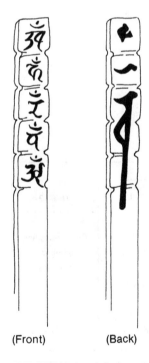

Shuji

Shuji (written characters) are visual symbols of the power of the various levels of vibratory energy, inscribed on the walking staffs of yamabushi (mountain warrior priests). The five characters (sounds—"ah, vah, rah, hah, khah") on one side represent the earth, water, fire, wind and void of the matrix realm material world. The single seed sound ("vahmm") on the opposite side is the symbol of the pure knowledge of the diamond realm. The construction of the staff attests to the ninja's belief that the two realms are mere reflections of each other.

(Front)   (Back)

The third area of knowledge required for mastery of nin-po mik-kyo's *sanmitsu* (three secrets of power) is the body's incorporation in the task of creating a reality from the intention formulated by the will and expressed through the voice as a vow. The *kuji-in* (finger entwining hand "seals") of ninjutsu are the same mudra hand postures of Indian, Tibetan and Chinese esoteric lore, and they represent the channeling of subtle energies, the transmitting of lessons in wisdom, and the affording of psychic protection to self and others.

In the electrochemical makeup of the human body, electro-polar channels (meridians) run through the tissues of the body. The hands and feet are thought to contain the sensitive ends and turnaround points of the channels. Ninjutsu's kuji-in (nine-syllable mudras) and their variations make up a power-generating system based on a balancing out or directing of energy through the hands. In this system, each hand and

Left Hand	Right Hand
Taizokai (material world)	*Kongokai* (pure wisdom)
Moon	Sun
Temporal reality	Ultimate actuality
Inner	Outer
Worldly beings	Gods
Healing	Power
In	*Yo*
Arresting the active mind	Realization of pure knowledge
Receiving	Projecting
Negative (-)	Positive (+)

Little Finger	Ring Finger	Middle Finger	Pointer	Thumb
Earth	Water	Fire	Wind	Void
Physical body	Emotions	Intellect	Wisdom	Communication
Rocks	Plants	Animals	Mankind	Subatomic particles
Stability	Adaptability	Connection	Freedom	Creativity
Chi	*Sui*	*Ka*	*Fu*	*Ku*
地	水	火	風	空

finger symbolizes a specific attribute of the body's makeup. Different energies of the personality are represented by element and structure codes. Concentration and stress on the various energies could result in an alteration of the body's mood, bearing and predominant capability at any given moment.

Nin-po mikkyo's *kuji goshin ho* (nine-syllable method of protection) is one of several mudra, mantra and mandala combinations perfected by the ninja for increased sensitivity to the workings of all around him or her. Effected before going into action or entering a threatening place, the nine hand poses and syllables work to sharpen the ninja's senses as a means for increasing the likelihood of success. Each of the nine hand poses, when used separately, has its unique mantra sentence and mind-setting procedure, which are not included in this volume.

The physical examples of the hand positions that follow serve as illustrations only. They are by no means complete lessons in themselves. Merely folding the fingers and making a sound with the voice will not produce any recognizable effect on the personality. Anyone wishing to develop a control over the subtle energies of the body must devote a considerable amount of study and concentration to build up skill in the kuji-in process. The crucial mind-setting and breathing routines have not been included here because they must be guided personally by a competent teacher. This series of hand positions and vows is presented here for its information value only.

"Rin, pyo, toh, sha, kai, jin, retsu, zai, zen" is the jumon vow that accompanies the weaving of the fingers for each of the nine steps, or "levels of power." Translated into working English with nine syllables, this means, "Here warriors all lined bold in front!"

Each of the syllables has its own hand pose, which in turn has its own jumon chant or vow that calls on a particular personification of some cosmic aspect or deity for assistance in directing power. The ninja selects a goal of emulation and then becomes that goal in thought, word and deed by attuning body, voice and mental imagery with the desired outcome. The entire personality then takes on the feel that the goal has already been accomplished and is merely awaiting the proper time to physically manifest itself.

Rin

Dokko-in (sign of the vajra thunderbolt)

The physical imitation of the mikkyo dokko or kongo (diamond thunderbolt) that represents the awesome power of wisdom and pure knowledge as it smashes through crudeness and ignorance, the dokko-in is used to inspire the strength for overcoming physical and mental trials and for prevailing over all that would crush the ninja.

Pyo

Daikongorin-in (sign of the great diamond wheel)

The physical imitation of an eight-spoke wheel, symbol of the power of knowledge that guides the eightfold path of personal development, the daikongorin-in is used to inspire all the body's nerve and glandular operational centers to foster full awakening.

Toh

Sotojishi-in (sign of the outer lion)

The outer lion hand tying signifies the successful blending with the forces outside of us, or attaining what we need while going along with whatever confronts us. By coming into attunement with the forces of fate, the ninja can develop ki-ai to foresee and go along with the scheme of totality.

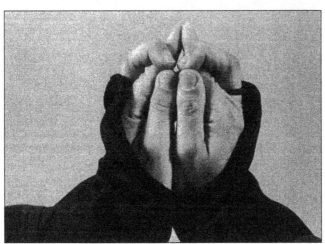

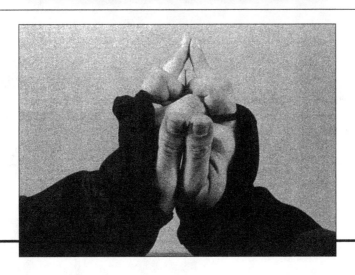

Sha

Uchijishi-in (sign of the inner lion)

The internal workings of our bodies are symbolized by the lion within. Our health can provide us with enormous power or can destroy all chances for accomplishment in this lifetime. The uchijishi-in, along with the proper jumon vow, is used to generate the energy for healing self and others, and to promote healthy surroundings.

Kai

Gebakuken-in (sign of the outer bonds fist)

The passions that bind us to illusions prevent us from receiving all that our consciousness is capable of taking in. The gebakuken-in represents the ninja letting go of the bonds of too tight conceptual thinking, and it is used to inspire an expanded awareness that will allow the ninja to feel the approach of a premonition of danger.

Jin

Naibakuken-in (sign of the inner bonds fist)

The mind's insistence on limiting its intake to physical sense data must be overcome before the ninja can employ the full powers of enlightenment. The naibakuken-in represents the ninja relying on the cosmic consciousness accepting the reality of intuition, and it is used to attune the awareness toward knowing the thoughts of others and projecting thoughts to others.

Retsu

Chiken-in (sign of the wisdom fist)

Mankind in the material world, represented by the upraised left index finger, is totally surrounded by the power and protection of the actuality of pure knowledge, represented by the right hand. The two hands together represent the oneness of the taizokai material realm and the kongokai spiritual realm, and the oneness of the individual and cosmic. The chiken-in frees the ninja from the limits of time and space, and it is used to assist the ninja in focusing on distant places and other times as sources of knowledge for application in the present time and place.

Zai

Nichirin-in (sign of the ring of the sun)

The triangular body of flame symbolizes the fire that must destroy all that is impure and stands in the way of sammaji, or the elevating of the mind beyond material reality to a plane where it is one with the unity of the universe. The nichirin-in is used to transport the ninja to a point of oneness with the source of all manifestation in the universe, where directions and physical forms of matter can be altered and controlled through the power of the will alone.

Zen

Ongyo-in (sign of the concealed form)

The ninja's power and perspective in life comes from an enlightenment that can be resented and scoffed at by lesser souls lacking enlightenment. Therefore, a part of that enlightenment is knowledge of the ways to become invisible. Along with the proper jumon recitation and mindset, the ongyo-in is used to obtain the protection of cosmic forces in order to become invisible to all lowly, resentful and evil people, and to vanish in the face of disaster.

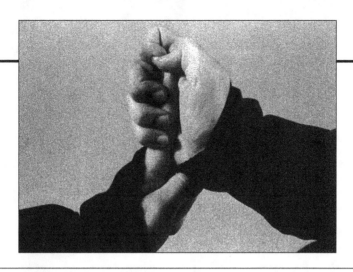

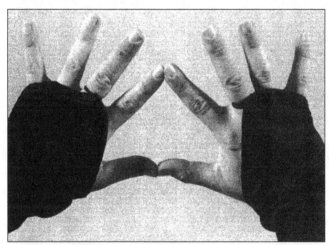

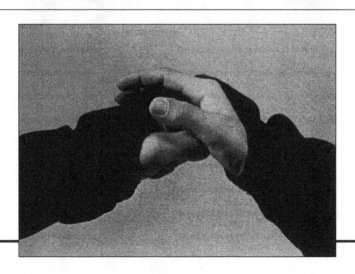

PART 3

Warrior Path of Togakure

CHAPTER 13

Brightness of spirit
  dwelling for eons so deep in its cavern
  awaiting the perfect moment
  for the truest seeker
  to pry open the door
  and the hidden knowledge once again
  illuminates the hearts of the worthy.

A PILGRIMAGE
TO TOGAKURE MOUNTAIN

Birth of the legacy

T he heat and humidity of Tokyo in June gave way to heat alone as we stepped from the Tokyu Express Liner in the *monzen machi* (temple city) of Nagano. A three-hour train ride had taken us north up into the high country far above Tokyo, and though the humidity faded with the increase in altitude, a shimmering haze of midsummer heat hovered over the grounds of the sprawling temple that formed the center of this ancient city.

Robed monks of the esoteric tradition stood in the noon sun, buzzing with their barely audible mantras, spoken in the language of ancient Himalayan kingdoms. Broad basket hats offered them some protection from the searing rays as they shook their six-ringed power staves in jangle rhythms, calling out for alms from strolling Japanese tourists. My wife and I passed by the temple. We were on our way elsewhere, on our own form of spiritual quest.

An open-windowed bus took us up into the mountains that loomed above the city of Nagano. On our left, we could see the simmering city in the valley below us, on our right, the cool blue-green forest that climbed the mountain ridges ahead of us. Rumiko and I were on our way to secluded Togakure Village, nestled up there somewhere in the harsh Joshinetsu Plateau.

The village of Togakure* was the childhood home of Daisuke Nishina more than 800 years ago. He had grown up in the rarefied air of these lofty haunted peaks, where he trained with the warrior ascetics of the Togakure Mountain *shugendo dojo*. Daisuke was later forced to leave his home, never to return again, and set out on a journey that would transform itself into the eventual founding of the Togakure Ryu of *ninjutsu,* the mystical art of Japan's legendary shadow warriors.

Years ago, I too had set out on a pilgrimage, equally compelled by some inner drive, or perhaps a greater outer calling unknown to me that had taken me from my boyhood home in search of the secrets of the warrior path of enlightenment. I was accepted as a direct disciple of the 34th grandmaster of the *ryu* that Daisuke had unknowingly created almost a millennium ago, and I had found my spirit's home here on the Honshu island of Japan.

Our bus moved slowly along the narrow winding roads that snaked over the hilly terrain of the area. A small cluster of weathered inns and storage barns, their massive thatched roofs towering five times as high as their gray wooden walls, sat waiting stoically ahead of us. Rumiko and I were surprised to learn that the little grouping of antique structures was the town center, so small was this tiny village.

A group of teenaged Japanese tourists milled about outside the bus. Though it was the middle of summer, they all wore the heavy black trousers or skirts and white shirts typical of Japanese high-school uniforms. They spotted me immediately, and their fascination over having a foreigner in that out-of-the-way village spread rapidly. My wife, Rumiko, was born and raised in Japan. She received little attention, while I received grins, waves, giggles and all sorts of attempts at English greetings.

I was amused that they thought it so strange to see a foreigner in Togakure. I smiled when thinking of what their reaction would be if

---

*"Toh gah koo rey" is the way the village and ninjutsu tradition were pronounced in ancient times. Today, the ryu still retains the original pronunciation of the Japanese kanji. The modern-day residents of the village, however, pronounce the written characters for the name of their home as Togakushi ("Toh gah koo shi"). Despite the difference in pronunciation, the meaning and form of the written characters are identical. For the sake of a feeling of historical continuity, the Togakure spelling has been used for the village name throughout this volume, instead of Togakushi, as it would normally appear in any printed material about the village.

they only knew why my wife and I were there. Rumiko and I had been given the responsibility of transmitting the authority, knowledge and power of Togakure Ryu ninjutsu to the Western world. And our trip to the founder's birthplace was a significant pilgrimage. This was no mere tour for the two of us. It was to be a homecoming.

The next day's dawn found us standing before a massive white stone torii bearing the Japanese characters for Toh Gakure. The seemingly ageless granite pillars and cross-piece straddled the path leading up to the Togakure Jinja Okusha (deep sanctuary), concealed high up on the side of Togakure Mountain. The air was clear and chilly, and the lush green of the fern-carpeted forest seemed to pull us onto the trail that led skyward into ancient history. Rumiko, the unborn daughter she held within her, and I began the ascent.

Songbirds chirped and twittered in their wooded abode, happily oblivious to the two strangers who walked along the graveled avenue in their midst. Sunshine poured from a deep azure sky, light winds moved the treetops, and a tiny brook rushed and tumbled along the northern edge of the climbing path.

The winding trail to the Okusha narrowed after 20 minutes of walking. Lofty cedars now shaded the increasingly steep pathway that unfolded between the mammoth trunks and sprawling roots. Only an oc-

Author Stephen Hayes and his wife, Rumiko, standing in front of the shrine atop Togakure Mountain.

casional patch of blue sky could be seen far overhead where the feathery branches parted in the wind hundreds of feet above the moss-covered path. Crows winged among the limbs above, calling out to each other, or perhaps to us, with their cries echoing throughout the valley.

This inner shrine was the most difficult of the three shrine levels to reach. The Hokoji (treasure of light) was the first one encountered when entering Togakure. The ornately carved structure sits high on a promontory looking out over the valley approach to the ancient mountain village. The Chusha (middle shrine) is the central focus around which the village lies. That is the grouping of sacred buildings that receives the most attention from visitors.

Rumiko and I had gone to the Chusha the day before. We had reached the top of the weathered wooden temple steps just as the late afternoon shadows began stretching out into the elongated forms that signal the onset of evening. The golden glow of sunset gave the temple yard a special, almost storybook feeling, as if we were moving through a vivid dream.

We stood and watched while the temple priests performed the sacred *okagura* on ritual drums, flutes and bells. The holy men re-enacted the story of how Ame no Yagokoro Omoi Kane no Mikoto had lured Amaterasu Omikami from her cave to return the light of wisdom to humankind eons ago. The legendary sun goddess of Japan felt betrayed by the dastardly behavior of her rebellious brother Susa no Oh no Mikoto and, in shame and penance, had concealed herself under the earth in a cave sealed behind a massive stone door. In remorse and fear, humankind had worked at bringing her back to their lives.

In the central hall of the Chusha shrine, the masked priests whirled about in intense drama, their orange, white, green and purple silk costumes and gleaming swords blending into the tale of how one wise and determined being persuaded the sun goddess to leave the darkness behind and return her gifts to the world. I was absorbed by the colorful spectacle as it unfolded before a low altar, which supported a large brush and ink rendition of the stone door to the legendary cave.

In an explosive climax to the performance, the symbolic stone door was pushed aside and one could look directly into the eyes of the knowledge of the ages. There before me was a bearer of the cosmic light and wisdom of the universe, and I laughed when I saw the figure in front of me. The irony of the message was at the same time humorously familiar and jarringly reawakening.

There on a pedestal was a round mirror, reflecting my own image back at me. There was the timeless celestial wisdom, wearing yellow cotton pants and a yellow hooded sweatshirt, staring out at me from behind a bearded grin. The flickering image was then joined by another smaller one in a pink running suit, and two smiles beamed in the late afternoon of Togakure Village.

Rumiko and I continued along the footpath that led up to the Okusha inner sanctuary. We talked of all we had seen, the significance of where we were at the moment, and the increasingly complex trail of events, coincidences and accidents that had brought us together and merged our paths, pursuing the heritage and legacy of Japan's original ninja. She and I talked and laughed, comfortable in the certainty that our yet undefinable lifework would, as the grandmaster had told us, eventually carry the endorsement of worldly significance in history.

Steps of rough stone took us up through a steep and winding neck of the trail, past a weed-tangled clearing that had once been the training grounds of warrior ascetic *shugenja* of Togakure Mountain. We moved between columns of towering cedars. I thought of the centuries of turbulent history that had unfolded while these giant trees grew patiently on this obscure mountainside. I thought of how young Daisuke, the original inspiration of our ninjutsu tradition, must have felt when he walked among these trees for the last time before fleeing to his unknown destiny in faraway Iga.

With a sudden and chilling start, it occurred to me that Daisuke Nishina had never walked among these trees; he had never seen them at all. These mighty and massive cedars, as ancient as they were, had come into being long after Daisuke had gone away forever. These huge pillars were the image of antiquity, and yet they were merely things to come in the distant future, back in the days of Daisuke. The thought was breathtaking. Someone had actually planted those trees long after Daisuke's departure, so old was the Togakure Ryu tradition.

By midmorning, we had reached the Okusha inner sanctuary of the Togakure shrine. High on a rocky outcropping near the crest of the mountain, fringed by the waving greenery of trees and ferns, sat the grouping of sacred structures that we had trekked so far to see.

An attendant in a utilitarian white kimono and *hakama* nodded to us in silent greeting and continued on with his work. Rumiko and I walked wordlessly through the tiny compound—the wind in the trees and faint chimes the only sounds that touched our ears. The sky was becoming slightly overcast, as a steel-gray color edged in on the brilliant blue overhead. The valley below us stretched for miles and miles before turning up into another ridge of mountains far away. Time seemed to have stopped, high up on that holy pinnacle.

Small cabinet-like buildings held picturesque tributes to the legendary holy figures in the spiritual culture of Japan. Like the Western world's Jewish prophets and Christian saints, the Eastern world's Shinto *kami* and Buddhist *bosatsu* were honored and revered for their significance in the universal scheme of bringing the peace of enlightenment to humankind.

In wordless contemplation there on that sacred peak above the village of Togakure, new insights glimmered and then glowed in my meditative consciousness. So many pieces of random knowledge that I had dismissed as coincidental or insignificant through my years of ninja training seemed to emerge again slowly, take distinct shape and fit together in a truly life-size jigsaw puzzle.

Toh Gakure, the "concealing door," the name of the village and the mountain, and the source of the warrior tradition that I had become a part of, stemmed from the legend of the cosmic light and wisdom glowing behind the stone door thousands of years ago. Like the concealing door

of Amaterasu Omikami, the Togakure Ryu had existed as a protective barrier throughout the centuries, maintaining the wisdom contained in the lifestyle of Japan's original mountain mystics until the course of universal history brought mankind to the point at which the knowledge was needed and could be understood again and embraced by a new age of humanity.

What if, as the grandmaster himself had suggested, the first 800 years of the Togakure Ryu were all devoted to laying the groundwork and the current generation would be the bridge to future generations during which the true essence of the knowledge and life ways protected by the ninja would blossom out from the shadows? What if the "golden age of ninjutsu" was not the period of turmoil in Japan 500 years ago but was actually yet to come in the future?

For the first time in my life, I could actually feel the physical weight and authority of more than 800 years of tradition, power and accomplishment that are the Togakure Ryu. As a martial arts instructor, I had always thought it exciting to be part of a system that old, that substantial and that historical, but I had never before realized how much more than a "system" our ryu was. I was startled to acknowledge that I had in effect given up the martial arts, in the sense of the term as it is used by the masses of *gi*-clad punchers and kickers worldwide, and taken on a life path on which physical fighting skills formed only the first step. I was numbed and shaken to the core with the impact of this new vision.

The teaching license given to me by my teacher took on new meaning in my thoughts. So much more than a paper rank or title, it was symbolic of my life fulfillment as I ventured further and further into the destiny of the Togakure tradition. The document given to me, with its seals and signature block imprints, was the tangible representation of all that had been granted me by fate and all that I had taken on.

Looking out across the mountains that shelter Togakure Village, hearing the ringing cries of the hawks and crows overhead, and breathing in the crisp pure air, I felt as if I had been born anew. How right it feels to be a part of this Togakure legacy. The warrior's spiritual quest has taken me so very far beyond what I had expected when I first entered my training half a lifetime ago. I could say that I was surprised, but in truth, something there in the heart of my soul has always known that this was the way it was intended to be. I was exactly where I had set out to be, and I was well on my way home.

CHAPTER 14

Those aspiring to enlightenment
are advised to hold in their hearts
the reassuring truth that
the inside of the universe is vast enough
to contain comfortably
all the paradoxes;
all the pieces of the puzzle
that we have not yet touched.

THE PATH

The warrior quest as a way of discovery

Each of us as a single spark of energy in the vast eternity of the universe has some piece of the greater lesson to be mastered and made our own in this lifetime. Despite the claims and promises of some of the more fundamentalist religions, we are not all here to gain the same insights. We are not all here with the same questions, and most certainly, the same answers will not satisfy the quest in all of us.

There are many paths of life available to us as individuals, along which we can progress toward personal fulfillment and enlightenment. There is the spiritual path, the healing path, the path of trade, the path of the artist, the path of the ruler and the path of the server. There are countless others, too vast to catalog here. In my own life, my teachers, my students and I have been sent forth on the path of the warrior.

The first, and for many the most difficult, step on the way is the discovery of the appropriate path itself. In ancient days, it was natural to simply accept whichever path circumstances of birth decreed. Today, with the increased freedom that the world allows individuals, finding the proper way of enlightenment can sometimes seem easier, or conversely, it can become a nightmare of indecision in a bewildering array of possibilities. For some, a life path is something realized and actively entered in childhood. For others, the experiences and environments encountered in later youth provide the means of recognizing and initiating a life path. Even middle or old age can be the period during which the path is discovered, resulting in a dramatic alteration of one's daily life. Some never find their path and live out their lives in quiet despair or disarrayed frustration, bitterness and confusion.

It helps to remember that the path itself is not the ultimate lesson but only the vehicle or the means of carrying ourselves to the significance of the lesson. The necessity of totally surrendering oneself to the path and the ability to see into the past, present and future all at the same instant of awareness reveal the importance of becoming an active element in the scheme of the universe—the result of any path chosen and adhered to with commitment and enthusiasm. The path is the way of attainment and not the destination itself.

Indeed, the eventual destination often turns out to be a complementary reflection of what the path was thought to teach, much to the surprise of the seeker. Those following the path of healing can discover the power of the personal will in maintaining one's own health; in truth, those refusing to be healed cannot be healed. Those following the path of service can discover that for a community and a world to move in harmony, each individual must develop his or her own powers to serve and sustain his or her own family. Those following the spiritual path can discover that the key to understanding the scheme of the cosmic can often be found in the workings of the mundane. Those following the warrior path can ultimately come to know the endless futility of conflict, and they can develop the strength and invulnerability that permits the freedom to choose gentleness.

Historically, following the warrior path of enlightenment usually involves, at some point, setting out on a *musha shugyo* (warrior errantry) quest. Musha shugyo takes the martial artist far from the comfortable, familiar surroundings of home and loved ones and exposes him or her to experiences that demand resourcefulness and ingenuity in order to find the key to survival. A set lifestyle, reliance on friends and family, the intellectual comfort of being on familiar turf, and perhaps even one's native language are forsaken and left behind when this way is undertaken.

Ironically enough, submitting oneself intentionally to the potential of frustration is the essence of growth in the warrior way of enlightenment. Because the wandering warrior must face strange and sometimes startling differences in daily living, all comfortable habits and ruts must be given up for more appropriate behavior under the circumstances. The musha shugyo forces the aspirant to look at new ways of doing things. At the point of surrendering our old limiting ways, we are freed and open to new insights. To cling to one's previous style in hopes of adding on new discoveries defeats the purpose of the time spent on the path. It is the shedding of all our barriers and reservations and diving into the total potential of power that is the warrior's goal during this quest. The musha shugyo is a time for letting go of constricting beliefs to gain freedom, not for taking on new burdens and restrictions.

Perhaps the most famous saga in the lore of Japan's wandering warriors is the musha shugyo of Musashi Miyamoto, the legendary swordsman who roamed 17th-century Japan in search of the essence of the warrior way. Only after a lifetime on this path and dozens of combat encounters did Musashi finally settle down in his later years to teach and guide others. His treatise on strategy, the *Gorin no Sho*, was dictated shortly before his death in the cave on Kumamoto's Kinbo-zan Mountain, where he lived the last two years of his life. Musashi's entire life was one of sacrifice and stark utilitarian existence in pursuit of the martial way.

From our own Togakure Ryu tradition, there are many stories of musha shugyo in each generation. Toshitsugu Takamatsu, the 33rd grandmaster and the teacher of my own teacher, spent years in China during the turbulent era of the early 1900s. My teacher Masaaki Hatsumi, traveled the length of Honshu Island to be with his teacher. The stories of my own journey and apprenticeship in Japan have been recounted in other books.

The Togakure Ryu was the result of a forced musha shugyo in the life of Daisuke Nishina, the originator of the ninjutsu system in the late 1100s. Daisuke had originally been trained in the ways of Togakure Mountain shugendo, a practice of warrior asceticism and power development in which attunement with and direction of the natural elements is gained. The mountain dojo of the Togakure shugenja practitioners had been established by the warrior monk En no Gyoja during the reign of Tenmu Tenno in the year A.D. 637. The teachings were handed down from one generation to another for 500 years until the young Daisuke found himself involved with the seemingly magical methods of self-protection attained by the warrior wizards of Togakure. With those wild holy men of the mountains, Daisuke exposed himself to the elements of nature, the demands of the body and emotions, and the intricacies of the intellect in order to transcend all and attain the spiritual heights that are said to lend one the "mind and eyes of God."

Throughout the seasons, the energetic Daisuke practiced the ways of physical and spiritual endurance taught by his hermit mentors high in the peaks of the Joshinetsu Plateau. Eventually, Daisuke's fascination with the ways of heaven, earth and mankind, as embodied by his fanatical teachers, was put to the ultimate test when Japan was plunged into a great civil war and the teenaged Daisuke sided with Kiso Yoshinaka, in the year 1181.

After a devastating battle, Daisuke was forced to flee for survival. He wandered in exile to the remote Iga province far away to the southwest of his original family home. There, he encountered the mystic warrior priest Kain Doshi, who further initiated the youthful Daisuke in the ways of warrior power. In complement to his experiences with the *yamabushi* of Togakure Mountain, Daisuke learned the *omote* (outer) and *ura* (inner) manifestations of worldly perspective as he moved through his training in the powers of light and darkness. The exiled warrior plummeted and soared through new levels of consciousness, awareness and perspective.

To commemorate his rebirth on a new level of living, Daisuke Nishina assumed the name of Daisuke Togakure, reflecting his roots and celebrating the flowering of his destiny. Thus was established the foundation of what in later generations would come to be known as the Togakure Ryu tradition of ninjutsu, the esoteric natural life ways made famous by the ninja phantom warriors of feudal Japan.

Diverse factors seem to combine to make the warrior way of enlightenment a difficult path to enter and follow. Perhaps the greatest impediment is the Western world's inherent resistance to total immersion in one single aspect of existence, no matter how much insight that immersion may provide toward the unfolding of a fulfilling life. We seem to be a culture that prefers dabbling over mastering. Amusement overshadows attainment. It is as if we are afraid of becoming too good at one thing. Dynamic characteristics such as enthusiasm, commitment and inspiration are all too often given derogatory labels like "fanati-

cism" or "narcissism." It seems so much easier not to make demands and simply move along in place where society deems it fashionable and comfortable.

The warrior way is exactly what the name implies; a *way* of directing the days of one's life to better produce the likelihood of encountering those experiences that will lead to the enlightenment sought. Donning a white *do-gi* and *obi* and writing out a check for the "yellow belt course" is not the same as setting out on the warrior path. While it is certainly true that the martial arts can be taken up for pleasant recreation, the dabbler is not to be confused with the seeker on the path. The warrior way is an all-consuming, all-illuminating, lifelong commitment that will tolerate no diversions. It is not a hobby.

Another difficulty for those who would take up the path is that there are very few people qualified to guide a student in the way of the warrior. As a collective group, contemporary martial arts teachers have very little personal experience in actual individual warfare. What are called "martial arts" are routinely taught as sports or exercise systems in Asia as well as the Western world today. Though it is controversial to say so, there seems to be very little "martialness" to be found.

To verify this, one need only visit a few training halls and watch the action, bearing in mind several basic questions. Do the attackers in the exchange drills move like real attackers would on the street, or are they following a mandatory stylized affectation? Are the students training with and against realistic contemporary weapons, or are things like knives, clubs and pistols prohibited in the training? Are the surroundings and training wear varied and typical of the environment of daily life, or are the training hall and the costumes alien to daily reality? Are the students forced to face all possible types of attack—strikes, grappling, armed assaults, multiple opponents, psych-outs—or is there an implied limit as to what the students will encounter?

How insignificant we have allowed the martial arts to become. What were once dynamic and vibrant ways of life, demanded by the unpredictability of fortune, have now in so many training halls become mere silly charades. Stagnant formal movement has taken the place of spontaneous creative use of nature. Overly structured contests have nurtured intensified egos and reliance on contrivances, wearing away or watering down the ultimate statement of unbridled, total intention. Without the immediate pressures of warfare, so many teachers have become lazy and have lost sight of the very meaning of the word "martial." The venerable warrior path has been abandoned for easier, simpler freeways, so convenient for the complacent yet ultimately leading nowhere.

The warrior's musha shugyo search could be compared with a journey to a holy shrine. As the trip begins, we hold in our hearts the knowledge that there is one true and appropriate route to the destination, and we take to the road with certainty and a strong resolve to reach the goal. As we proceed, however, other roads that seem to be more attractive, more enjoyable or shorter become apparent. In our confusion, it can soon appear that these tangential roads better match the superficial appearance of what we think the path "ought" to look like. Instead of following the true route to the shrine, we then find ourselves wandering in all directions with our energy scattered, racing after what entertains us at the moment and forever losing the possibility of reaching the shrine. We never find our way home.

As a spiritual anchor to prevent drifting with the currents of illusion, the warrior aspirant can take refuge in the threefold power of the martial tradition. The act of taking refuge does not mean hoping that someone will stoop down and save us or take away our hardships for us, nor does it mean believing that something special will enter us or take us over and make us different. To take refuge in the martial tradition is to acknowledge the possibilities of our own resourcefulness in light of the inspiration provided by our mentors. Our refuge is our reference point, there to ever remind us of the true path we seek to follow.

The first refuge is the historical ryu itself, personified by the head master for each generation. The title *soke* is given to the person who has the responsibility of transmitting the knowledge gained from his teacher (the past generation) to his followers (the future generation). As such, the soke is a bridge between the tradition's history and the tradition's destiny. Though always operating in the present moment, the soke has the power to see backward and forward in time simultaneously. The grandmaster therefore has hundreds of years of experience on which to draw for inspiration and guidance. In a warrior ryu, the grandmaster carries the weight, power and authority of all those masters who have gone before him. For every successive grandmaster and his generation, there is yet a new layer of power given to the ryu and its members.

An authentic martial art ryu is not something lightly or easily established, nor is it a mere avenue of convenience for a would-be "master" who is simply unable to fit in with any other system around at the time. In the case of ninjutsu's Togakure Ryu, the martial tradition was not established or known by any name until well into its third generation. Only then did the followers of Daisuke Togakure feel justified in referring to their life ways and budding tradition as a ryu and begin to call themselves warriors of the Togakure Ryu.

Therefore, to take refuge in the ryu is to know complete trust in and belief in the teacher who embodies the essence of the ryu. The teacher's gift is his inspiration and the collective power of the generations past and present. He represents what we can become with proper training.

The second refuge is the greater truths embodied in the training methods taught by the ryu. From the days of the founder through the present, the master teachers of the ryu have spent centuries collecting

Historical perspective and contemporary application form an important part of ninja tradition and training. Here, a single swordsman engages two spearmen in a classic battle.

only those techniques, approaches and strategies that brought success-ful results. In the ancient days, when life-or-death combat clashes were common parts of daily living, false technique or inappropriate appli-cation would surely result in the ninja's death. Therefore, only proven methods would make it back from the battleground to be incorporated into the ryu's combat training program. Untested techniques of dubious practicality would die with the warrior who attempted them in battle, thus purifying continuously the principles of the fighting method.

In a similar manner, the teachings for the guidance of the practitioner toward enlightenment have gone through the same test of time over the generations. As centuries of master teachers' work unfolded, their life spans tested and refined over and over again the methods of attaining the *satori* (transcendent harmony) available to all humankind. The ways of cultivating the wisdom that leads to enlightenment could only be a product of lifetimes of research.

Therefore, to take refuge in these methods is to know complete confidence in the life-protecting skills developed, refined and perfected throughout generations of actual warfare. The combat and enlighten-ment methods of an authentic historical martial ryu will bear the tests of time—they are not untested theories from the imagination of one single individual.

The third refuge is the community of followers who have become a part of the ryu who work together in search of knowledge. Each grand-master creates a community of seekers around him, because without a family of practitioners, the ryu cannot be a living thing. As the powerful tradition of winning builds up over the generations, the community of practitioners begins to have a strong spiritual life force of its own. All who find it their destiny to become a part increasingly feel the power working in their lives. Like a huge, vibrating tuning fork that causes other tuning forks to buzz and hum in unison with it as they draw near, the ryu becomes more and more a great chord into which the lives of the members fall in harmony. Power comes from power. Residing in the presence of success propagates success.

Becoming a part of the community means taking one's place in the dy-namic and colorful panorama of personalities who have joined together on the same warrior path under the authority of the master teachers of the ryu. Senior members are regarded with respect and support in light of the progress they have made and the responsibility they carry.

Junior members are regarded with love and guidance in light of the faith, loyalty and determination they demonstrate. All fellow members, regardless of rank, are appreciated for the uniqueness of their individual personalities and are acknowledged for the strengths and talents they bring to the community.

Therefore, to take refuge in the community is to know complete openhearted acceptance of one's fellows in the search and to be totally willing to offer and accept the love and encouragement of the family.

To wholeheartedly take refuge in the ryu tradition (the teacher), the *ho* (ultimate truth of the techniques) and the *ichi mon* (family-community) is to know the power that comes from a complete involvement in following the way of the warrior path. Anything less than a total three-part commitment reduces one's warrior art to the level of a mere hobby or pastime and can actually create a dangerous imbalance in the practitioner's life.

Those who direct all their attention toward the ryu and grandmaster alone, ignoring the community of fellow students and the actual skills that require years to develop, face the danger of becoming warriors in name only. These are people who use the reputation of the ryu for their own self-promotion. The established community of followers and the work required to master the methods are seen as annoyances to be brushed aside.

Those who direct all their attention toward the physical techniques while ignoring the tradition of the ryu and the support of the community are entering into a most dangerous delusion. Centuries ago, the art of ninjutsu was driven into disrepute by many factors, one of which was the splintering off of *genin* (agents) from the wisdom and guidance of the *jonin* (family head). Ninjutsu is not a collection of mechanical skills that can be picked up or made up by anyone who wishes to call him or herself a ninja. Those dwelling in the realm of physical technique alone face the danger of moving through life in confusion, without guidance, direction or purpose. It is all too easy for these people to find themselves boxed in by circumstances that they never dreamed could materialize. It is no exaggeration to warn that this lack of greater awareness can often be dangerous, even fatal. This has been proved time and again throughout history, and it continues to be just as true even in the modern martial arts scene of today.

And finally, those who direct all their attention toward the community while ignoring the ryu and the teachings face the danger of becoming no more than mere groupies for whom personal power and identity are totally dependent on acceptance from the active members of the ryu. In its extreme form, this reduces the way to the level of a womb-like cult.

Unless the practitioner is under the guidance of a capable master teacher, progress is slow and tortuous at best, if at all. The hindrances, false methods and temptations are countless. There are so many mistakes that the unguided can make, that the possibility of going astray into outmoded or impractical martial systems is far greater than the possibility of accidentally happening onto true martial power and enlightenment. Without being in the company of those who have been along the path and who have experienced training in the pragmatic techniques and approaches that have a proven record of results, mastery of the warrior way is almost impossible to reach. The intellectual mind can create so many tempting delusions—neatly packaged (yet incomplete) explanations or comfortable short-cut rationalizations—it seems to require superhuman effort to resist all the hybrid martial arts fads and toys that are waiting to divert the potential warrior from the truth. To take refuge in the master teacher and his ryu, the community of seekers, and the universal laws embodied in the techniques is to form a solid and reliable foundation for personal growth and expansion through the pursuit of the warrior ideal.

With the power of the ryu and the guidance of those who have gone before, we can take to the road with unshakeable confidence. We can be firm in the knowledge that all difficulties and trials to be faced can be mastered and transformed into our own insights that will assist us in discovering the enlightenment we seek.

CHAPTER 15

It is an exhilarating discovery
to realize that
your soul's heart
is the most knowledgeable priest
that you can find.

ENLIGHTENED CONSCIOUSNESS

The goal and process of warrior training

Enlightenment is a heavily loaded word in our Western culture. It is so easily bandied about and yet so difficult to pin down with a definition. Often, enlightenment is thought to be a feeling, or a kind of super-understanding, or a state of solemnity and holiness, but at its truest and most essential level, the quality of enlightenment is none of these lesser states. Enlightenment is not the result of emotional, intellectual or even most religious processes. It is not possible to "figure out" enlightenment because words come nowhere near the experience and, in many cases, actually block the seeker from the enlightened consciousness sought.

Enlightenment can be pursued and does occasionally surprise the pursuer by actually blossoming in him or her. More often, however, the keys to the enlightened state lie in letting go of this ambitious struggle for the prize and losing oneself in an all-consuming activity or situation. This feeling of selflessness can be the product of merging with glorious surroundings or highly meaningful events, or it can result from letting go of all restraints and merging with a simple activity in a mind-releasing way. At first, one seems to observe one's own participation, perhaps even to the level of acknowledging the enjoyment experienced, but then the observation deepens, until there is no longer any feeling of separateness between the observer and that which is observed. When one recalls such a moment, it is remembered as one of awe, joy, total involvement and aliveness. At the time of the experience, however, the merging is so total and the mind is so relaxed that descriptive thought is temporarily transcended.

The state of enlightenment is an inner phenomenon that comes when all the unnatural darkness and heaviness that cloud and weigh down life are shed. It produces an altered view of things that also can cause an altered mode of living or behaving, once clear sight is attained. For the warrior mystic, enlightenment is the realization of one's ability to see through the illusory surface of things. This aspect of enlightenment often includes the startling perception that everything, no matter how "evil" or "good" by conventional labels, is *right* and *appropriate* for the universe and all therein. There is great comfort and power in this breakthrough of understanding. Before the enlightenment experience, of course, this thought is felt to be impossibly confusing and contradictory, even absurd.

This realization necessarily entails a departure from the fears and helplessness of the Dark Ages, in which people were taught that they were mere playthings in the hands of gods and devils, totally incapable of, and certainly morally prevented from, moving out of their place in life, no matter how miserable that place might be. There were political and religious (and therefore, ultimately economic) reasons for holding the masses in ignorance of their own power. There was far less turmoil and social unrest. Unfortunately, the price paid was intense misery, suffering and abuse, and the vast majority of living souls on the planet had no personal identity, dignity or freedom.

One of the traditional means of approaching the ideal condition that facilitates enlightenment is to allow oneself to let go of limiting attachments. These hindrances are symbolized in the attachments to "name, the elements and the Void." Upon setting out on a musha shugyo, the warrior embarks on a journey toward greater knowledge by cutting through the illusions that have been taken to heart over the years.

First of these three influences to be acknowledged is your "name," or simply "who you are right now." Generally, this is tied to the past and entails all the details of what you have done and what has been done to

you up to this point in life. It is sort of a cosmic balance sheet of all the events that seem to have occurred with no conscious cause-and-effect relationship.

This influence could be characterized as being those things in your life over which you may feel that you had no control. It is all those physical, social, familial, cultural and genetic aspects you inherited automatically when you were born. It is all your natural abilities, talents and inclinations. It is your personality, physique and emotional makeup that you describe as "only natural." This first major influencing factor is referred to as your name because it stands for all you are.

The second influence you must acknowledge and work through is the effect of all the outside elements in your life. Generally, this is tied in with the present and relates to the future. This is how you are affected by all the events that occur with a recognizable cause-and-effect relationship.

This influence could be characterized as being those things that interact with your life to make up your day-to-day activity. It is who your friends and enemies are, what weaknesses and strengths you have developed, and the way you operate in relationships. It is the effect of all your decisions in the cultural, economic and political fabric of the current day. It is your ability to work with all the obstacles and opportunities that arise in life. This second major influence is referred to as the "elements" because it stands for all those things that shape your life.

The third influence you have to acknowledge is your own responsibility for all that was, is and will be in your life. Generally, this means a willingness to accept your share of the situation you find yourself in. You have to know and believe that you are the only one who can do anything about affecting your life.

This influence could be characterized as being the degree to which you are willing to engage your personal creative power in order to guide your own life. You are responsible for all the problems and triumphs in your life. You allowed them to materialize or allowed them to come about by not actively preventing them. You must accept them for what they are—teachers you created to help you grow and advance. This third major influence is referred to as the "Void" because it stands for all the undefined potential that is your future.

Therefore, to believe that you have a controlling influence over what you know as reality, you must acknowledge the effects of all you were born with, all you interact with and all your potential power for direct-ing your life. At the same time, you must give up your attachment to all the limitations that are inherent in these three aspects of personality.

By giving up attachment to name, elements and the Void, the seeker on the warrior path can attain the freedom to see life as it actually is and gain the spontaneous adaptability that will allow him or her to ex-ercise fully the power that dwells in each moment of living. When those aspects of life symbolized by name, elements and the Void no longer control the warrior, he or she is returned to the "zero state"—perfect neutral resourcefulness. This return to zero provides the ability to relax and flow with any circumstance life presents.

"Name" symbolizes all you were born as. Therefore, giving up your attachment to your name means giving up your personal limitations and weaknesses you thought you were saddled with for life. This may be tougher than it sounds because it means giving up a lot of comfortable excuses and self-limiting habits of behavior and thought.

The "elements" symbolize all your standard methods for dealing with anything you encounter. Therefore, giving up your attachment to the elements means giving up your unthinking, habitual responses that may not be appropriate for the situation at hand; preconceived judgments that limit your possible routes of action or thought; opinions that work to stop you before you even get started. This is difficult because it means giving up outgrown concepts of understanding life, as well as abandon-ing or altering personal ideals that no longer produce the results that you need in the present.

The "Void" symbolizes all the power you have to direct and shape your life. Therefore, giving up your attachment to the Void means giving up your futile attempts to reduce all actions, plans and interactions to the realm of rational and mechanical principles alone, and letting go of the insistence that all experiences fit and conform to your personal intellectual model of how things ought to be. This is extremely difficult because it means learning to balance your views of accomplishment and destiny, your personal direction in life, with the greater workings of the cosmic scheme of totality. Imbalance in this area can be a two-way trap with dangers at either extreme. You can hopelessly battle through your days because of your inability to determine or even conceive of the cosmic cycles and seasons of life. At the other extreme, you can sink into the helplessness of waiting and wishing for the ghosts, celestial

Seated Meditation Postures

For meditation work, any seated posture that allows the back to remain in a straightened position will work. Perhaps most traditional for the Japanese martial arts is the seiza (kneeling) posture and the crossed-leg seated posture. To reduce unnecessary tension in the lower back, which could distract from meditative concentration, a folded towel or small pillow can be used to lift the hips off the ground slightly.

imaginary friends or mythical beings from childhood's beliefs to do the work for you in attaining enlightenment or so-called "salvation." Both extremes have disappointment built in.

The warrior's enlightenment cannot be gained by merely reading a book or by following a set routine of mechanical steps. There are no doctrines or exercises that can make you enlightened. All that a book of this nature can do is suggest that the possibility of dropping heaviness and darkness does exist for all and provide some guidance for obtaining an idea of what the enlightened state could be like.

The following exercises are offered as examples of ways to catch a fleeting glimpse of the enlightened state of being. In effect, they can allow you to create a given feeling or temporary way of seeing or acting. The exercises are not to be confused with the actual attainment of enlightenment itself, however.

For the following meditation exercises, sit in a comfortable position with your back held in a naturally straight posture. The crossed-leg position, *seiza* (kneeling) and sitting in a straight-backed chair are of equal benefit for novices. The important thing is to allow the breath to move in and out of the lungs freely in a nondistracting manner. Shade or close your eyes, lower your chin slightly and relax your hands in your lap. Direct the conscious awareness inward, and focus on the mental work to the exclusion of external distractions.

EXERCISE ONE

For insight, from the *chi no kata* (earth) level of consciousness, meditate on the frailty, ever-degenerating vitality and impurity (incompleteness) of the human body. Work for realization of the futility of centering your ultimate awareness and priorities on the physical machine alone. Mentally look around at all the examples of human bodies in a variety of age and health states. The unpredictability of disease, the demands of the appetites, the awkwardness of youth and the unresponsiveness of old age can be seen simultaneously to better understand the limitations of the body.

EXERCISE TWO

For insight, from the *sui no kata* (water) level of consciousness, meditate on the delusions and deceptions of the sensations. Work for realization of the destructiveness of centering your awareness and judgments on the wayward-leading qualities of your sense stimuli. Mentally observe all the examples of tricks that the senses can play on your perception of reality. Consider the limited scope of what can be explained through so-called rational, objective analysis.

EXERCISE THREE

For insight, from the *hi no kata* (fire) level of consciousness, meditate on the impermanence and inconstancy of the mind's thoughts. Work for realization of the ever-shifting unreliability of the mind in flux. Reflect on how the mind abandons old ideas once firmly defended and adopts new concepts resolutely, as if those new temporary ideas contained the final truth. The mental process of forming beliefs regardless of the objective mind's inability to determine universal truth, the turmoil of stress as the mind works to live in surroundings that it finds totally inharmonious, and the phenomenon of misunderstanding physical and emotional actions can be seen from the meditative state in order to better understand the limitations of the mental process of discrimination.

EXERCISE FOUR

For insight, from the *fu no kata* (wind) level of consciousness, meditate on the fleeting transiency of the self in the universal scheme. Work for realization of the magnitude of the story of our planet from dim past through far future and the relatively brief moment that any self can affect the total epoch. Consider the overall significance of personal troubles, disappointments, strivings and triumphs experienced by the self in the grand picture of the history of the cosmos.

EXERCISE FIVE

For calmness of mind, from the chi no kata (earth) level of awareness, meditate on the tendency of worldly materialistic life to take over and consume the individual in order to enlighten the mind to the effects of passion and greed.

EXERCISE SIX

For calmness of mind, from the sui no kata (water) level of awareness, meditate on sympathy and empathetic identification with other people in order to enlighten the mind toward the elimination of anger.

EXERCISE SEVEN

For calmness of mind, from the hi no kata (fire) level of awareness, meditate on cause and effect in order to enlighten the mind to the effects of ignorance.

EXERCISE EIGHT

For calmness of mind, from the fu no kata (wind) level of awareness, meditate on the diversity of realms in order to enlighten the mind to the validity of differing standpoints and to eliminate limiting, selfish views.

EXERCISE NINE

For calmness of mind, from the *ku no kata* (the Void) level of awareness, meditate on the flow of breath as a means of neutral concentration in order to enlighten the mind to the effects of mental dispersion.

EXERCISE TEN

Imagine you are in the future looking back at the present, which will appear as the past from your viewpoint in the imaginary future. Work at seeing yourself right now through the eyes of the self as you will be in the future as a means for guiding decision-making and action planning.

EXERCISE ELEVEN

For perspective on action, meditate on the ability to look forward into the future from the immediacy of the present moment of action. Work at seeing the potential results to be generated from current second-to-second consciousness.

CHAPTER 16

Just as your own body
  turns against and eradicates
  diseased tissues
  that would choke out the possibility
  of continued vibrant life,
  the ninja moves stealthily and resolutely
  against the poisonous elements
  of the communal body of humankind,
  ridding us all
  of that which would corrode and corrupt.

NINJA INVISIBILITY

Ways of undetected influence

Throughout those periods of Japanese history in which the legendary ninja were active in the clandestine methods of protecting their homes and families, it is highly likely that the black suits and masks so often seen in Japanese movies and comic books were actually worn much less often than the conventional dress of the time. Common sense alone tells us that to be caught moving through a castle corridor or village alleyway while wearing a costume that erased all doubt as to the illegal purpose of one's presence would be akin to suicide in an age when ninjutsu was considered the method of terrorists and assassins.

Of course, there were those times when the *shinobi shozoku* or *nin niku yoroi* outfit so often associated with ninjutsu would be a tactical or even psychological advantage. Subdued tones of faded black, dark blue or gray were often perfect for clothing that would fade from sight in the shadowy corners and recesses of a Japanese fortress or castle. The traditional ninja suit could even cover a disguise of conventional clothing that would later aid the ninja in escaping safely. As a psychological ploy, even those hired warriors not associated with the actual ninja clans of south central Japan would occasionally don the trappings of the ninja in order to add to their potential shock value in combat. With the reputation for treachery, coldblooded ruthlessness and amoral commitment to goals ever a part of the samurai's perception of the ninja, being confronted by a masked, black-clad figure twisting his fingers into symbolic knots while rasping some mysterious sutra in a monotone was often enough to cause hesitation, whether the accosted was actually a true ninja or not.

It was often more prudent, however, for the ninja to adopt more subtler ways of disguising his or her presence or concealing the body from view. Historically, the ninja's ways of creating the illusion of invisibility were a highly developed science that combined an understanding of what we would today call physics, psychology and physiology. Despite the passage of the centuries, *onshinjutsu*, the ninja's unique "art of invisibility," remains a valid principle to aid police, investigators, antiterrorist groups and military reconnaissance units in modern society.

The quality of invisibility can be approached from a number of different angles. The demands of the situation, the amount of lead time needed for preparation and the severity of the price of failure determine the best tactics for any given situation.

The first method of invisibility is to prevent light rays from reflecting off the subject. Total darkness, reduced or altered lighting, and colors or shapes that blend with the background are examples of invisibility that result in the inability of the perceiver to detect the subject. Like a glass that reflects nothing and yet the object is definitely there, one can't be seen because one sends back no distinguishing light clues.

A second method of creating the effect of invisibility is to take away the perceiver's capability of sight. This method includes smoke bombs and smoke screens, chemical gases and sprays used as eye irritants, *metsubushi*, or blinder clouds of ash, sand and iron filings, and intense flashes of bright light, all of which render the perceiver's sight temporarily useless.

A third principle of invisibility is employed in the *shichi ho de* (seven ways of going) system of ninjutsu. With this method of moving unseen, light impressions are reflected from the subject and do register in the eyes of the perceiver, but the stimuli does not trigger a response. In this application, the ninja's image enters the perceiver's field of vision in such a way as not to be noticed, even though fully exposed to the adversary.

In short, by assuming the guise of something or someone who is of no concern to the enemy, the ninja can move unhindered in full view of those who would otherwise attack him.

Daily life is full of hoards of little gray people who enter and depart from our lives uneventfully, leaving little or no traces in our consciousness. The larger the city in which we live or the more regions through which we travel, the more of these seemingly nameless, storyless, characters one encounters. Though in truth every living being on our earth has his or her own unique history, personal feelings, fears, dreams and hopes, through sheer overload alone it is so easy to overlook all the fascinating facets that make up even the most seemingly mundane of individuals. In our modem intercity, interstate and international society, we all come in contact with so many people that conscious intellectual acknowledgment of everyone is overwhelming, if not impossible. As a means of countering this barrage of potential for interpretation, classification and judgment, our minds simply tune out all but what seems crucial to daily personal survival. We operate under a mental "automatic pilot" until something that seems important or demanding comes along.

For those studying the warrior ways in the modern world, it is crucial to note that this state of mental numbness is a product not of boredom but of overstimulation. When the frame of reference stretches beyond the mind's capability to note and discern, normal sights and even some outstanding things can vanish even as our eyes scan across them. A masterpiece of oil painting can so easily disappear from sight when placed on a wall alongside other masterworks in a huge gallery of art. Though the painter's work itself is no less expressive, it readily fades from view when made a part of a massive collection. A single breathy note from a reed flute, so meaningful and soul touching as it resonates through a deserted wooden temple, would seem lost among the surging tones generated by a full orchestra in crescendo.

From this perspective, it is easy to see how the majority of people who contact us in daily life could disappear into the background as we search for the highlights. With our eyes on the clock and the speedometer or our minds engaged in the search for that special contact, fugitive, associate or lover, it is easy for all those people who serve us and contact us to fade into invisibility. This tendency for the minds of others to *allow us to disappear* is the key to the effectiveness of ninjutsu's shichi ho de method for the attainment of invisibility.

When required to infiltrate a city, fortress or camp, the ninja can use this reliable technique of blending in with the surrounding community so as to be undetected by the enemy. During the civil turmoil that characterized the Sengoku Jidai (Warring States Period) of 16th-century Japan, a system of seven disguises was developed for the operatives of the ninja families fighting for survival in those harsh times. The seven cover identities of the ancient shichi ho de were the following:

Akindo	Merchant or tradesman
Hokashi	Musician
Komuso	Itinerant priest
Sarugaku	Entertainer, "monkey trainer"
Shukke	Buddhist monk
Tsunegata or ronin	Wandering samurai for hire
Yamabushi	Mountain warrior ascetic

CONTEMPORARY CHARACTER TYPES

The seven characters of the shichi ho de were perfect for the Japan of 500 years ago, in which religious men and warriors alike moved through communities and countrysides in such broad spectacle that their conflicts became commonplace. For the practice of the shinobi arts today, however, such antique impersonations would hardly be congruous with contemporary society. Obviously, moving through the street in a robe with a reed basket over one's head while playing a bamboo flute is not the best way to blend in, even in remote rural Japan. This in no way invalidates the usefulness of the shichi ho de concept. The methods of ninjutsu are timeless, although the details of its application may change through the ages. This is true of the physical combat training, spiritual work and military strategy.

Behind the physical details of the shichi ho de system concept lies a twofold structure. *Hensojutsu,* the art of disguise, is the way of altering one's appearance or bearing in such a way as to disappear from view by blending in with the surroundings. Through disguise, the ninja can become invisible by concealing those cues that would trigger recognition in the consciousness of the enemy. *Gisojutsu,* the art of impersonation, is the way of assuming another personality or identity in such a way as to operate in full sight or even with the cooperation of the enemy. Through impersonation, the ninja can replace those psychological cues that would put the enemy on guard and can even create an imbalance in the mind of the enemy that leads him to vulnerability. At times, the two arts overlap in application.

A more contemporary version of the shichi ho de method would include the following character types based on the *kotsu* (principles) of the historical system.

Scholastic

This category includes students, professors, researchers, technical specialists, writers, artists and, in some cases, radical or activist types. In-depth research will be required for anyone attempting to impersonate a character in this category. If possible, it would be best to impersonate an individual with whom there was some common academic background.

All people in this category will have a specific campus, school or facility with which they are familiar. The more well-known the institution, the more likely it will be to meet others who were there once, making familiarity with the physical layout and atmosphere crucial. People in this category also will have an area of expertise in which they are well-versed intellectually, whether it be a classical European composer, nuclear reactors or economic theories. It is necessary to be more than a little familiar with the topic for which one is posing as an authority. Artists and writers will have to be able to create, or at least display someone else's work as their own creations. Radicals and activists will have a specific cause, ideal or movement with which they identify.

Business

This is an extremely broad category that ranges from salespeople, merchants and office workers to secretaries, accountants and consultants. In terms of disguise, the basic uniting factor in this classification is business attire and grooming, and it should be noted that business roles are the most readily assumed identities in modern Western society.

Basic business skills and attitudes can be obtained through vocational schools, on-the-job training or personal interviews with sympathetic associates. Actual positions as typists, clerks and salespeople are always available through newspaper classified advertisements or agencies that offer temporary office help. Convincing-looking business cards and stationery for an assortment of character roles and identities can be printed inexpensively and can be produced as needed. Offering a card as a vice president of manufacturing operations, the ninja might be able to open doors, capture attention and gain access to the right contacts or facilities. On the other hand, offering a card as a self-employed recruiter of salespeople for a shady-sounding pyramid organization, the ninja might turn off quickly those people who pay too close attention when discretion is needed.

Explosive smoke grenades are used as blinders to assist the ninja in the mechanics of becoming invisible.

The explosive metsubushi (sight removers) are applied against attackers.

Rural

In this category are farmers, ranchers, migrant workers and any other personalities commonly associated with rural or country settings. The smaller or more remote the town or community, the more difficult it will be to fit into that location anonymously.

Farmers and farmworkers have specific crops or livestock with which they deal and naturally have the knowledge that comes with experience in the field. Ranchers are competent on horseback and have a working knowledge of animals. Ranchers and farmers also should be familiar with and capable of driving standard shift trucks and vehicles associated with their areas of work. Ninja posing as loggers should possess and know how to carry the gear and equipment appropriate for the role assumed. Hunters should be aware of hunting season dates, appropriate caliber weapons for specific game, and logical approaches for stalking the prey they claim to be hunting. Fishermen should have the appropriate tackle and bait, and they should know the types of fish indigenous to the area. Hunters and fishermen must possess a proper license for the game they are stalking and the region in which they are operating.

Religious

This narrow classification includes priests, rabbis, evangelists, missionaries and even some types of social workers. Religious personages are often given special respect, or at least tolerance, by society in general, even by those people not belonging to the religious organization represented.

Obviously, a ninja posing as a religious figure must have knowledge of the religion being assumed, or at least a basic familiarity with the core doctrines of that religion. Behavior traits are perhaps the most critical areas where mistakes can be made by the less than cautious. Small details can be deadly. It is unlikely that a fundamentalist Christian evangelist on tour would order a beer, whereas a Roman Catholic priest might find nothing wrong with having a mug of that beverage. A Jewish rabbi might sit down with a cup of coffee, but that is something that would be totally out of character for a Mormon missionary.

Public Figures

Another broad category, this character group includes entertainers, actors, musicians, sports figures, politicians, reporters, models or anyone with an interesting life story to tell or live out. An aura of notoriety, glamour or even infamy is the uniting factor in this classification. It is an interesting paradox to note that being in the center of the spotlight can sometimes be one of the most effective ways of concealing from others one's true purpose or aims.

All people in this category would have a particular claim to fame around which their identity would revolve. Some considerations for impersonation would be that a sports figure must have an appropriate physique, a model or actor will have a portfolio with pictures, a musician must be able to perform, a political figure will have a party and a constituency that he or she represents, and an author will have a subject on which he or she is an authority.

Labor

This classification can include construction workers, painters, gardeners, truck drivers and plumbers, or any other occupation in which people provide services through their physical skills. Working ability in the occupation being used as a cover would be necessary for the ninja.

In terms of disguise, the laborer is often identified simply by the clothing style worn or the equipment carried. Paint-spattered white clothes, a carpenter's tool belt, suntanned arms and grass clippings on the pants cuffs, engine oil ground under the fingernails—all are symbols of labor that in the right places trigger an instant unconscious acceptance in the minds of observers who might otherwise take undue notice of a stranger in their area.

Uniformed

Similar to the labor category, this character group covers repairmen, meter readers, security guards, janitors, nurses, police officers and military ranks. Other uniform types could include clown clothing with makeup—even Santa Claus suits or amusement park characters when working a crowded street, park or market area. The uniting factor in this category is some sort of uniform that creates a feeling in passers-by that the ninja in his or her assumed identity is "supposed to be there," whether taking apart a revolving door or roping off a no-parking area.

A person in uniform can be a very powerful psychological cue. When confronted by occupation soldiers, MPs or police officers on patrol, feelings of acquiescence can be triggered. Doctors, nurses, repairmen and guards project images of "making things all right." One also can create the subtle impression of a uniform by wearing simple monochromatic clothing in dark colors.

PERSONALITY ASPECTS

The contemporary ninja is by no means limited to these seven identity groups alone. If more appropriate or necessary, any role that will accomplish the purpose at hand will be employed. The shichi ho de structure is a convenient way to catalog methods so that something normally obvious is not overlooked during times of stress. As a tool of the ninja, the "seven ways" is used to assist, not to limit or hinder.

A kunoichi uses a wall panel as an entrance to a secret passageway, creating the illusion of quickly "disappearing."

A kunoichi disappears into a specially constructed danden gaeshi (wall trap door) beneath a mikkyo shrine.

It is important to bear in mind the purpose of employing the hensojutsu and gisojutsu methods of ninjutsu in each specific situation. In general, disguises are used to facilitate blending in and disappearing as a part of another required action. Impersonations are used to gain direct control in a given action. To observe a specific pedestrian traffic pattern, for example, one might choose to sit at the edge of a construction site and eat a sandwich from a metal lunchbox while wearing a plaid wool shirt and a hard hat. No real knowledge of building a skyscraper would be required. On the other hand, to infiltrate a construction site in an investigation would require the extensive research that would permit the ninja to actually become one of the crew. Merely donning a disguise would be dangerously insufficient in that case.

Ninjutsu's *hengen kashi no jutsu* is the method of totally becoming a new character for as long as necessary. The ninja is rendered invisible by leaving behind "ninja-ness" and taking on the personality aspects necessary to blend and thereby vanish. More than just pasting on a false mustache or stuffing a jacket, the theory of hengen kashi (immersion in the illusion) requires alertness at several different levels.

Appearance

For tasks of impersonation, try to pick an identity in which you appear to fit readily. Extended impersonations run the risk of having an artificial disguise discovered, making a dramatic cosmetic change a dangerous gamble. A young person would find it difficult posing as a business consultant or high-ranking religious personage, whereas an older person would find it awkward taking a college student or army private role without drawing attention. Naturally based alterations of appearance are best for impersonations. Hairstyles and color can be changed easily. Weight can be picked up or dropped with sufficient advance notice. Facial hair (or the lack of) can create a variety of looks. Adjustment of posture, bearing and stride is also a major aspect of making a character fit others' expectations. The purpose of an impersonation is to convince target personnel that you are who they want you to be.

Techniques of disguise include makeup, costumes and physical movement, just like in a play or movie. However, unlike theatrical entertainment, a less than convincing performance could result in the imprisonment or death of the ninja. Considerations for possible points of disguise include the following:

Gender
Race
Height, weight and build
Age
Speech quality and accent
Facial features
Hair color, style and length
Scars or tattoos
Deformities or injuries
Right- or left-handedness
Walking stride and pace
Clothing details and badges

Theatrical makeup supplies can be found in nearly every city. Secondhand stores and charity thrift shops are excellent sources for worn-looking clothing and uniforms in all sizes. High-quality wigs and elevator shoes can be purchased from appropriate specialty retailers.

Knowledge

All character types assumed have specific bodies of knowledge that go naturally with their roles. When assuming some identities, physical abilities or skills are mandatory. Other personalities require intellectual expertise or background knowledge. Whenever possible, select a suitable role in which your own personality or background can be used without great adjustment or massive research efforts that might require more time than is available. Obviously, some impersonations will demand more knowledge than others. Posing as a state auditor, for example, will require more study and background than will impersonating an ice-cream vendor at a carnival.

Libraries, campus bookstores and paperback study guides for high school, college or vocational school courses are an excellent means of getting a quick overview of most conventional knowledge areas required for an impersonation.

Language

The highly trained and experienced ninja will use as few words as possible, realizing that the more he or she ventures into conversation, the greater the chance of the listener detecting a mistake in details. Supply answers and comments to questions posed only when there is a danger of discovery by not commenting, and avoid suggesting things that the questioner had not thought of asking himself or herself. Voice quality and language used must be appropriate for the character being assumed. Accents, dialects, slang and technical jargon should be observed and studied so as to guard against misuse.

Because of language and idiom complications, foreign identities are difficult to assume. With sufficient study of a language and minimal use of conversation in the area of infiltration, a ninja can successfully deal with required foreign activity, however. Though the intelligence information he or she would be able to gather under such circumstances might be limited, there is much that could be done by restricting or structuring encounters with native elements to avoid compromising the project. As another consideration, it can involve great risk to portray a foreign person in one's own country without a fundamental knowledge of the nuances of accent and language of the assumed homeland.

Geography

Some character roles require a familiarity with places and customs as a part of their makeup. It is wise to select a background with which you have a natural tie because details can be deadly if you are uncertain. A ninja posing as a security guard at a stadium had better know where the first-aid station or men's rooms are. A ninja posing as a real estate agent in Chicago had better know the layout of the city's neighborhoods in terms of income, home prices and ethnic makeup.

Another aspect of geography means knowing the way about one's area of operation. Map-reading and map-drawing skills are essential. It cannot be stressed enough that a crucial key to the success of an action is a thorough casing of the potential area of operation one or more times before actually going in. Moving into an area cold is inviting the unforeseen to create problems. The ninja should have a working knowledge of streets, corridors, gates, forest tracts, bodies of water, security systems, and transportation routes and means, as well as several preplanned escape routes and emergency procedures, before setting out on any covert action.

Psychology

When employing a false identity from the shichi ho de, whether for purposes of disguise or impersonation, the most important psychological factor to keep in mind is to maintain alertness while appearing outwardly calm. Do not overplay the role in an attempt to convince the target that you are the new personality. Smooth and natural adoption of the character style often means actually *underplaying* the role. Locksmiths do not try to act "locksmith-like"; they are just individuals who work on locks to earn a living. Police officers rarely sit around formally discussing casework while off-duty on a coffee break; instead, they are human beings in a relaxed and probably jocular moment of their day. The telephone repairman does not consciously style his behavior while on the job; he is a person with his own unique personality who just happens to be in that occupation. Avoid the danger of being too stereotypically posed when affecting a temporary illusion.

When you assume an identity, you must actually become the new character, down to the last idiosyncratic detail of personality. You may be forced to do, say, or allege to have done things that are totally unacceptable to your own true personality. Often, that entails appearing foolish, cowardly, weak, immoral, mentally unbalanced, perverted, or in many other ways contradictory to what you might believe your true self-essence to be. This kind of commitment is not as easy as it might seem. The goal takes precedence over the image of the agent, and the ninja must be perfectly comfortable with creating the impression of failure in order to ultimately achieve success.

The following exercises introduce some basic practices that will help reinforce the principles of onshinjutsu.

EXERCISE ONE

When you find yourself in a restaurant, airport, shopping mall or any public area with a crowd of strangers, quickly look over the crowd in an alert yet not deliberate frame of mind. Pass your eyes over them in a casual scanning motion just to see who is there. Maintain a curious but not investigative mental attitude.

After one or even two surface scans, go back and really examine the area and the people you just observed. Look closely and critically this time, noting that person or people who initially caught your attention as you ran your eyes across the crowd. What was it about them that caused you to notice them more than the others around you? Be very specific in your analysis, and make a note of your findings on what causes people to stand out in a crowd.

Again, go back and re-examine the crowd. This time, observe closely and look for that person who *least* caught your eye the first time. You may have missed him or her completely and be mildly surprised to notice that person at all. What was it about that person that allowed him or her to move about in plain sight before your eyes and yet remain unnoticed by you? Again, be very specific in your analysis. Make a note of your findings on what allows people to vanish into a crowd before the eyes of observers.

Compile your findings as you repeat this exercise over and over again during the coming months. Look for significant correlations in terms of body poses, color and style of apparel, position in the room, sex and age, actions, and all other similarities that became increasingly obvious to you. Study the ways that you can use this self-taught knowledge to stand out from or disappear into a crowd at will.

EXERCISE TWO

Whenever you find yourself a part of an audience situation, whether it is in a lecture hall, school classroom, church congregation or political rally, experiment with your physical bearing, eye contact and personal presence to see how easily you can capture or totally avoid the attention of the person addressing the crowd.

To gain and hold attention, work at becoming a part of the speaker's thoughts. Immerse yourself in what the speaker is attempting to put across, tuning your mind to what his or her mind is holding. Make deliberate eye contact and maintain an assuring, encouraging expression on your countenance. From these obvious starting considerations, work at discovering what you can do with mental imagery and nonverbal communication to channel his or her lecture into a personal address to you. Make a note of what you can do to turn on and enhance your own personal magnetism.

Reverse this procedure to disappear into the crowd. Direct your thoughts elsewhere, or create disjointed mental "white noise" in your consciousness to prevent being tuned in to. Alter your body position and mental attunement to avoid direct notice. Work at experimenting with all possible mind tools as a means of discouraging attention in subtle ways. You are looking for a way of vanishing in a crowd without giving off those telltale cues of one who is noticed by trying too hard to be inconspicuous.

Study your results through repeated experiments and note the significant items and techniques that work for you. Compile your own methods of forcing yourself into the mind of another or willfully remaining unknown and unseen.

EXERCISE THREE

For reasons of investigative work, personal privacy or security, or professional need, comb through your own background to find the root characteristics that will permit you to create three distinct, alternate identities for yourself.

Step One

Begin by determining and listing names, physical descriptions, background histories, career paths and personality traits for each of the three individuals. Collect personal items for these characters whenever you have a few extra moments. Continuously scan printed material, conversations and documentaries for background details that would fit your alter identities.

Step Two

Collect a wardrobe of appropriate garments and accessories for each character. Include items that will pad, heighten or otherwise alter your physical bearing, as well. Along with the clothing, assemble all necessary wigs, glasses and makeup elements necessary for transformation into this alternate identity.

Step Three

Establish a "paper" background for each of your characters. Start with business cards, stationery, club memberships and mail drops. From there, move on to establish credit histories for each of the three, setting up bank accounts and charge accounts, bearing in mind that separate federal identification numbers will be required for each personality.

Step Four

Set up residences and places of business for each of the three identities. Personal furnishings, down to details like scrapbooks, baby pictures and high-school trophies, can be obtained easily at flea markets and garage sales.

Step Five

Cultivate friendships and personal contacts for each of the three personalities. Personal involvements should be widespread and not limited to the identity's professional sphere of activity alone.

Follow the suggested steps of this exercise as far as necessary in your life. Readers with just a superficial curiosity in ninjutsu will probably be content to stop after completing Step One as an intellectual exercise. Professional investigators, police, reporters, couriers, bodyguards and the like may need to carry the exercise on to the levels implied beyond Step Five in the series.

CHAPTER 17

Would that all who encountered us
could show and receive love and acceptance.
A noble ideal indeed,
but one not yet practical
nor safe,
in the unfolding saga of humankind.

KEN TAI ICHI JO

The body and weapon are one

he attainment of a spiritual lifestyle can only be possible after the physical dangers and demands of daily living, and the fears they generate, have been overcome. This is often misunderstood by those who condemn the practice of the martial arts as being antisocial or promoting violence in an already fractured and alienating society.

Indeed, there are those schools that do dwell on their own narrow approaches to physical mayhem while totally ignoring the higher powers of the warrior, or the grander perspectives that allow the warrior to know when it is inappropriate to engage combat skills. These *michi dojo*—traditionless, masterless "street schools"—actually infect their students' lives with the physical danger and emotional stress they pretend to alleviate. Instead of encountering life-promoting warrior sages in positions of instruction in these training halls, one finds bitter men with threatened egos and attitudes that constantly seek out the negative in life and interpret all actions on the part of others as insults or threats. "Respect," as they define it, is more important to these teachers than the quality of love, and they never attain peace in their lives.

By contrast, the practice of the true warrior arts as a life way promotes peaceful communities through cultivation of the personal power within each individual. Strength, resourcefulness and responsibility replace fear, helplessness and dependency as one meets challenges and finds solutions to them. It is one thing to shrink back docilely in terror while pretending to choose acquiescence willfully. It is altogether a different thing to choose gentleness freely because, having attained the skills of devastation, one has removed the fear of angering or displeasing others. Only the truly powerful, or those who have nothing to lose, can be totally gentle with a free and unhindered heart, for they are invulnerable.

In these confusing and highly competitive times, there is much that induces fear in the hearts of the benevolent. Therefore, the physical combat methods of ninjutsu, or *nin-po* as it is known in the higher order, by necessity include a wide array of skills for handling every conceivable situation of self-protection. The goal is survival at the least and supremacy whenever possible. To attain it, one applies appropriate, continually responsive action that always takes a dangerous situation exactly where the ninja wants it to go. By conscientiously applying this principle in daily ninja training, the practitioner gains the experience of mastering through physical agility, creative thought, and a firm and directed will.

Because of this emphasis on spontaneous decision and creative ability, the concept of *kata* as solo action prearranged patterns of movement is not a part of the *jutsu* combat methods of nin-po, at least not in the ordinary sense of the Japanese word kata. The omission of solo action kata floor routines—a training method so fundamental to other Japanese, Chinese and Korean martial arts practiced today—was determined more by the history and purpose of ninjutsu than by any decision or mere preference of a given teacher or master instructor.

Historically, the concept of solo action floor routine training in the martial arts grew for two distinct reasons. First, kata were used as a means of transmitting a school's combat techniques and principles from generation to generation during a relatively peaceful era, following one of continual warfare. With no means of gaining combat experience firsthand (and no pressing need to spend the time necessary to develop spontaneous killing skills), the samurai of later feudal Japan employed the kata as a means of suggesting the feel of battle and providing the essence of combat methods that had proved successful in the past.

Peacetime tampering or revision of the kata was strictly forbidden in most of the classical *bujutsu ryu*. The second purpose of kata was to provide a set, nonchanging routine that could be memorized for the practice of Zen moving meditation. The ultimate purpose of the Zen arts, however, lies not in training for the overcoming of enemies but in the perfection of one's own character and the attainment of the peace of enlightenment.

Neither of the two foregoing methods fit the purpose of ninja warrior training in history or in modern application. A kata based on set, memorized techniques is an inappropriate way of training warriors who will face actual combat in the field or on the street. Changes in weapon construction, use or availability and evolution in wearing apparel, building construction and technology could render any kata totally obsolete even within its own generation. Zen kata are also inappropriate for warrior training. The elimination of options and decision-making requirements, which make the kata so effective for Zen training, is counterproductive to the preparation that the ninja warrior requires for actively improving his or her ability to adapt and survive in hostile environments.

As a further historical note, ninja training methods for the development of warrior powers were established 13 centuries in the past. The techniques pioneered by the warrior wizards of Togakure Mountain, which later evolved into the clandestine ways of ninjutsu, predate the kata tradition by centuries. The approach to enlightenment endorsed by the warrior ascetics of Togakure is also more akin to the practice of tantra, in which inner visualized action is the tool for attaining mastery. In a sense, esoteric tantra is the philosophical opposite of Zen.

Example 1

Rigid, stylized methods of unarmed defense were developed as a special means of dealing with very specific types of attack. The straight-line defensive action depicted here works fairly well as long as the attacker restricts his onslaught to the same style as the defender.

Example 2

If the attacker is angry or otherwise intent on harming the defender, however, he can circumvent these defenses, and the rigid straight-line defense against angular or circular attacks will fail due to the following:

—*Improper timing because of required setup before delivery*

—*Improper angling that forces a weaker weapon position to resist a stronger force*

—*Improper strategy that leaves the defender in a position highly vulnerable to follow-up techniques*

Instead of set techniques or specific movements, the combat training methods of ninjutsu rely on the active understanding of principles as the way of gaining prowess. The principles are universal and are manifested in all aspects of contention: physical survival in the wilderness, emotional confrontations in the home or office, or armed conflicts on the street. Though it may require a greater amount of time to internalize and make personal a principle than it does a technique, once the principle is mastered, all related techniques are immediately possible.

Example 3

Sporting methods that have developed ways to take advantage of the protective characteristics of boxing gloves can create dangerous habits in field or street combat. Covering actions that crowd an opponent's punches work fairly well as a means of temporarily stalling a fight to catch one's breath or regroup in the ring. Both contestants wear padded gloves, which create the buffer zone.

Example 4

When the fighters are not wearing gloves, however, there is no cover provided by merely raising the hands or bowing the head. The upraised hands themselves become vulnerable targets (A), and the bowed head is open to low attacks (B). Crowding as a defense will fail because of the following:

—*Improperly passive nature of the defense, which cannot possibly harm the attacker and yet leaves the defender open to unlimited abuse*

—*Improper distancing, in which offensive, forward-moving footwork is used even though there is no intention to attack with the movement*

—*Improper strategy that leaves the defender virtually sightless and trapped in a space where the maximum possible punishment can be dealt to him*

One of the major principles taught in the ninja *taijutsu* martial art is *ken tai ichi jo,* or literally, "the body and weapon are one." More than just a body that moves a weapon around, or a weapon that determines how the body must be used, the combat method of the ninja fuses the two parts into a whole. It is a concept far beyond the overused admonition, "The weapon is an extension of your body." In nin-po combat, the body is the weapon.

Example 5

The effective use of the ken tai ichi jo principle of taijutsu creates knockdown power without having to rely on superior muscle to accomplish the job. If pursuit is necessary (A-D), the torso does the job of chasing, leaving the limbs free to inflict damage. The taijutsu unarmed combat method relies on the fluid coordination of motion, extension, sinking and accuracy to develop explosive power from what appears to be relaxed movement. The weapon and footwork become one. The weapon moves at its own speed, and the body in motion increases the speed while adding substance to the strike.

Because the training involves such a wide variety of weapon types to be mastered (including hands, feet, elbows and knees, blades, sticks, firearms, chains and cords), the process of coming to know each new weapon takes on more importance than it would in a specialty art dealing exclusively with punches, pistols or samurai swords—in which weapon familiarization takes place only once in the practitioner's career. For this reason, ninjutsu training places great emphasis on a four-step process of weapon mastery that is used many times during the student's years in the art.

The logical starting point is to become familiar with the new weapon to be mastered. Familiarity leads to relaxation, which leads to confidence. You might learn to form a special fist, then set your feet appropriately and discover the ways the arm can be extended to deliver the strike from varying angles. You unsheathe a new blade and get a feel for its grip and balance, then move the weapon in practice slashes, stabs or cuts. In similar fashion, a foot, a cane, a chain-sickle or even a can of tear gas must go through this essential breaking-in period during which familiarity is acquired. This should be a very personal process and not a stage that is passed through fleetingly with token acknowledgment.

After attaining familiarity with the new weapon and making the weapon a part of the way you move, you can then progress to the second stage of the series, which introduces the footwork that will allow you to deliver techniques with total effectiveness. Distancing and angling, aspects crucial to applying any fighting technique, are determined almost exclusively by footwork.

Maai (interval) refers to intervals in timing and distancing. Successful timing is a feel for the rhythm needed to mesh with and overcome an assailant, and an ability to fit in with the "breathing" of the fight. Correct use of rhythm and timing actually replaces the necessity for speed of motion. The maai of distancing does not merely imply how far you are from an assailant but the grander perception of how the effective placement of your body can prevent the attacker from succeeding while giving you the ability to conquer. Efficient striking depends on proper distancing—a product of footwork—and not just bending or extending the body.

Doai (angling) is another footwork skill. Taijutsu, which is the unarmed foundation for all ninja combat methods, relies on the principle of moving the body in such a way as to avoid the damage of an attack while *simultaneously* injuring your attacker. This "defensive attacking" takes advantage of angles that allow the defender a safe zone from which to launch counters, and it replaces the need for the rather crude and dangerous system of blocking *before* striking.

Example 6

The effective angling, distancing and timing method of the ninja's taijutsu allows the defender to flow with the angle of the attack as appropriate. By shifting back from the attack, cutting to the inside of the attack and sinking below the attack (A), the defender has taken himself out of the attacker's range while remaining close enough to apply a damaging counterstrike (B) to his arm. The taijutsu sui no kata defensive footwork and body dynamics can handle any variation of attacking angle, from straight shot to looping hook punch, because the response takes the defender into safe territory. There is no need for a block as such. Even if the attacker attempts to recover with an immediate cross from his trailing hand, the defender is still immune to the attacker because of the appropriate angling with his first move. Again, the defender does not need to block and can therefore concentrate on damaging counterblows.

In ninjutsu training, all footwork is based on a series of four models, whether the fight involves fists, sticks or blades. Instead of developing a complex system of technical movements that would take the body decades to acquire, you can rely on the indisputable logic of pure feeling as a means of instruction in the proper use of the feet and body in motion. In any given conflict or confrontation, you can respond instinctually in one of four distinct and fundamental ways:

Chi no kata Earth mode	You find yourself holding your ground solidly, neither needing to retreat nor wanting to attack.
Sui no kata Water mode	You feel the need to reposition and find yourself angling strategically.
Hi no kata Fire mode	You want to take control of your assailant and find yourself pulled forward by the strength of your own intention.
Fu no kata Wind mode	You have no need to fight, and you find yourself evading and redirecting the attacker's energy by going with his movements.

The system is simple and can be picked up quickly because it is based on following your natural, emotional "gut feeling" that arises in any type of conflict. Recognizing and going with the feeling becomes a more important priority than developing the ability to perform specific stylized techniques.

Example 7

If aggressive footwork is the mode the defender chooses, effective use of tai-jutsu distancing will take the fight to the attacker. Crowding is used to optimum benefit. Rather than merely covering, the defender damages or at least stuns with his forward motion. By keeping the spine in the universally erect posture characteristic of taijutsu, the defender can execute a devastating zutsuki (head butt) as a byproduct of his forward-closing motion.

Example 8

The taijutsu hi no kata attacking footwork and body dynamics are well-suited to moving inside the comfortable fighting zone of a larger adversary. From inside the adversary's punching range, damaging strikes can be directed aggressively against his limbs as they move in an attempt to adjust to the change in fighting distance.

Example 9

The ninja must be aware, however, that close-quarters fighting almost without exception turns into grappling. Fists become claws, elbow strikes become lifts and kicking is replaced by sweeps or leveraging.

The third step in the development of reliable combat survival skills through ninjutsu training is the crucial aspect of *actually applying* the punch, cut, thrust or any other offensive or counteroffensive technique. A technique is only as good as its application at the moment, no matter how well someone else can do it or how well you have done it at other times. Theory and tradition aside, the simple test of a technique's effectiveness is to try it out against a realistic striking target. When it comes to living through a murderous attack, the ninja's fighting system emphasizes simple, pragmatic applications of well-tested, target-seasoned blows and cuts. Actual application becomes the primary method of study because it is essential to practice the exact skill that you wish to perfect. If your goal is to be able to knock someone over with a punch or kick, you must train *repetitively* by striking objects with your fists, feet, knees and elbows. Shadowboxing or sparring with padded equipment can be helpful, but they are not nearly as important as slamming a realistic target over and over again with full-bodied power—*if* powerful blows are what you want to develop.

This applies to blades and sticks, as well. Slicing or flailing the air with a sword, pole or chain may give you the feeling that you have perfected the technique. Put a real and resilient target in the path and the weapon rebounds away from your target or misses altogether.

Example 10

Demonstration or performance-oriented methods often stress blinding speed and flurries of stinging punches, kicks or weapon strikes. The trap-smack-rap-slap action depicted here works fairly well as long as both combatants maintain the required distance and do not engage in any but the most minimal footwork.

Example 11

In the throes of actual life-and-death combat, however, training theory often goes out the window as the more gut-level emotions of fear, vengeance or fury take predominance. Because the defender is not used to employing footwork and body dynamics to deliver powerful strikes, he will be vulnerable to the temptation to chase his elusive adversary with his moving weapon alone. Against a skilled fighter, speed hits that reach with the arm or leg (A-B) alone will fail because of the following:

—*Improper use of body mechanics, which causes the lower body to remain frozen in place while the weapon should be advancing*

—*Improper dynamics that create the ineffective habit of moving the upper body after or apart from the action of the foundation, producing a dangerous one-two motion for every single action executed*

—*Improper strategy, which robs power from hits that land without the body mass behind them*

Remember that merely standing in place and beating, kicking or slashing in rhythmic cadence is of limited effectiveness in terms of preparing you for combat reality. You will not plant your feet and hack rhythmically on the street or in the field. Therefore, *do not do it in training either.* Alter your angle toward the target constantly, shifting your balance each time you strike, just like you would in an actual combat encounter. Be aware of the proper breathing method, as well.

Familiarity and confidence with each weapon, appropriate footwork and body positioning, and experienced timing and distancing for target impact lead the student practitioner to the fourth step in the mastery of any weapon, which is the total body power of ken tai ichi jo.

The concept of total body power reflects the ninja warrior's preference for the body mass in motion, rather than mere tensing of the limbs, as the primary source for power in strikes, throws and cuts. This method transmits a "slamming" feel to the hits instead of a "stinging" feel. This ken tai ichi jo approach allows any technique applied to have a knockdown quality to it, even in applications in which the moves themselves are somewhat lacking in technical finesse because of the unpredictability of combat in natural surroundings. The following examples of ninjutsu combat techniques against possible attacks illustrate many interpretations of the principles of maai, doai and ken tai ichi jo. The examples are not necessarily set kata but suggestions of where the spontaneous action might have gone in an actual life-or-death situation.

Hanbo: Defense Against Stick

The attacker swings his weapon downward at the defender's shoulders and neck with a diagonal aim (1-2). The receiver crouches while adjusting his angle outward and counterstrikes (3) the attacker's moving arm. (This action is aggressive, not a defensive block or parry, and should injure his arm.) The defender immediately shifts his weight forward, rolls his wrist over to align the lower end of the hanbo with the attacker's ribs and (4) slams the tip of the cane into the attacker's ribs, just below the arm. If this is not enough to end the fight, the defender slams the tip of the hanbo upward to meet the attacker's arm again (5). The defender (6-7) shoves his cane forward over the attacker's arm and pulls back to act as a lock across the attacker's wrist (8) while using his upper torso to exert pressure against the back of the attacker's elbow for restraint. The defender follows up with a strike to the attacker's face and a knee smash (9) to the back of his leg to force the attacker to the ground.

Kyoketsu Shoge: Defense Against Sword

The defender observes as the attacker stalks him with a raised sword, getting a feel for the subtle timing displayed by his adversary (1). As the sword bearer makes an adjustment in posture, the defender sends the steel ring flying (2) at his adversary. By projecting his weapon with his entire body, the defender can generate sufficient power to damage rather than merely sting or slap. Precise footwork

and cord "reach" allow the defender to hit his adversary whether he moves forward, back or holds his ground. If the attacker manages to avoid the strike (3-4) and counters, the defender temporarily abandons the ring end of his weapon and allows the blade to do the work. Using retreating pivotal turns, the defender brings the blade up (5) to meet the attacker's sword hand while he regroups

continued on next page

the steel ring end (6) by pulling the rope tightly between his outstretched hands. The defender pivots again (7-8) and smashes the steel ring into the base of the attacker's

skull. The defender steps back and reaches down with the blade (9-10) to hook the ankle of his attacker and topple him to the ground.

Unarmed Defense Against Club

The attacker lunges forward with a club swipe at the defender's head (1). The defender angles back and to the side (2-3) and punches the outside of the attacker's weapon arm. The defender immediately jams his leading leg (4) into the shin of the attacker and rocks forward (5-6) with his bodyweight to force the attacker to the ground. If necessary, the defender drops forward, plunging his elbow into the attacker's breastbone or solar plexus (7-8).

Kusari-Gama: Defense Against Sword

As the attacker approaches, the defender pivots his body (1) and slings the weighted chain at the attacker's ankles as a snare (2). The attacker leaps into the air to avoid the chain, which could put the defender in danger if the chain drops into a position from which it is difficult to sling the weight again immediately. As the attacker moves in for the kill, the defender (3-4) lifts his foot with a pivotal body twist and sends the weight out (5) at the attacker's hands, causing him to recoil. The chain is stopped by the defender's trapping foot action (6). The defender now uses an outstretched body pivot while sweeping his leg forward (7) to send the weight back at the attacker. The weighted chain finds its target (8) and ensnares the attacker's lead foot. The defender then pulls the attacker off-balance with a backpedaling motion (9).

Unarmed Defense Against Kick

The attacker moves forward with a front kick (1-2). Timing his move, the defender angles away and counters with a stamp kick (3) to the attacker's groin and hip joint. (The move is purely coun-

teroffensive because there is no attempt at blocking.) The attacker recoils (4) back from the impact but attempts to gain time by charging in (5) with a body tackle.

continued on next page ▶

Again, the defender angles with the attack, this time applying a rising knee smash (6-7) to the attacker's face. The defender now redirects his kicking leg and stamps

the attacker's trapped knee to knock him to the ground (8). The defender can press down on the attacker's leg to control him (9-10).

Sword Against Sword

The attacker raises his sword with a two-handed grip and initiates a downward diagonal slash (1). The defender closes in, rather than retreat, and uses a reverse grip to unsheathe his own blade as he moves (2). As the attacker's arms descend, they encounter the rising slice of the defender's blade as it leaves its scabbard (3). The defender

then pivots, maintaining his position close by the attacker's side and away from his sword (4). Continuing to use the reverse grip, the defender shifts forward (5-6) and projects his sword's cutting edge along the side of the attacker's neck while stepping into the attacker to force him to the ground.

Kyoketsu Shoge: Defense Against Kusari-Gama

As the attacker lashes out with a kusari-gama (1), the defender drops into a protective forward roll to get low enough to move inside the range of the attacker's weapon (2-3). The defender rises on one knee (4) with a stabbing lunge to the attacker's sickle hand. As the defender immobilizes the attacker's weapon hand, he executes a knee strike (5) to the attacker's leg while covering the path of the adversary's sickle. The defender then loops the cord behind the attacker's neck (6-7) and around his arm to immobilize him for an armbar throw (8-9) to the ground.

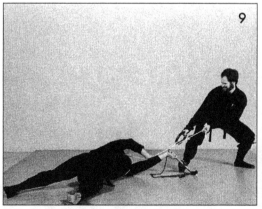

Shuriken:
Infighting Defense

The attacker grabs the defender by the lapel of his jacket and attempts to strike him with a club (1). While dropping back into a defensive posture, the defender reaches into his jacket (2) and pulls out a four-pointed senban shuriken. The defender then pivots by throwing his leading leg to his rear, simultaneously jabbing (3) the shuriken into the back of the attacker's grab-

bing hand. (See inset 3A.) As the attacker tumbles forward with the pain and pressure, the defender reaches up and over the attacker's head (4) with the shuriken, embedding the point in the attacker's scalp. (Inset 4A shows how the shuriken is held flat, pulled forward and down.) The defender then ends the fight with a rising kick (5-6) to the attacker's midsection.

Hand-to-Hand Defense

The attacker initiates his offense with a leading leg kick (1-2), which the defender stops with a trapping stamp kick (3). The attacker immediately counters with a rising punch from the other side (4). The defender intercepts the uppercut (5) with a jamming punch to the attacker's upper arm while moving in and applying a head butt to the attacker's face. The defender then pivots away from the attacker, hooking his arm (6-7) through the elbow and behind the shoulder to gain control, and throws the attacker forward (8) onto the ground.

Shuriken: Defense Against Choke

An attacker approaches the defender from the rear and applies a chokehold to restrain him (1). The defender reaches into his jacket and grabs a shuriken (2), then reaches back over his shoulder (see inset 2A for detail) with his shuriken hand and embeds the point of the blade (3) in the attacker's clothing or skin. Dropping his bodyweight, the defender maintains pulling pressure on the blade and slides his feet between the attacker's legs (4). The defender then turns his shoulders (5) to throw the attacker over his back.

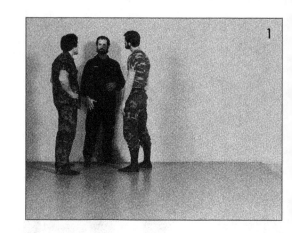

Defense Against Two Opponents

Two attackers move in to corner the defender (1). The defender jerks his shoulders and hands up momentarily (as if to punch) to startle or distract his attackers and delay their attack (2). The defender drops immediately by flexing his legs (3) and executes a double boshi-ken thumbfist attack (4) to both attackers' midsection as they move in. As the attackers pull back or fold with the stabbing strikes, the defender dives between them (5-6) and rolls to a safe vantage point (7) from which he can either escape or continue the fight on his own terms.

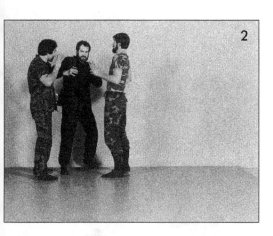

Grappling Defense Against Kick

The attacker moves in and throws a high right roundhouse kick (1-2). Instead of endangering himself by attempting to block a moving boot or leg with the smaller bones of his arm, the defender drops forward (3-4) and under the kick, diving at the attacker's supporting left leg. The defender's shoulder rams the attacker's left knee at a damaging angle. As the attacker tumbles to the ground, the defender turns his tackle (5-6) into a forward shoulder roll and brings the bottom of his left foot down (7) on the attacker's face. If necessary, the defender can follow up with a right heel shove/kick (8) under the attacker's chin.

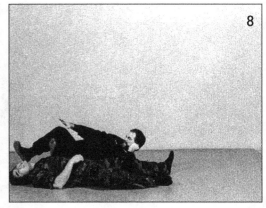

Defense From the Ground

The attacker moves in to pin or kick the downed defender (1). The defender times his move to coincide with the attacker's approach (2), and he kicks behind the attacker's leg with his own inward-turned foot (3). With a simultaneous pull from behind the attacker's leg with one foot, the grounded defender (4-5) executes a stamping heel kick to the attacker's knee joint. As the kick slams into its target, the defender twists his hips to increase the push-pull action on the attacker's leg. As the attacker topples, the defender sweeps an attempted counterkick aside (6) and executes a heel-stamp kick to the groin (7).

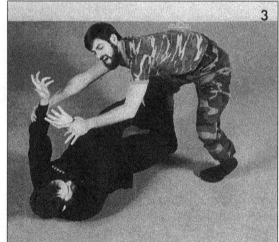

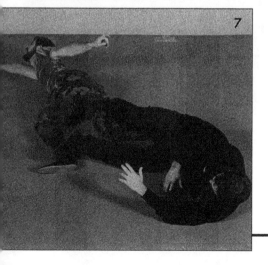

Knife Against Knife

The attacker and defender approach each other, both gripping knives in their right hands (1-2). As the attacker initiates an inward slashing cut to the defender's midsection (3), the defender angles in to close the distance and uses his right fist (gripping the knife) to punch the inside forearm of the attacker. (This is an attacking move and not

a block. Note that the fist stops the arm without cutting the attacker. Attempting to grab the attacker's knife arm or hand before striking is extremely dangerous at real fighting speed.) The defender immediately grabs the attacker's arm (4-5) and strikes the side of the attacker's head with the handle of his knife.

continued on next page ▶

The defender uses his entire body and not just his hand, adding force to the strike and moving his body inside the attacker's free hand. The defender then rolls his knife out and over the back of the attacker's neck (6) and pulls

down sharply (7) using his entire bodyweight. The back of the blade forces the attacker down (his right arm is gripped firmly) without cutting him (8). The attacker is then pinned (9-10) in an armbar submission and his knife is taken away.

Regaining Control of a Weapon

As the attacker stalks the defender with his knife, the defender raises his hanbo for a strike (1). The attacker begins a cutting lunge but stops short to grab the defender's descending weapon at the wrist (2-3). The defender kicks the attacker's knife hand away to prevent being stabbed (4-5), and then he reaches under the attacker's grabbing wrist (6) to secure a two-handed grip on the hanbo. The defender steps back (7-8) with his rear foot to angle away from the attacker's knife and then binds the attacker's arm into a lock. (See inset 7A.) The defender backs away from the attacker, levering down on the trapped wrist (9) by lowering himself into a crouched position.

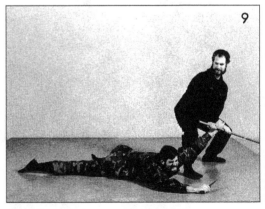

Hanbo: Defense Against Knife

The attacker, wielding a knife, grabs the defender by the shoulder to push him off-balance and cut him (1). The defender angles backward to avoid the cut while striking the attacker's lead leg behind the knee (2). Continuing his backpedaling motion, the defender (3) covers the attacker's grabbing hand using his free hand and slams the hanbo (4) underneath the attacker's outstretched arm at the elbow. The cane under the attacker's upturned elbow creates an armbar (5), which the defender uses to pull the attacker forward by applying his bodyweight and pivoting (6). The armbar is used to throw the attacker to the ground (7).

Kusari-Gama: Defense Against Sword, With Backward Throw

The attacker approaches with a sword (1). The defender responds by striking out with the weighted end of his kusari-gama (2). The attacker pulls

his hands back to avoid the flying weight and angles in (3-4) with a countering cut. The defender reverses his spiraling body motion and punches (5) the attacker's lead arm.

continued on next page

Before the attacker can recover, the defender raps the sickle hand (6-7) into the attacker's face and moves the handle in front of his neck while moving into position behind him. The defender crosses his wrists

behind the defender's neck to apply a chokehold from the rear. The defender then pivots, lifting the attacker (8-10) into position for a neck-breaking, backward throw.

Unarmed Defense Against Knife

The attacker advances with a knife in his right hand and initiates a ripping stab to the defender's midsection (1). The defender angles to the outside to avoid the cut as the attacker makes his move (2). Immediately after shifting his feet, the defender punches down into the attacker's ribs and continues on around behind the attacker, leaving his punching (right) arm hooked in the crook (3) of the attacker's (right) elbow. As the attacker attempts a flailing pivot to escape the arm-hold (4), the defender reaches over with his free hand (5) and secures the attacker's left arm. The defender then pulls in and back on the attacker's elbows to immobilize him and grabs the knife-hand wrist (6) from behind with his left hand. The defender can then wedge apart the attacker's feet to take him to the ground (7-9).

CHAPTER 18

Dynamic power lies inert in the core
of all the ten thousand things.
By attuning with all things
and excluding none
the ninja can avail himself of
the collective power of the cosmos.

The alignment and activation of
thought, word and deed
is the bridge to these powers.

KUJI-KIRI

Directing the power of the surroundings

A DARING TEST

During his historic visit in 1982 to the United States to meet the students who studied his ninja arts with me, Masaaki Hatsumi provided me with an inspiring lesson in the power of our ryu traditions. My own understanding of the essence of our martial method, and why our system is so removed from the more popular martial arts of today, was expanded a hundredfold as a result of a few seconds in the woods of Ohio on that summer day.

A group of visiting students asked Masaaki Hatsumi *sensei* about the often-misunderstood powers of the ninja's *kuji-kiri* and *kuji-in*. The grandmaster's reply was, in essence, that the kuji would only work for those fully initiated into the living history of the ryu. There is no way to create mechanically the effect of kuji without being an integral part of the tradition. The way to approach kuji power, admonished Hatsumi sensei, was to train even more diligently in the taijutsu principles of combat so that one can gain the kotsu (essence) of what has worked for ninja warriors over the generations. From this merging with the original source of power comes the budding command of kuji-kiri and kuji-in.

Though spoken from the heart, the words did not seem to register intellectually with the students.

Masaaki Hatsumi suddenly turned to me and ordered me to punch him in the back of the head from behind whenever I was ready. Perhaps he detected a look of horror on my face, for he laughed and said he would take all responsibility for whatever happened. I was again ordered to punch my teacher without warning. With that, he turned his back to me and casually waited for my strike. He continued to talk to the crowd, and seemingly without any preparation or setup whatsoever, he slipped to the side as my fist sailed through the air where his head had been a fraction of a second before. There is no way he could have seen or heard the punch coming.

The master then scanned the stunned crowd and announced flatly, "That is kuji." I could barely believe what I had just witnessed, although I had been an active part of the event.

Some thought it was a trick or rehearsed act. That is all that those people were ready to see. Others were amazed and thought the event to be a demonstration of the *sakki* (killer force). Again, that was not the point. There was no killer determination because I had no intention at all of harming or killing my teacher.

Though I did not intend to injure my teacher, the punch was nonetheless very dangerous at several levels. Obviously, it would have knocked the man out if I had connected with the base of his skull, regardless of my intention or lack thereof. The grandmaster moved at just the right moment, having somehow perceived the imperceptible, and spared himself the impact. At that level alone, it was pretty impressive.

At a deeper level, one more in touch with my own life and the destinies of my own students, the punch represented the potential *death* and *end* of the 34 generations of Togakure Ryu. If my fist, in all its speed and well-trained power, had hit Masaaki Hatsumi from behind, it would have signified the end of our tradition for all eternity.

If the ninja arts I studied were authentic and have an actual predestination for existing in this present and the future, there would be no way that the grandmaster could fail such a severe public test. Imagine what would be left of the reputation of the tradition if the grandmaster of the ninja had ordered his student to punch him in the back of the head and had then found himself regaining consciousness in the dust at his shocked student's feet. It would have been impossible for a master failing such a test to ever show his face in public again without drawing savage ridicule and laughter. It would have been impossible for the students of that master to ever again teach their art with confidence and credibility while the whole world knew the embarrassing truth. The ryu would in effect be as dead and cold as the ashes of the original founder of so many generations ago.

It is as if the spirits of all the past grandmasters stand behind the man who now carries the title and guide him through these dangers in ways that the master himself admits he cannot explain scientifically. The master teacher is but the current moment's manifestation of the collective power and consciousness of all that the ryu has been, is and will be. The warrior becomes one with generations of power created by his ancestors. That is the secret of the power of the seemingly magical kuji. That is the overwhelming significance of having an authentic teacher with a lineage of successful warrior sages behind him.

MIND SCIENCE BEHIND THE MYSTERY

The ninja of history were often feared by conventional warriors with limited combat experience and actively superstitious minds. Known to be an underground culture prevented by law from openly engaging in honorable defense of their communities and recognized as the silent

The more superstitious people of feudal Japan thought the tengu was a demonic ancestor of the ninja.

protectors of the *mikkyo* temples dedicated to the teaching of mystical Buddhism, the ninja were the targets of fear and dread because of the lack of understanding in others. Rather than combat the accusations of being in league with *maryoku* (dark powers), malevolent ghostly *yurei* and demonic *oni*, the ninja chose to allow these fears to stand and indeed fueled the fires of terror in the hearts of their oppressors by actively playing along with their maligned image. When vastly outnumbered and overpowered, any weapon or ruse becomes a means of attaining victory.

Fear and superstition can be powerful tools when employed skillfully by people of clarity and knowledge. Stories told of the ninja's descent from *tengu*—a half-crow, half-man demon—were probably a cultural adaptation of the legendary *garuda* of the Himalayas. The ninja were known to have been influenced and inspired by the fanatical shugenja ascetics of the mountains, who were said to have taught them how to walk through fire, move unclothed through freezing waters, control and command the weather, and summon the powerful kami (spirits) that dwelled in all parts of nature. Yogic and tantric teachings imported from the far off Himalayas and interpreted by the secret mikkyo doctrines were thought to have given the ninja the ability to become invisible at will, read the mind of others, and change the course of history from remote locations through the power of intention alone. Because the enemies of the ninja families believed the ninja did possess such powers, it was a simple process to allow these beliefs to work toward the clan's goals.

As with most legends, however, there is a basis in fact around which these incredible tales grew. Frantic tales of the ninja's ability to curse, hex or jinx an enemy and cause his downfall are also matched by stories of how the ninja could enhance, empower and strengthen others to improve the odds of outcome in a dangerous situation. At the core of these superstitions lies the often exaggerated and misunderstood power of the ninja's *kuji no ho* (method of the nine syllables) and the related *juji no ho* (method of the 10 syllables) symbolism.

The numeral "9" has great significance in the practice and understanding of ninjutsu. Known as the "universal number," it depicts the universe in its completion. As three multiplied by three, nine reminds us of the *san-go* (three planes of action): body, mind and spirit. Each in turn is experienced on a physical, mental and spiritual level of consciousness. Mathematically, nine is as high as one can go before reaching zero again. Ten is beyond completion; the numeral "1" is in a new column and a zero is placed where the "9" used to be. Therefore, the number 9 finds itself in use as a symbol of ultimate power in the ninja's kuji no ho.

The *kuji goshin ho* (nine-syllable method of protection) of nin-po mikkyo is a system that includes nine voiced oaths or *jumon* (mantras), nine corresponding hand configurations, referred to as the kuji-in (nine-syllable seals) and nine distinct processes of concentration. As a system, the *kuji goshin ho kestu-in* are used to alter a ninja's body and personality makeup in order for the ninja to be best-suited for any task at hand.

The cryptic nine syllables themselves are derived from a Chinese interpretation in which the nine written characters form a sentence meaning, "Before the battle, all the warriors are assembled in ranks in front of the fortress." In ancient China, military strategists often blended their knowledge of martial methods with esoteric power studies known as *juho* to ensure successful battles. The Chinese phrase *"Ring p'ing to ze chieh chen li zai chien"* is pronounced *"Rin pyo toh sha kai jin rets' zai zen"* in the Japanese language and is understood to mirror a spectrum of nine distinct levels of divinely inspired power inherent in every man or woman.

Nin-po's juji no ho carries the power inherent in the kuji system to symbolic extremes by representing an intention of the will carried out to a strength even beyond that of the universal power. In this case, the 10 represents a degree beyond perfection and completion. Ten can be seen as the "zero state" one returns to by advancing through all the demands and lessons of life, taking the practitioner full circle in his or her development from zero on up through zero. Used to intensify and enhance the ninja's total commitment to a given outcome, the juji letter or graphic symbol is affixed as an addition to one of the kuji no ho power methods.

No matter how materialistically one wishes to view the world, unexplainable or mysterious occurrences continue to exist. People find their health miraculously cured, they are prevented by coincidences from being on a jetliner that crashes, and they are shot at point-blank range and not wounded. Ignoring these phenomena, or pretending that they do not exist, simply because they do not fit in with a desired scientific or rational approach to living is to leave a major part of any potential outcome up to raw chance, which is a highly dangerous attitude for anyone really needing to employ the skills of life protection embodied in the art of ninjutsu.

Granted, the employment of seemingly magical devices such as the ninja's kuji or juji as charms, curses or blessings can be seen as setting into motion predictable psychological reactions on the part of your adversary. The "voodoo doll" effect, wherein the victim grows weak or ill because of the power of suggestion alone, certainly cannot be discounted. In the feudal ages, people trained in rank-and-file warfare would naturally lack the sophistication needed to look through superstitious beliefs without being affected. If they feared the ninja's power and the wrathful deities said to be in league with the ninja, common warriors could actually fall into weakness through the self-engendered powers of their own minds.

On the other hand, however, it could be the case that blessings, curses and prayers actually create an effect when properly employed, regardless of our inability to interpret or explain the process in a scientific, intellectual manner. Even among the higher classes of modern society today, jinxes and blessings are often regarded as realities. The power of prayer, common to most Western religions, is relied on by many for strength and insight in difficult times.

A ninja evokes fear in his superstitious enemies through the use of a carved wooden demon mask.

A kunoichi demonstrates one of ninjutsu's kuji no ho ketsu in finger entwinings for the channeling of internal energy. These mystical hand "seals" are part of the higher, more esoteric aspects of ninja training today, just like in centuries past.

As a first step in developing ninjutsu's kuji to "direct" the will, it is important to realize that to be effective or productive, each specific thought or intention must have a unique vehicle to isolate it from the usual jumble of thoughts that swirl around in our conscious minds. Beginning students often confuse their intentions with mere wishes and desires, which from past experience seem hopelessly far from the actual end sought. From a Western psychological standpoint, something that stays within the mind seems to have little acknowledgeable reality or potential for affecting external conditions. Therefore, a definite verbal utterance is spoken to give the intention a vibrant entity of its own. The spoken word works to give actuality or form to the intention that it would not otherwise possess. The intention becomes a unique "thing," separate from the warrior who sets it in motion.

Intense thoughts, when expressed with deep emotional feeling from the core of one's very being, arouse an energy or a form of "spiritual kinetics" known as a neuromuscular discharge. The more feeling there is behind the words, the more likely it is that the utterance will be accompanied by some outward physical manifestation of the intention. Pointing with the finger, punching a fist into the palm of the hand, shifting or stamping the feet, or setting the facial expression are examples of gestures we affect unconsciously in order to confer a dynamic certainty on our intention.

This dynamic (and sometimes dramatic) engaging of the powers of the *sanmitsu*—thought, word and deed—forms the first three steps of employing the kuji no ho of ninjutsu. First, the ninja isolates the intention. Next, he or she gives it a vibrant, verbal reality. Third, the ninja makes it a dynamic physical actuality.

There are few people who have not had the experience of being in a place or in the presence of certain people where a distinct feeling of disharmony was sensed. Many people notice this feeling of uneasiness when walking into a room, a building or even a geographical area, where it seems that the vibrations there are discordant, depressing, draining or agitating. Often there is no satisfactory explanation for these impressions. There is just an uncomfortable feeling associated with the location or person.

If discordant vibrations can indeed exist and remain in a place or around a particular person or group, it must be true that some thing, action or effect is responsible for the presence experienced as inharmonious. If it is possible to create the discord from an originally neutral or perhaps even positive situation, it also must be possible to alter the negative vibrations which themselves are a product of a previous alteration. The heavy, discordant feelings can be replaced by harmonious vibrations, if it is important enough to us to dedicate our energy toward altering our surrounding environment rather than endure it.

There are physical and psychic aspects in the transformation process. Physically, the ninja can employ appropriate sounds that will create an altered vibratory state. Through proper psychic and mental focusing, the ninja can maintain harmony with all types of vibration required and assist in the continued existence of those vibrations.

As one of several means of combining these physical, mental and spiritual aspects of altering the surroundings, the ninja practitioner in the higher levels of training is taught to use the power of the kuji-kiri (nine-syllable grid of slashes). Said to have been handed down from the divine warrior guardian Marishi-ten, the esoteric power formula of the *kuji goshin ho kuji-kiri* is used to invoke the power to overcome evil, illusion, ignorance and weakness, and to enhance and protect the ninja in any environment.

With a sincere and unhesitating spirit, the ninja symbolically duplicates the flaming sword of Fudo-myo, the fearsome mythical protector of the will, law and integrity of the universe. The positive-power right hand and the negative-receiving left hand are brought together in front of the chest in imitation of the wrathful deity's sheathed sword while the incantation of Fudo-myo is repeated a set number of times, each repetition stressing the vibratory effects and intensity of the jumon to a greater degree than before.

From this position, the ninja steps forward with the symbolic drawn sword to cut through the air with a grid of alternating horizontal and vertical slashes. The spiritual blade moves from left to right and high to low while the ninja recites the nine power syllables of the kuji goshin ho. The 10th syllable (juji) can be added while the energy grid is dispersed with a punching wave of the hand before the symbolic sword is sheathed.

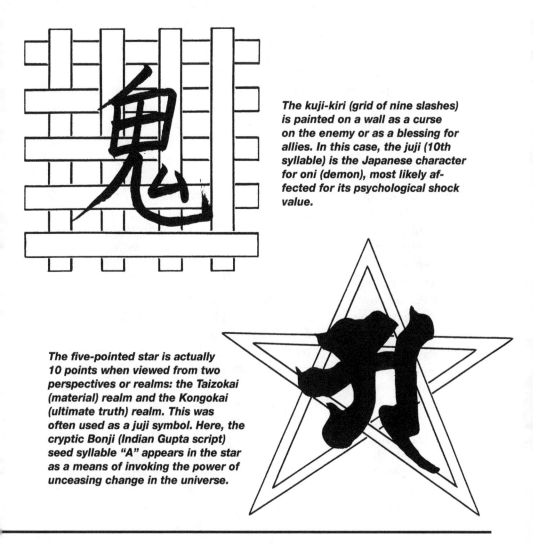

The kuji-kiri (grid of nine slashes) is painted on a wall as a curse on the enemy or as a blessing for allies. In this case, the juji (10th syllable) is the Japanese character for oni (demon), most likely affected for its psychological shock value.

The five-pointed star is actually 10 points when viewed from two perspectives or realms: the Taizokai (material) realm and the Kongokai (ultimate truth) realm. This was often used as a juji symbol. Here, the cryptic Bonji (Indian Gupta script) seed syllable "A" appears in the star as a means of invoking the power of unceasing change in the universe.

As recorded in the *Kuji Denjyu no Makimono* (scroll for the transmission of the nine-syllable power method), this ghostly grid of protective power forms a wall of intention projected by the ninja warrior. The scroll goes on to compare the grid procedure with the power of a great sword. In the hands of a skilled warrior, the sword is awesome in its effectiveness. In the hands of a small child, the sword becomes a useless burden that consumes power instead of projecting it. According to the scroll, people with less than total commitment and faith will actually harm themselves when attempting to invoke the kuji-kiri because confusion, hesitancy and scattered energies will result, leaving them even more vulnerable than before they invoked the grid. A partial grid is worse than no grid at all. It would be far better to simply avoid those places or people with which discord is felt or to employ physical means to endure them until the ninja's personal power and endorsement from previous generations of ancestors are at a level at which the kuji-kiri can command results.

Historically, these methods were transmitted secretly to prevent individuals from harming themselves through improper practice and incomplete skill development. Furthermore, the entire process could be printed in a step-by-step series and the method still would not work for the person who has not been initiated in the subtle nuances of the kuji and juji power teachings—nor been granted the authority of the ages to make them work (thereby eliminating any fear of people using the kuji-kiri or kuji-in for "evil" deeds).

Though perhaps far less dramatic than sworn secrecy or concern over deadly misuse of raw power, the simple truth is that key sections of the energy channeling methods have been withheld to prevent the curious from "playing around" with the process. Halfhearted idly curious attempts at trying out or testing the kuji goshin ho will almost certainly produce no discernible results. The more often a person repeatedly stumbles through the steps and gets nothing in return, the more confused and desensitized he or she will become and the more diluted the essence of the method will become. Eventually, these unprepared people thoroughly convince themselves that "this stuff doesn't work" and forever lose the opportunity to learn and use these very real powers.

The same line of reasoning can be followed and observed in the more apparently physical aspects of ninja training. Students will observe the conspicuous lack of "nuts and bolts" specifics in the descriptions of the fighting clashes that serve as examples in the volumes of this series. There has been no attempt to teach the timing elements and body dynamics so crucial to successful results in the ninja combat method. As with the more subtle spiritual teachings, the fighting system deletions are not because of a need for secrecy or a fear of dangerous misuse. Even at its most base physical level, it is not possible to teach ninjutsu in a mechanistic context. Unlike the vast majority of the more popular forms of martial arts today, nin-po is a path that must find a balance between the practitioner's physical realm, intellectual realm and spiritual realm from the very first lesson.

The kuji-kiri is described here for informational purposes only in order to serve as an inspiration to those people who are ready to seek out this knowledge. The power exists. However, like other powers such as electricity, solar radiation and gale-force winds, it cannot be transmitted as an experience on the printed page. The kuji goshin ho can only be described here conceptually. The actual initiation and empowerment can only come from personal interaction with a teacher who is experienced in the method. The kuji powers are gifts to be presented to the student only at the right moments on the warrior path of enlightenment.

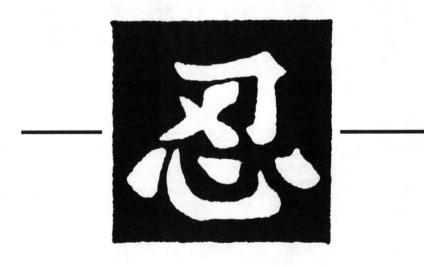

PART 4

Legacy of the Night Warrior

CHAPTER 19

Yours is a legacy of service to those in need,
  protection to those in distress
  and strength to those who are overpowered.
Your guide is nin-po
  silent means of working your will without actions.
Your reward is spiritual growth
  and an active role in the scheme of totality.

THE UNFOLDING STORY

In ancient times, he is a military adviser, a bringer of good fortune

The historical art of Japan's invisible ninja warriors of the night has its roots woven deep in the ancient past of the enigmatic island nation of the Rising Sun. Unlike the more conventional and easily accessible sport and recreation martial arts that are so popular in our modern society, it is almost impossible to determine an exact time or place or founder associated with the birth of *ninjutsu*. Korean *taekwondo* can be traced back to its founding in the 1950s. Japanese judo can be traced back to its origins in the late 1800s. Even the majority of the traditional sword arts and sports of Japan have documented founders and births traceable to the 1500s.

ANCIENT HISTORY

The art of ninjutsu, however, reaches back over a millennium to an age in Japan's antiquity. The body of knowledge that later came to be called ninjutsu, or *nin-po* in its higher order, was at first regarded as merely an unconventional way of handling life situations and accomplishing the necessary. What eventually went on to become a highly systematic and scientific method of combat, espionage and danger prevention began as a shadowy counterculture, a forced reaction against the mainstream of Japanese political, military, economic and social traditions.

Forerunners of the Ninja

The art seems to have developed from an entwining of religious and military backgrounds to produce a uniquely Japanese approach toward using nature, cosmic laws, human psychology and physiology, and the inevitable cycles of history as a means of ensuring physical and spiritual survival. The forerunners of the ninja included *sennin* and *gyoja* (warrior hermits), *yamabushi* and *shugenja* (mountain mystics), refugee Chinese Taoist sages and military officers, as well as unfortunate Japanese *bushi* who found themselves homeless and masterless after their forces had been routed by others.

The First Ninja

The original people who were later referred to as ninja filled advisory roles in the camps of military rulers vying for control over the various regions of Japan. The true ninja was a "bringer of good fortune" to those who had the power and influence to assist the ninja's families in finding peaceful and stable lives. Because of the original ninja's closeness with nature and inclinations toward what others described as "occult" powers, they could provide valuable perspectives and counsel to those who were more familiar with conventional politics and warfare. The ninja had trusted contacts or direct subordinates who could move into areas closed to conventional forces for reconnaissance, and they also possessed an insightful mind that could see into the future to evaluate any currently formulating plans.

In most cases, ninjutsu *ryu* (traditions or systems) came to be formed as one generation after another carried on the stealthy methods of survival handed down from the elders of the family to the younger members. The ryu would not be "founded" as such but rather would evolve itself up from seemingly unrelated fragments of history in the making. The Togakure Ryu of ninjutsu, for example, was well into its third generation before its members began to refer to their body of developing knowledge and tradition as a documented ryu based on the experiences and teachings of their ancestor Daisuke Togakure in the late 1100s.

The Gyokko Ryu ninja system of *koshijutsu* (unarmed combat) evolved for many generations in the Iga region of Japan before the members of that particular martial tradition decided to name their method after the Chinese refugee warrior Cho Gyokko, who had first introduced his revolutionary concepts of unarmed fighting to the rural Japanese locals aiding him in his new country of political exile.

Formation of Ryu

Other ninjutsu ryu came into existence as the tides of Japanese economics and politics became more turbulent from the 1300s onward. Ryu were often formed as families that found themselves outside the mainstream of military and political developments, in which creative thinking and action were the last remaining possibilities for guaranteeing survival. Other ryu were only temporarily established for the purpose of aiding the cause of a specific regional lord, military group or religious order and then later disbanded when no longer needed. Some ninjutsu ryu were regional in nature and came together as a result of geographical politics. Still other ryu were based around extensive bodies of knowledge, experience and wisdom collected by one specific individual.

The documented historical ninja ryu of Japan varied in size and importance from small collections of a few family members to vast regional networks involving hundreds of people who often did not even know each other and were connected only through their common loyalties to a single overseer. The following names are a partial listing of a few of the more influential or historically significant ninjutsu ryu and their founders, regions of operation or military and political affiliations:

- Nakagawa Ryu ninjutsu was based in Aomori Prefecture, organized by Nakagawa Kohayato.

- Haguro Ryu ninjutsu was based in Yamagata Prefecture and was said to have been developed by the warrior ascetics of Haguro Mountain.

- Uesugi Ryu ninjutsu was established for Uesugi Kenshin as a military espionage organization by Usami Suruganokami Sadayuki in Niigata Prefecture.

- Kaji Ryu ninjutsu was founded by Kaji Ominokami Kagehide, a student of the founder of Uesugi Ryu, but was also linked to the roots of Iga's Hattori Ryu ninjutsu.

- Matsumoto Ryu ninjutsu was based in Tochigi Prefecture.

- Matsuda Ryu ninjutsu was based in Ibaraki Prefecture.

- Koyo Ryu, Ninko Ryu and Takeda Ryu ninjutsu, founded by Takeda Shingen for intelligence gathering, used wandering monks and merchants as agents.

- Fuma nin-po, based in Kanagawa Prefecture, established by Fuma Kotaro, specialized in guerrilla warfare.

- Akiba Ryu and Ichizen Ryu, based in Aichi Prefecture, were established by Hachisuka Koroku Masakatsu, who was a famous ninja from this area.

- Mino Ryu ninjutsu, based in Gifu Prefecture, was developed during the rule of Saito Dosan and included the Kurokawa ninja group of Koga.

- Echizen Ryu ninjutsu was established in Toyama Prefecture by Iga ninja fleeing the attack of Oda Nobunaga.

- Yoshitsune Ryu ninjutsu, based in Fukui Prefecture, was developed for Yoshitsune Minamoto as a blend of espionage methods taught by Ise Saburo and yamabushi teachings.

- Koga Ryu ninjutsu was a regional tradition made up of more than 50 families.

- Iga Ryu ninjutsu was a regional tradition made up of several key families, most notably the Hattori and Momochi clans.

- Negoro Ryu, founded by Suginobo Myosan, firearms master; Saiga Ryu, firearms and explosives specialists; Natori Ryu, founded by Natori Sanjuro Masatake, author of *Sho Nin Ki* ninjutsu reference work; and Kishu Ryu ninjutsu were based in Wakayama Prefecture.

- Bizen Ryu ninjutsu was based in Okayama Prefecture.

- Fukushima Ryu ninjutsu, transmitted by Nojirijiro Jirouemon Narimasa, was based in Shimane Prefecture.

- Kuroda Ryu ninjutsu was based in Fukuoka Prefecture in support of the Kuroda family government.

- Nanban Ryu ninjutsu was based in Nagasaki Prefecture.

- Satsuma nin-po was based in Kagoshima Prefecture in support of the Shimazu family government.

The vast majority of ninjutsu ryu,* all save a small handful, died out long before the Meiji Restoration in 1868. Once unification and enforced peace came to Japan in the 1600s, the need for extensive intelligence-gathering networks and thorough training in the brutal arts of life or death all but vanished. As the need for the skill of ninjutsu dwindled, so did the numbers of practitioners who devoted their energies to living the *shinobi* arts. Just like there is no French underground resistance movement now that there are no longer German occupation troops holding French territory, the urgency of the original ninja families also faded with time and with the establishment of new Japanese governmental policies.

Today, the remains of most historical ninja ryu can be seen on public display in museums and galleries throughout Japan. Scrolls of grand-master authority, weapons and even battle garb, in some rare cases, can be found as silent testimony to their system's demise.

Once a ryu died out, the last remaining grandmaster was expected to destroy the tradition's scrolls and manuscripts to prevent the ryu's name and reputation from being dragged into disrepute. In some cases, the material was left behind or sold off by heirs who did not understand the significance of the contents.

MODERN HISTORY

In the middle of the 19th century, the island nation of Japan opened up to foreign trade and influence. The once-powerful Tokugawa family, who had ruled Japan as military dictators for more than 200 years, relinquished control over the government. The elite samurai class that had provided law, order and stability to Japanese life for almost 700 years was abolished, and Japan raced to adopt the newly discovered

*Author's footnote:
These ninjutsu ryu names are a part of the past history of Japan, just like the names Sitting Bull and Francis "Swamp Fox" Marion are part of American history. Anyone claiming to be teaching the methods of any of these ryu will of course have to possess extensive documentation to prove that the scrolls donated to the museums are actually frauds and that he has indeed inherited the authority of the ryu, which Japanese historians and scholars have verified as dead. Students beware! Would you really want to model your life after that of a person who would lie to you about his credentials in order to coerce your respect or get some of your money?

Western modes of culture.

During the Meiji era that followed the opening of Japan in 1868, two important government slogans changed the face of life in Japan. The *fukoku kyohei* stated the new government's aim was to "enrich the nation and strengthen the military." The second slogan of *bunmei kaika* provided the means of building up the country by "opening up the culture" to the influence of foreign ways. The old traditions like the warrior skills of individual combat came to be seen as *yaban* (barbaric), and the military leaders of Japan turned to Europe for guidance in modern military tactics.

As one result of this cultural upheaval, the martial arts were stripped of their martial significance and transformed into sports and personal development exercise systems. Battlefield methods of life-protecting combat were fractionalized into pieces of ritual movement with one specific weapon, or games of skills with a limited set of body movements. Comprehensive warrior training covering a broad scope of applications was seen as a relic from the dead past, something useless in the modern age.

Those martial artists who pioneered the change from warfare to self-improvement are now legendary. Judo's Jigoro Kano, *aikido's* Morihei Ueshiba and karate's Gichin Funakoshi captured the hearts of their nation with their new, safer, limited and sanitized versions of what had once been rough-and-tumble combat methods in which injury was quite often a part of the training. The new martial systems were heralded as "gentlemanly" adaptations of the old and obsolete warrior methods.

Not all master teachers of the martial arts embraced this change in approach, however. Many of the old warriors cautioned against the rush to abandon what had been their legacy for generations. For the large part, however, their pleas fell on deaf ears, and they gradually faded into obscurity with progress into the 20th century.

Ishitani Trains Takamatsu

Such was the case of Takakage Matsutaro Ishitani, whose ancestors had been high-ranking *chunin* ninja in the troops of Iga Ryu ninjutsu *jonin* Hanzo Hattori three centuries earlier. As the 26th grandmaster of the Kuki Shinden Ryu *happo biken* (secret weapon arts) of ninjutsu, a system originally founded by Izumo Kanja Yoshiteru, Ishitani refused to dilute his method to appeal to the masses now more interested in sporting competition or Zen movement.

Obscurity for Ishitani was being relegated to doing security work at the Takamatsu family's match factory in Kobe, the closest thing he could find for application of the clandestine specialties he had inherited from an older and less secure age. Without students or a *dojo*, the grandmaster of Kuki Shinden happo biken resigned himself to living out the rest of his life as an anachronism from another time. He was prepared, like other ninja masters before him, to destroy all his secret scrolls and weapons before his death. If there were no worthy heir, the legacy would be taken to the grave with him.

Through his work at the Takamatsu match factory, Ishitani came to meet the young son of the factory's owner. A special relationship soon developed, and Ishitani knew that he had found the heir he had been seeking in the young Toshitsugu Takamatsu. Already an experienced practitioner of Koto Ryu *koppojutsu* and Shinden Fudo Ryu *dakentaijutsu*, as taught to him by his grandfather Shinryuken Masamitsu Toda, the young Takamatsu leapt at the chance to learn the specialties of the Kuki Shinden Ryu from his new mentor Ishitani. In an age that had outgrown the true warrior ways, it was a perfect matching of student and teacher.

Covers of antique Japanese ninja novels held at the Ninja Yashiki Museum in Iga-Ueno City, Japan.

Ishitani first taught Takamatsu the eight-part *happo* method that included the following:

1. *Taijutsu* (unarmed combat), *hichojutsu* (leaping), *nawanage* (rope throwing)

2. *Koppojutsu* (bone-smashing technique), *jutaijutsu* (grappling)

3. *Yarijutsu* (spear technique), *naginatajutsu* (halberd skills)

4. *Bojutsu* (long-staff fighting), *jojutsu* (cane technique), *hanbojutsu* (stick fighting)

5. *Senban nage (shuriken* star throwing), *tokenjutsu* (knife throwing)

6. *Kajutsu* (fire and explosives), *suijutsu* (water techniques)

7. *Chiku jo gunryaku heiho* (military tactics and fortress design and penetration)

8. *Onshinjutsu* (art of invisibility), *hensojutsu* (disguise)

Next, the young disciple was taught the *hiken* (secret sword) method, which included the Kuki Shinden Ryu approach to handling *ken* (swords), *kodachi* (short blades) and *jutte* (anti-sword truncheons).

Takamatsu trained hard and assimilated the teachings, and he was eventually granted the scrolls, weapons and title of 27th grandmaster of the Kuki Shinden happo biken tradition. Ishitani had found his heir.

As a child, Takamatsu had been shuttled through a succession of nine foster mothers. His childhood had not been a happy one, and security was but a fleeting concept in his young life. Takamatsu had grown up tough and determined, as evidenced by a Kobe newspaper report of the 14-year-old having soundly thrashed a gang of older attackers in an alleyway. The young Takamatsu therefore came to rely on his grandparents as the single point of stability in his life.

Takamatsu's grandfather had been the supervisor of sword teachers for the Tokugawa shogun's government school in their home region. Much less well-known was the fact that Toda was the 32nd in the line of grandmasters of the Togakure Ryu ninjutsu tradition. Following his instruction of the Koto Ryu and Shinden Fudo Ryu methods, the grandmaster began to train his grandson in the esoteric art of the Togakure ninja warriors. Climbing, stalking and evasion techniques were introduced along with the weapon and unarmed skills that the young Takamatsu had been practicing since late childhood.

Ineligible for military service in the early 1900s because of a ruptured eardrum carried as a souvenir of a fight during his teen years, Takamatsu took off on his own when he was 21. A career at the match factory paled in comparison with the thought of the adventure that waited across the sea in China, then considered the land of fortune in Japan's future. Journeying from the vast country, Takamatsu found numerous opportunities to rely on his warrior skills for the protection of his life.

After the rough-and-tumble years in China and a period of living in the wilderness of the mountains in Japan, Takamatsu returned to his home in 1919 to study and be ordained as a Tendai-shu *mikkyo* (esoteric) Buddhist priest. By age 30, Takamatsu had straddled the two realms of warrior invincibility and spiritual power as a master of both.

Takamatsu Trains Hatsumi

Masaaki Hatsumi began his martial arts training at age 7, when he began practicing with his father's *bokuto* (wooden sword). From that point, he went on to train in all the popular Japanese martial arts of the wartime era, eventually earning teaching ranks in karate, aikido and judo. The martial arts and theater arts were the passions of his life in his teen and young adult years.

During the postwar years in Japan, however, the young Hatsumi was shocked to see how quickly and skillfully the American occupation soldiers he taught picked up the technique of judo. The huge Americans used their size and natural athletic inclinations to learn in months what it took the Japanese years of training to obtain. What was the use of training in a system if others could surpass your efforts by mere size alone? There had to be some sort of ultimate warrior system for all situations, thought the young martial arts teacher.

Through his *kobudo* (ancient weapons) teacher, Hatsumi learned of a teacher named Toshitsugu Takamatsu of Kashiwabara City to the west of the Iga region in Japan. As a last hope at finding someone who could teach a living warrior art and not a recreational sport or system of rigid lifeless *kata*, the young Hatsumi traveled across Honshu Island to find the teacher he had been seeking for a lifetime.

The veteran battler Takamatsu was well into his 60s when he met the young man who would eventually become his spiritual heir and the next grandmaster of ninjutsu. For Takamatsu, that first meeting was more of a reunion than an introduction. In a poem to Hatsumi,

Takamatsu wrote the following:

> *Long ago, I was an accomplished warrior*
> *of the koppojutsu tradition.*
> *I was courageous and as intense as the flame,*
> *even in battle against violent animals.*
> *I have a heart that is like the wildflowers of the meadows,*
> *and yet straight and true as the bamboo.*
> *Not even ten thousand enemies can cause me fear.*
> *Who is there in the world who would keep alive*
> *this will of the warrior's heart?*
> *There you are, this one sent to me by the warrior gods.*
> *I have been waiting for you*
> *through all the ages.*

For years, Hatsumi suffered his rough apprenticeship under the direction of the ninja grandmaster with a heart like wildflowers and hands like a tiger's. Eventually, he went on to inherit the title of grandmaster of the nine warrior traditions carried by his teacher Takamatsu.

CHAPTER 20

In the lessons of nature
    there is wisdom for the ninja.
The mystical combatant becomes
    the whisper of the leaves
    the smell of the earth
    the taste of the sea
    in order to accomplish what must be done
    and live to celebrate
    yet another day.

THE FIVE ELEMENTS OF ESCAPE

His close communion with nature gives him the wisdom to survive

The legendary Japanese warrior art of ninjutsu developed in mountain and marsh wilderness territories far remote from the feudal capital. Because the historical ninja had to face overwhelming odds, with the enemy often being government troops who were far better equipped, stronger in numbers, and official representatives of the legal establishment controlling the region, physical survival often entailed a working familiarity with the forces of nature and the cycles of the seasons as a means of increasing the likelihood of success for these outlawed economic and religious rebels.

As a means of passing on skills to younger family members and preserving the knowledge in a manner that would allow seasoned operatives to recall vital instructions even in moments of extreme life-threatening stress, the ninja of south central Japan developed a series of working models from nature. The models were used as codes to simplify the process of understanding and remembering. They were not employed in attempting the impossible task of classifying all potential methods with all their physical details.

In the nature lore of ninjutsu, there developed two distinct systems that today are commonly referred to as "five element" theories.

Go-Dai

Of great importance in understanding the ninja combat method, one theory, the ninja's *go-dai* (five major elemental manifestations), derived from the *nin-po mikkyo* Himalayan tantric spiritual teachings, includes the following codes:

Chi—earth (solid matter)
Sui—water (liquids)
Ka—fire (energy transformation)
Fu—wind (gases)
Ku—primordial ether (subatomic source of all elements)

Go-Gyo

Another "five element" theory, the *go-gyo* (five-element transformations), stemmed from Chinese Taoist teachings that found their way into feudal Japan by way of authorized cultural exchanges, as well as covert instruction provided by refugee Chinese generals and priests seeking sanctuary in Japan following the destruction that accompanied the collapse of China's Tang dynasty in the 10th century. Unlike the go-dai system that cataloged the elements during the ever-continuing formation of the universe, the go-gyo system stems from the *in* and *yo* (*yin* and *yang* in Chinese) polarity theory and catalogs the cycle of transformation that continuously takes place in the realm of material objects. The five elemental transformations include the following contraction and expansion codes:

Sui—water (dissolving)
Moku—wood (growing)
Ka—fire (evaporating)
Do—earth (solidifying)
Kin—metal (hardening)

These five elemental codes were developed as symbols typifying the stages through which all matter passes. They are not meant to be limited to literal classifications of trees, rocks, water and so forth. All phenomena continue to pass through these transformations in a cyclical pattern, for which the five codes were assigned as a means of better understanding. The five do not exist as five separate entities in themselves but rather reflect the quality of blending or emerging from one state into another. The cycle has no real beginning or end, either. The observer will note that the cycle seems to begin at that stage in the rise and fall of energy wherever he or she happens to first direct attention.

Each stage of the transformation process leads naturally into the next in a series of never-ending supporting relationships. Water (sinking condensation) produces wood, wood (up-reaching growth) produces fire, fire (expanding free energy) produces solid earth, earth (compacting) produces metal and metal (hardening) in turn produces water. This natural five-element code system works equally well whether used for medical healing and strengthening purposes or applied as a means of analyzing the destinies of nations.

Goton-Po

Rationally, the symbols also can be followed in a series of destructive or inhibiting relationships by altering the perspective or progress of the flow. Water (melting) can put out fire, fire (rising energy) can soften metal, metal (hardening) can cut down wood, wood (growing) can break up earth and earth (solidifying) can dam up water. This subduing symbolism is in turn the basis for the historical ninja's *goton-po* (five-element escape method).

Because the ninja families of ancient Japan were part of an underground counterculture that existed at the annoyance of the established bureaucracy power structure, self-protection and the prevention of danger often entailed covert actions by mere individuals opposing the might of major troop formations. These tremendous odds made winning through conventional honorable warfare impossible. Therefore, all approaches to survival, from psychological deception to homemade black powder to blending with the elements of nature, had to he considered by the ninja.

At face value, the ninja's goton-po could, of course, serve as a guide for vanishing from the sight of the enemy. The night warrior could imitate or blend in with the rocks and earth, trees, bodies of water, or use fire and smoke or metal objects as a means of enhancing his or her chances of successful escape. This is the more obvious application of the goton-po five-element theory.

Dotonjutsu is the use of the earth element to aid in escape. This application includes knowledge of the geography of the area of operation,

the use of natural terrain features for concealment, and the strategic employment of terrain as a means of hindering and discouraging the enemy's pursuit. Skills of land navigation, efficient walking and running methods, and a working knowledge of how to operate a wide range of vehicles are also parts of ninjutsu's dotonjutsu.

Suitonjutsu is the use of the water element to aid in escape and evasion. This application of the go-gyo theory includes the use of still or moving water as a means of penetrating or leaving enemy territory, the use of water for concealment, and the use of streams, bodies of water and even induced flooding as a means of detaining or hindering pursuers. Methods of water navigation, stealth swimming and underwater action, and knowledge of boat and flotation device operation are also parts of the ninja's suitonjutsu.

Katonjutsu is the use of the fire element to assist the ninja in escape actions. This interpretation of the goton-po five-element tactics includes the use of smoke and fire as cover or distraction, as well as knowledge of the preparation and employment of explosives. Also part of ninjutsu's katonjutsu since the 16th century is a working ability with all types of firearms that could be used by or against the ninja and his or her family.

Mokutonjutsu is the use of wood and plants as a means of aiding the ninja to evade an enemy. Trees and brush could be used for concealment or undetected viewing posts, or could be employed to hinder large groups of armored or mounted troops attempting pursuit. The use of plants as natural medicine or poisons also constitutes an aspect of ninjutsu's mokutonjutsu as does a working knowledge of structural configuration and carpentry.

Kintonjutsu is the employment of metal objects to assist in escape and evasion. Metal applications include all tools needed to gain access or escape from locked and barricaded structures, climb or perch on high structures or natural formations, or fight off the attack of an enemy who would restrain the ninja.

Less obvious is the deeper symbolism of the goton-po as a series of lesson blocks dealing with the transformation of energies in a natural manner so as to be able to guide and overcome the enemy's attack. Sometimes that meant creating a false and yet totally believable perception of reality in the enemy's mind. Growing, rising energy (wood) leads to free-moving expansive energy (fire), unless it encounters factors of hardening (metal), which inhibits or stops growth. Melting, newly flowing energy (water) leads to growing, rising energy (wood), unless solidifying tendencies (earth) inhibit it. In a combat scenario, free-moving expansive energy (fire) that manifests itself as speed and power will eventually run out, which leads to a need to slow down (earth) and scientifically hold ground, unless the reliance on speed is inhibited by energy-conserving tendencies that turn the fighting action into scientifically tactical flowing motions (water).

It is important to emphasize that the ninja's five-element go-gyo theory of using natural cyclical tendencies is based on a series of graphic symbols from nature and does not represent a system of literal interpretations of the so-called elements. "Metal produces water, which produces wood, but is conquered by fire, which is in turn conquered by water," is really a coded way of reminding ourselves that hardness eventually softens, and softness produces upward-rising energy, but the tendency toward hardness is inhibited by aspects that would lead to lighter, freer energy, and expansive rising energy is in turn brought down by qualities of melting or flowing. As with all else that is ninjutsu, the go-gyo five elements are powerful tools that can lead to the understanding that produces enlightenment, if only we can reach behind the surface and grasp the hidden significance.

DOTONJUTSU (Use of Earth)

Concealment in a Rock Formation

Using a rock and the shadow it casts is a good example of dotonjutsu (earth escape method). Blending in with the desert surroundings, you can avoid detection (1). The severe contrast of light and shadow also helps to hide you from sight even when you begin to

move out if you are wearing dark clothing (2). Dark shapes are difficult for the eyes to distinguish in a shadow if the surrounding light is stark and intense. In this way, you can remain hidden until it is safe to leave your hiding place entirely (3-4).

Concealment From a Guard

In this example of doton-jutsu, you become a part of something familiar to the bored guard, such as a rock grouping (1-4). He has walked this route many times before without incident, and his at-

tention is not attracted to benign landscape features he is accustomed to taking for granted. Such "boring" objects make excellent cover in which to conceal yourself.

Concealment in Low Vegetation

Using dotonjutsu, you can use a washed-out area on a slope as a place to remain out of sight, staying close to the ground and allowing the low vegetation to conceal you in the same way it conceals the ground, until the proper

time comes to move (1-4). Blending in and becoming part of the environment so as to remain undetected is also a matter of considering the nature of the particular element you have chosen to use as your method.

Climbing a Rock Face

To scale a rock face, the body (1) is flattened out and allowed to relax into the surface of the rock. The limbs stretch out so that bone, as well as muscle, carries the load of the shifting weight. You must hold three points secured (2) while you move a fourth, either hand or foot, into a higher position (3-6). That way, your body will have a better chance of holding firmly should the new hand or foot position prove to be unstable. The three-point method also aids in quieter climbing.

447

Scaling a Wall

To escape capture or avoid a needless confrontation, dotonjutsu can be used to run right up a wall in order to evade a pursuer (1). By generating enough speed, the momentum of your body

carries you into the wall, giving you enough force against it to enable you to use your feet to propel your body upward (2-4) along the surface of the vertical obstacle and facilitate your escape (5).

SUITONJUTSU (Use of Water)

Concealment in a Pond

To avoid detection or as a means of escape, water can be used as a hiding place (1-2). Again, because one does not normally think of water as a good hiding place, it makes an excellent one. You are able to hide below the surface of a pond by breathing through a thin tube that has the appearance of a reed, becoming yourself a part of the water by being calm, and therefore not creating any movement that would disturb the natural appearance of the water under those particular conditions.

KATONJUTSU (Use of Smoke and Fire)

Distraction and Intimidation

(A) The use of smoke and fire created terror in an age when all structures were made of wood, rice paper and straw. (B) The use of firearms and explosives was also a crucial aspect of the ninja's fire approach to escape and avoidance.

MOKUTONJUTSU
(Use of Wood)

Climbing a Column

As a means of evading discovery, proper tree- and column-climbing techniques from the ninja's use of wood for escape are taught to contemporary age students. Note that your body is held upright and close to the tree trunk so that the feet can wedge in by using the body's weight, not muscle tension, to hold the position (1-2) while your hands reach up for a higher hold (3-4). Then the feet are brought up to a higher position (5).

KINTONJUTSU
(Use of Metal)

Tools and Weapons

(A) The kaginawa (the ninja's rope and grappling hook) is used as a climbing aid or for transporting gear and equipment. (B) The Togakure Ryu ninja's shuko (hand claws) are hooked over objects to be climbed and never slammed straight into solid surfaces. Contrary to modern belief, the shuko were not tools common to most ancient ninjutsu ryu but rather were secret inventions of Iga province Togakure family ninja. (C) The shuriken

Kaginawa

Shuko

(throwing blades), perhaps the most famous of the legendary ninja tools, are a prime example of the ninja's creative thinking in applying the principles of the kintonjutsu. (D) Tetsubishi (iron spikes) are yet another example of the kintonjutsu principles of using metal to aid escape. Thrown in the path of pursuers, the spikes impede the enemy's pursuit. (These are on display in the Ninja Yashiki Museum in Iga-Ueno City, Japan.)

Tetsubishi

Shuriken

CHAPTER 21

Swiftness of fist
power behind the kick—
the vast collection of techniques.
These are but the first step
of the journey to warrior invincibility.
Why then are so many content to stop learning
and put down roots
at the entrance to the path?

FLOWING ACTION

Living in the flow of action, his success is the most natural outcome of combat

Once a student of the warrior arts completes his or her training in the fundamentals of physical self-protection combat, it is then time to go on and personalize the art so as to make the fundamentals an integral part of the personality. In effect, the basics are "forgotten" as special and separate in and of themselves.

This process can work in two ways. The student can adapt his or her ways of moving so as to conform to the art. The movements are internalized and the body ends up with a new way of moving, as in the kata (form) method of training. On the other hand, the student can adapt the art to fit his or her ways of moving. The purpose and details of the techniques are internalized, and the body ends up with additional possibilities for ways of moving, as in the *waza* (technique) method of training.

The kata method of dramatically altering the way the student's body moves from the inside can cause frustration because of the rigid manner in which the body's natural movement patterns are ignored or disrupted.

The waza method of quickly altering the way the body moves from the outside by supplying new ways to handle familiar situations can

provide frustration through the unstructured manner in which the body's learned movement patterns are expected to adapt freely to the new material.

For balanced growth through training in the warrior arts, one must change from the inside as well as the outside. To restrict training to only one of the two methods is to encourage only half the growth possible. Although for a brief period results do seem to appear more quickly, this is simply because the contrasting half of the training process is not present to cause doubts in the body or mind.

Kotsu

The key to progress in the self-protection methods that character-ize the art of ninjutsu is a *kotsu* (essence) approach to training. By combining aspects of training in movement principles and application concepts, the student can develop a balanced ability that blends skills of effective body dynamics with practical responses to attacks. With that kind of training approach, even from the first few instruction sessions, the student will come away with some useable concrete results that he or she can rely on while at the same time begin a lifetime of personal refinement of natural body movement that will continue to unfold as he or she progresses through all the stages of growing older.

Nagare

One of the fundamental principles emphasized in ninja training is the concept of *nagare* (flowing) action. The idea of a flow refers equally to the movement from one action to the next, the body dynamics that deliver the movement, the physical logic that determines the appropri-ate movement, and the actual course of progress toward the desired outcome of the conflict.

For those students to whom the concept of nagare is foreign or even confusing, it is perhaps an effective educational device to reverse the concept and examine the results derived. Without an overall flowing quality, the student finds his or her moves to be unrelated single units quite independent structurally from other moves in the string of actions making up any given technique. Without flow, the student may struggle to force a technique to fit a situation that somehow seems awkward, or find that the conflict has ended up in areas or shapes that had not been counted on. The absence of flowing grace forces fighting movements

to rely on the muscle and bone power of the limbs alone, which is a dangerous habit for the one who is less strong in a combat clash.

Ritsudo

Closely related to the quality of flowing adaptability is the concept of fitting in with or riding along with the *ritsudo* (rhythm) of the actions that make up the fight. This rhythm is an inherent part of any activity that involves the interrelated body dynamics of two or more individuals in motion. The rhythm of the actions of a conflict also can be described as the "breath" of the fight. One phase leads into another in a back and forth of projecting and receiving that resembles the mechanics of breathing.

Ritsudo is an awareness of rhythm at several levels. At one level, the defender must fit in with the movements of his attacker in order to gain control of the direction of the fight. Another level of rhythm is characterized by the emotional fluctuations of both fighters from second to second. Another rhythm is evidenced in the movements and muscular contractions that propel the bodies of the combatants. Perhaps ultimately, ritsudo manifests itself as the progressing interplay of cause and effect in a fighting encounter. The defender's initial attack causes the effect of his angling back away with a counterstrike or grab, which then becomes the cause of the effect of the defender's attempting a follow-up lunge, which is then the cause of his next move as an effect ... and the rhythm of the opposing forces continues until stillness is once again reached.

Total Training

In learning to handle a fighting situation well, and thereby ultimately learning how to transcend the limitations of needing to rely on physical defensive action, the student of the warrior ways can observe a triangular interrelation of three major aspects of winning a conventional fight. Though each of the single aspects themselves could possibly be relied on as a point of training focus, such narrow approaches will ultimately fall short when compared with total training.

Mechanics—the most efficient ways of moving the body in response to attacks; includes proper physical fundamentals such as footwork, angling and distancing, proper employment of body weapons, and effective techniques and strategies.

Dynamics—the most efficient means by which the mechanics are employed; includes proper applications of energy, rhythm and flow, strength and flexibility, speed relationships, and the ability to "feel and fit into" the action of the technique exchange.

Intention—the total commitment of the mechanics and dynamics toward the clearly recognized goal of victory; includes proper motivation for the application of violent methods, will to win that transcends normal fears or limits, and a mindset that not only sees victory as the single possible outcome but also has no concept of the possibility of losing.

As a means of training to apply this awareness of three-way interaction, the student can practice with two distinct methods of approach: training drills and fighting scenarios.

TRAINING DRILLS

Training drills isolate a particular movement, limb or feeling and then allow the student to repeat the desired experience over and over again without concern for danger or the possibility of his or her technique being interrupted. Drills are purposely abstract so that the student can concentrate on the piece of the action to be perfected without being distracted by the grander scope of what would happen in the totality of an actual fight. These abstract training drills allow the development of skills necessary for the application of techniques through the second training method of fighting scenarios.

Single-Action Repetition

The trainee repeats a single action from a potential fighting response, working at eventual mastery through continuous experience. Again and again, the trainee works at blasting his training partner's attacking

arm out of its course toward him. As the attacker lunges with a blow toward the face (1-3), the trainee steps to the side (4), intercepting the attacking arm, deflecting the blow (5) and knocking the

continued on next page

arm completely out of the way (6). The exercise isolates and repeats the same attack with no attempt at a follow-up or counter (7) as the attacker again comes forward with a

blow toward the face (8), and the defender blocks it (9), punches the attacker's arm (10) and drives it out of the way (11).

Defense and Counter Repetition

Any given technique series can be practiced for perfection through drills. As the attacker attacks (1-2), his punch is knocked away with a strike to the arm (3), and then the defender follows up with an open-hand strike to the neck (4-7). The attacker assists his defender by supplying the standard attack each time and makes no attempt to trick or overthrow the response of the defender.

Strike and Defense Exchange

The defender and his attacker take turns exchanging an identical kicking attack and counter back and forth in continuous flowing succession. Strikes or punches could just as easily be drilled with this method. As the attacker kicks (1-2), the defender intercepts with his leg and kicks the attacking leg aside (3-4). The defender in turn provides a counter-kick to the other side (5-6), which the attacker parries (7). The exchange is repeated again (8-11).

469

Multiple-Strike Succession Exchange

Both training partners take turns repeating an identical multiple-part flow of attacks and counters. As the attacker leads with a left jab (1-2), the defender knocks it away (3-4), then parries another lunge punch to the face (5-8), sweeps

continued on next page

aside an uppercut by guiding it away from his body (9-11) and counters with his own body punch (12-13). He immediately dives right back with the same attack pattern, this time as the aggressor, and the exchange continues on with the roles reversed (14-16).

Grappling Flow Exchange

With a flow drill using a wrist twist as the technique to be perfected, both training partners take turns applying the throw and rolling out as a means of escape. Note that each time one of the partners is thrown, he retains control of the thrower's hand (as shown in detail in Step 4) by squeezing down on his fingers to hold him in place for the counter-throw. The defender applies a wrist twist (1-2) and throws the attacker (3). The attacker, by squeezing down on the defender's hand to retain control and rolling (4) back up to a standing position (5), reverses the situation by applying a wrist twist on the defender (6), and the defender falls (7), rolls out of the wrist twist (8), trapping the attacker's fingers in his hand and standing up (9), reverses the hold.

474

2

3

5

6

8

9

continued on next page ▶

The defender throws the attacker again (10). The attacker rolls out of the wrist twist, retaining control of the defender's hand (11-12), and comes back up to a standing position with the grip reversed (13). He throws the defender on his back (14-15). The defender rolls out of the wrist twist (16-17) and reverses the hold on the attacker (18), and the procedure is repeated.

Weapon Grappling Flow Exchange

A continuous flow of grabs and throws uses the ninja's hanbo (cane). The attacker thrusts (1), and the defender steps to one side and intercepts the attacker's lunge (2). Then he uses arm and leg leverage to execute a defensive throw and disarm the attacker (3-6). With roles now reversed (7), the original defender

continued on next page ▶

becomes the attacker and executes a thrust (8), which the defender sidesteps and intercepts (9). The defender then executes a defensive throw and disarms the new attacker (10-12). The roles are again switched as the original attacker, now once again in possession of the hanbo, executes a thrust, and the drill is repeated (13-14).

FIGHT SCENARIOS

The fight scenario recreates the fight in full detail, with accurately acted out body dynamics. Though fight scenarios can be drilled and abstract drills can resemble the action of a fight, the two types of exercise serve different purposes.

Defense Against Knife Lunge

The attacker advances with a stab to the defender's midsection (1-2), which the defender avoids with a last-second body shift and counterstrikes against the attacker's weapon hand (3). The defender then continues with a punch to the ribs to unbalance his attacker (4-5) and then a counterpunch against the attacker's attempt to punch (6-7).

continued on next page ▶

The defender steps under the attacker's held arm while applying a rising forearm strike to the attacker's chin (8-9). The defender's body movement provides the windup for a throw that stuns the attacker (10-11) and holds him in place for the defender's knee to the face (12-13) and disarm (14).

Flowing Action in Unarmed Defense

With motion flow, the defender avoids his attacker's punch (1-3). The attacker grabs the defender's shoulder (4-5) and attempts to kick (6-7), which the defender blocks (8-9). As the attacker moves in with a punch (10-11), the

2

3

6

7

10

11

continued on next page ▶

defender counters with attacks to the limbs (12-17). As the assault continues, the attacker manages to gain control once again (18) and attempts to throw the defender to finish the fight (19). The defender does not try to force the technique but instead goes along with the throw while securing the attacker's arm, using his rear body drop to propel the attacker's face into the ground, knocking him out (20-22).

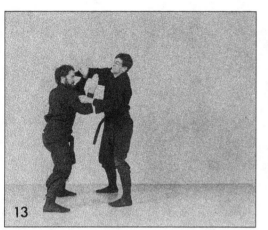

13

14

17

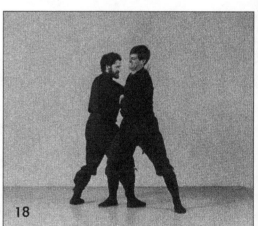

18

21

22

Body in Motion to Create Knockdown Power

The defender uses her attacker's pull on her arm to propel her body forward with a shoulder slam to the upper arm of the attacker (1-6). Her elbow-lock armbar holds the attacker in place (7) for a rear sweeping throw that forces the attacker facedown to the ground (8-10). The defender then stretches the attacker's arm between the top of one knee and the bottom of the other to create arm-breaking leverage (11).

Evasive Flowing Body Action With Counterblows

The defender evades his attacker's kicks and punches by means of flowing footwork and body angling while simultaneously applying counter-strikes. As the attacker kicks (1-3), the defender steps to the side (4) and counters with a blow to the face (5). The attacker's follow-up strike to the face (6-7) is sidestepped by the defender (8-9).

continued on next page ▶

The defender punches the attacking arm out of the way (10-11). The defender then grabs the attacker behind the ears, uses his thumbs to gouge the attacker's eyes (12-15) and, gaining a superior position by flipping him (16-17), gouges his face with clawing hands (18).

Flowing From High to Low
With Defensive Counters

On rough terrain, the defender drops below his attacker's clubbing swing (1-3) and rises to punch the attacking arm (4-5), and again he drops low to avoid the attacker's roundhouse kick (6-7). From his low vantage point (8), the defender moves in and tackles the attacker's knee (9)

continued on next page

and drives him down onto the ground (10-11). To prevent the attacker from kicking with his free leg, the defender pulls back and down on the attacker's captured leg, dragging him across the surface of the rocks (12-14). A sharp kick to the face (15-17) and a knee-wrenching twist to the held leg prevent the attacker from continuing the fight (18-19).

Flowing Along With Technique Interruption

The defender evades the attacker's leading-hand punch by shifting back and to the inside with his entire body (1-2). The defender then shifts to the inside of the stronger follow-up punch by the attacker (3-4) while executing a counterpunch to the attacker's exposed wrist (5-6). A similar response then handles the third punch (7-10).

continued on next page ▶

The defender counterattacks with a shikanken (extended knuckle punch) into the shoulder joint (11-12) and a forearm slam into the side of the head (13-14), stunning the attacker and setting him up for a shoulder-damaging arm twist (15-17). When the attacker attempts to pull out of the arm twist (18), the defender goes with that flow of action and follows along with a kitenken (hand-edge strike) to the attacker's neck (19-20)

continued on next page

and then a knee slam to the ribs (21-22). As the attacker drops to the ground, the defender braces the extended arm (23-25) and steps across the falling body (26-28), using his hips in motion to break the attacker's shoulder (29-30).

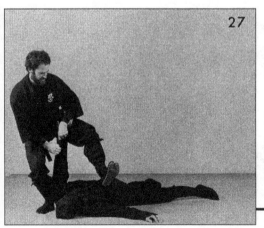

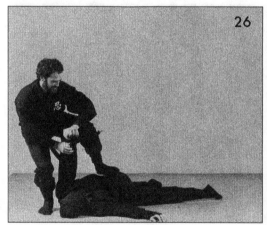

Use of Environment to Assist Flow

The attacker stabs at the defender, who is up against a rock (1-2). The defender fades inside the lunge (3) and pulls the attacker into an elbow slam to the chin (4). He steps under the attacker's arm and directs his head into the rock with an armbar body slam (5-7). He twists the attacker's arm with an arm lock and hits him with an elbow strike to the temple (8) before dropping his weight onto the attacker's leg to damage his knee and disarm him (9-11).

Arm-Entrapping Defense

The attacker grabs the defender to hold him in place for a punch to the face (1-2). The defender slips to the inside of the punch while executing a distracting shakoken (palm-heel strike) to the underside of the attacker's jaw (3). The defender then applies an armbar (4-6) and a leg kickout to force the adversary to the ground (7-9). Bodyweight pressure across the attacker's outstretched arm breaks his elbow.

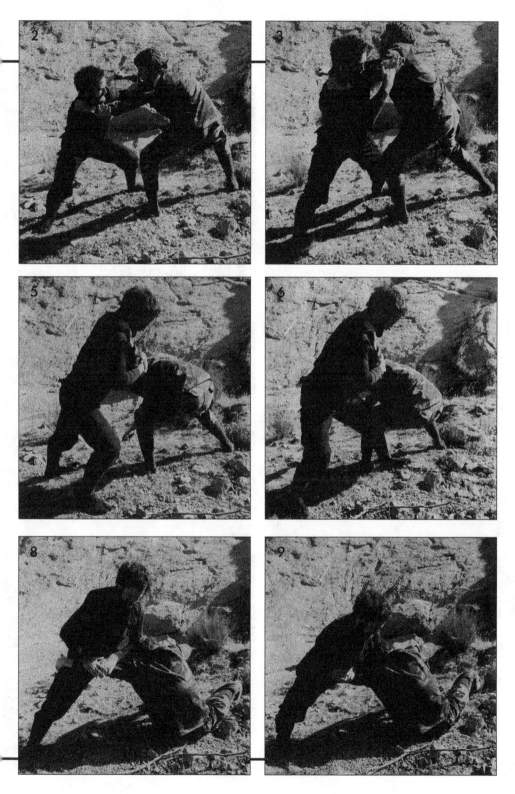

Striking and Grappling Flow

The attacker attempts a leading punch, which the defender knocks away with an outside clubbing strike (1-3). The aggressor follows with a front kick (4-5). The defender evades to the outside, with a simultaneous kick to the attacker's leg (6). The attacker grabs the defender to pin him down (7-8). The defender leaves the attacker's hand in place to facilitate a lunging kitenken (hand-edge strike) to the neck (9-10). Grabbing the attacker's hand (11), the defender

continued on next page

then applies an uragyaku (inward wrist twist) to the attacker's trapped arm (12-13). The attacker tries to free his hand (14-15), but the defender flows right on to an omotegyaku (outward wrist twist) (16) and a hooking kick to knock the attacker down (17-19). The defender then drops his weight on the bent wrist to damage the arm (20-22).

513

CHAPTER 22

There are times when
yielding is power,
laughter is strength,
and a gentle touch is
the blow that subdues the assassin.
These too are great lessons
to be learned by even the mightiest of warriors.

KUNOICHI, THE DEADLY FLOWER

She fights alongside her brother ninja, defeating even those of greater strength

The Japanese warlord Moritoki Mochizuki was killed in the famous battle of Kawanakajima in 1561, and his widowed wife Chiyome was left in the care and custody of her husband's uncle, the powerful Shingen Takeda. Rather than retire to the secluded life of a nun as might have been expected under the situation, Mochizuki's widow went on to play an active role in support of the great *daimyo* Takeda. At Takeda's request, Chiyome agreed to undertake the establishment of one of the most effective and yet undetected networks of *kunoichi* (female ninja) agents in the history of the Sengokujidai (Warring States Period) of Japan.

Takeda's idea was to have Chiyome set up a group of trained *miko* (female shrine attendants) who would act as spies, observers and messengers throughout Takeda's Kai region (present-day Yamanashi), as well as the Shinano territory (present-day Nigata), which was the prime target of conquest for Takeda and his rival Kenshin Uesugi. Takeda had always made good use of ninja in his own domain as well as those of other lords. The kunoichi would be yet another means of gathering needed intelligence or verifying reports from other sources and agents. The young female shrine attendants could easily travel around the area and interact with the local residents without arousing much suspicion at all, thereby adding to the overall strength of the Takeda family.

Chiyome established her underground academy in the village of Nazu, in Chiisa-gun of Shinshu (present-day Nagano), and went to work as the headmistress of her school for female ninja agents. Because the miko were always young unmarried girls, Chiyome began recruiting appropriate candidates from the ranks of the countless children rendered homeless by the all-consuming civil war that raged throughout the island nation of Japan. Takeda's kunoichi trainer became foster mother to any orphaned, abandoned, runaway or lost girls who found themselves in the Shinshu region without anyone to turn to. To the citizens of the region, Chiyome appeared to be nothing more than a kindly compassionate woman who was working to provide some comfort and spiritual value to the lives of certain young girls who would have otherwise been relegated to a life of misery and wretchedness.

First, the girls were instructed in the duties, manners and knowledge of the miko vestal virgins who served the priests of the Shinto shrines of the land. Second, in addition to the standard training, however, the young charges of Chiyome were also given a thorough grounding in a mindset perception that would later guarantee their loyalty in all situations. By continuously prompting and reminding the girls of the source of their salvation from a life of misery, Chiyome worked to bind the girls to her. The girls were encouraged to examine their previous lives over and over in the same way. What had led them to their misery? Who let them down? Who found them and saved them when all seemed lost? The girls eventually came to believe that the only way to survive in the world was to depend on their strong ties with their fellow sisters from the academy and to demonstrate total loyalty to Chiyome.

As a third step in the girls' education, Chiyome taught them how to obtain information valuable to her, how to analyze and evaluate situations, how to cause confusion and dissension through the planting of rumors, how to recruit reliable messengers who could pass on information to other kunoichi miko in the network, how to disguise themselves, and how to use their feminine charm to manipulate men when appropriate. Once completing the course of indoctrination and training at the ninja academy in Nazu, the girls were sent out to become

a part of Chiyome's female agent group.

Chiyome gathered her intelligence from all over the two target provinces of Kai and Shinano, also picking up knowledge from travelers who had journeyed in from outlying areas, and passed her findings on to Takeda directly. To protect the efficiency and integrity of the kunoichi ring, Chiyome's role in Takeda's scheme was disclosed to nobody and remained a secret for the life of the great general.

The history of feudal Japan is filled with such stories as that of the female ninja of the Mochizuki family. All members of the family were ready to do whatever was required to ensure the security and safety of

their clan, women as well as men, and each person had his or her roles and specialties. Women could often move undetected and unsuspected in circles where male agents would find it difficult or impossible to fit in, which made them especially valuable for purposes of espionage that would better enhance the family's chances for survival.

Kunoichi Training

Historically, the kunoichi was trained in a manner similar to her male counterparts, although the instruction of the female ninja did emphasize the more subtle aspects of personal one-on-one warfare. Small unit battlefield tactics that would be taught to her brothers would have been less important than skills of psychology and the manipulation of another's personality or perspective through behavior modification and the channeling of her intuition, all of which were emphasized in the historical kunoichi training. The preparation of kunoichi for active fieldwork did of course include basic instruction in the ninjutsu combat methods of taijutsu (unarmed self-protection), bojutsu and hanbojutsu (staff and cane fighting), *tantojutsu* (knife techniques), *sojutsu* (spear usage) and *kenjutsu* (sword methods). The tactics, however, were designed to fit the specific situation of a smaller woman contending with and escaping from larger male adversaries rather than situations of commando-type attacks against guard positions or sentry outposts.

This same emphasis on pragmatic approaches toward using the body's structure and dynamics in a scientific manner continues to guide the training of current-day female members of the authentic Japanese ninjutsu tradition. With a working ability to apply the principles of naturalness of motion and adaptability to the elements of the situation through taijutsu, female practitioners can use their generally smaller stature and natural grace to successfully handle any life-threatening or potentially injurious situation. As with all other aspects of ninjutsu, what more conventional thinkers would label as "weaknesses," the ninja sees as tools.

Accommodations must of course be made for the realities of female self-protection in the current age, just as was true in eras past. Footwork dynamics must be adjusted to the normal daily dress and footwear of the female practitioner. Skirts and dresses that wrap around the legs in a binding manner and shoes with straps or elevated soles pose the same problems that wraparound kimonos and *zori* (slip-on sandals)

and *geta* (wooden clogs) once created for the historical female ninja. Strength ratios between average female defenders and male attackers also must be acknowledged, rendering self-defense tactics that rely on power punching, kicking or throwing virtually useless in realistic life-threatening encounters.

Another crucial aspect of self-protection for female ninja is the woman's potential for employing what seem to be brutal tactics against a fellow human being. In the contemporary Western world, just like it was in ancient Japan, female members of society are subtly taught that their demeanors ought to be gentle and refined. Stereotypically, little boys are taught to be tough and competitive on the sports field, while little girls are taught to be accommodating and sociable in the home. From ancient history right up to today, men have generally been regarded as the contending breadwinners, while women have generally been regarded as the appeasing peacemakers. This cultural or perhaps biological-hormonal orientation toward uniting tendencies can often interfere with the realization that a life threat from an attacker has materialized in all its malevolent darkness. Unfortunately, all too often it takes the civilized victim, whether woman or man, too long to come to the realization that the attack is indeed real and that protective action is demanded. That deadly hesitation for the thought, "It really is happening to me!" to pass through the conscious mind is all it takes for the attacker to gain complete control of the situation.

The teachings of the historical Togakure Ryu ninjutsu suggest that cruel attackers be regarded as nonhuman demonic forces or crazed savage animals that must be dealt with by any means required for a successful outcome to the unfortunate encounter. Just like any human body is capable of producing healthy cells for growth of the body, as well as deadly cancerous cells that could destroy the body if unchecked, humankind seems to produce its own images of "growth" and "cancer" beings. Each such being must be recognized for its inherent value and handled with appropriate means. Any person considering himself or herself worthy of living a happy and healthy life of meaning must realize the deadly folly of regarding dangerous killers and maimers as fellow humans worthy of consideration. Such vicious entities are "fellow" only to other such cancerous beings.

Nin-Po Taijutsu Methods of Kunoichi

The following examples show a few of the ninja taijutsu methods appropriate for a person of smaller stature, of less relative strength, occasionally wearing restrictive clothing—typical in a situation in which the female ninja must contend with a larger male assailant.

Defense Against
Rear Forearm Choke

In this example of taijutsu training for women, the defender is attacked from behind by an assailant who applies a rear forearm choke to cut off her air and pull her backward onto the ground (1). She responds by stabbing backward over her shoulder with her straightened fingers to distract her attacker from the pressure of his choke (2-3). As the attacker reaches up to move the defender's hand away from his eyes (4), the defender uses the moment to shift her body into a more stable position (5).

continued on next page

She immediately lowers her weight down and back onto the attacker's extended leg (6-7), either breaking the knee or forcing the attacker to the ground (8). The defender then shifts her bodyweight behind an elbow armbar in order to drive her attacker's face into the ground (9-11).

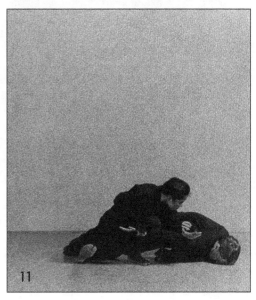

Knife Retention in Clash

A stronger attacker attempts to wrest away the knife that the defender has taken up in her defense (1-2). His greater strength prevents her from employing any sort of wrist-leverage move, and her kimono prevents her from freeing her leg for any sort of kicking defense. The defender allows her arm to be held in place and shifts her hips back and down with a crouching pivot away from her own knife (3). This action causes the knife to cut across the attacker's wrist without the defender having to apply any great power and, at the same time, takes her out of range of any possible retaliatory kicks (4). Again shifting laterally on crouching knees, she moves across her attacker to capture his power and continues to direct his movements in such a manner that he cannot get to her. As the defender moves, she allows the back of her blade to capture the attacker's wrist while she pulls back and across with her bodyweight in motion for power, slamming her elbow into the attacker's temple (5-7). A palm-heel strike directing her bodyweight into the back of the attacker's outstretched arm breaks his elbow and forces him to the ground in submission (8-9).

2

3

5

6

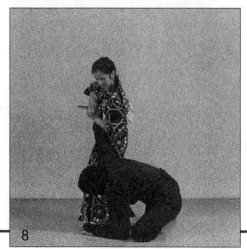

8

9

Defense Against
Wrist Restraint and Choke

The attacker has grabbed the female defender by the wrist and throat in an attempt to choke her (1-3). Rather than resist his strength and leverage as he might have expected, the defender charges in with an urashuto kitenken (knife-edge hand attack) to the attacker's throat, using her assailant's pulling motion to her own advantage. The nin-po taijutsu shuto strike uses the thumb to brace the extended fingers for more support, allowing the hand increased strength. Unlike the conventional straight-fingered "karate chop" as shown in most self-defense books, the ninja's kitenken (angled-finger strike) pops open from a closed fist on impact with the target (4-8).

continued on next page ▶

The defender then takes advantage of the momentarily stunning blow to free her arm from the attacker's gripping hand (9) and moves her body into position for relief of the choke (10). The defender then pivots back toward the attacker while punching up into the underside of his arm and peeling his weakened hand loose (11-14). A rising forearm strike to the attacker's groin then knocks him back and away to allow her to escape (15-16).

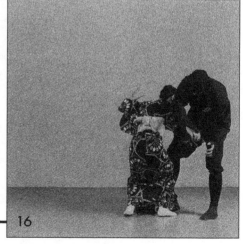

531

Defense Against
Wrist Restraint and Slap

The female defender is held in place by her male attacker, who holds both her smaller wrists in one hand and slaps across and down at her face with the other (1-2). She responds by leaving her wrists in place while dropping around to the side of the assailant's gripping arm to avoid the strike (3). Once in place behind her attacker, the defender slams her knee into the back of the enemy's knee with a sinking leverage action (4-6), forcing him to the ground in an effortless

continued on next page

manner (7). The defender allows her back to remain erect so that the attacker will have to release his hands to break his fall rather than hit his face or shoulder on the floor. The female defender immediately follows up her escape with a swinging shin kick to the attacker's face (8-12).

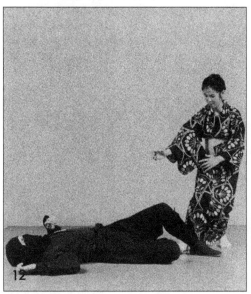

Hanbo Defense Against Roundhouse Kick

The defender confronts an assailant with her hanbo (cane) poised for a strike (1). The attacker attempts to avoid the cane by using his superior size and reach in a karate-style roundhouse kick (2-3). Rather than resist the shock of the impact, the defender drifts in toward her attacker's center with a cane-tip strike to the underside of her assailant's chin, eluding the kick (4). She then lifts the trailing end of the cane from beneath the kicker's extended leg (5) to topple him with assistance from a foot sweep (6-7). Forward-binding pressure from the cane then damages the attacker's leg to prevent him from regaining his footing to continue the fight (8).

Defense From
Against the Wall

The defender is restrained by both wrists and shoved toward a wall (1). In response, she lowers her hips and quickly pulls her leg up to aim at the assailant's rear leg (2), which she knocks out with a forward heel-stomp kick (3-4). As the attacker falls forward, the defender meets his face with shakoken (palm-heel strikes) to the jaw (5), which turn into thumbnail rips along the attacker's upper gums (6) and then

continued on next page ▶

a two-handed thumb-hook tearing action across the assailant's mouth (7-8). As the enraged attacker lifts his head to relieve the pain, the female defender executes a zutsuki (forehead smash) into his nose and upper lip. It is important to note that the head-smash action is derived from the entire body in motion and not a mere nodding snap from the neck muscles. The defender then plants her foot on top of the attacker's leading foot to pin it in place (9) and uses a knee-ram action against the attacker's immobilized knee (10) to topple him with a fall that will cause his pinned ankle to break (11-12).

Defense Against Body Pin

The defender is restrained with a tackling action that works to hold her in place (1-3). Bracing the attacker's head with one hand, she uses her other hand to apply a fingernail cutting action (4-5) into the cartilage folds in the attacker's ear (6). As the assailant lifts his head in response to the pain (7), he is met with an elbow smash to the temple (8-9).

continued on next page

543

The defender pulls back against the bone and cartilage of the nose with a finger-hooking action to expose the attacker's throat (10-14) for a hand-edge strike that collapses the assailant's windpipe (15-17), and then she knocks him to the ground (18).

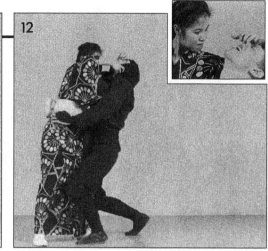

Defense Against Arm Twist

An attacker grabs the defender and twists her arm up behind her back in an effort to control and direct her (1). She shifts forward with the foot on the side of the twisted arm to relieve the pressure by altering the angle, as well as pull the attacker off-balance (2). Note: This move would probably be appropriate only for people with sufficient training in the ninja's junan taiso (flexibility exercises) or some other yoga-like system that emphasizes suppleness of the body. Self-protection be-

gins with good health. The defender suddenly shifts her body in the opposite direction, trapping the attacker's guiding arm by lifting what was her trailing hand (3). She then leans forward with a crouching shift of her knee against the attacker's leg, damaging his knee (4), and taking him to the ground with the twisting pressure of her bodyweight against his trapped leg (5). Once the attacker is down, the defender has the advantage (6). Keeping her eyes on the attacker at all times,

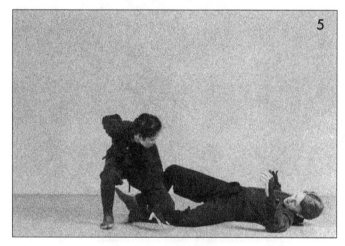

continued on next page

the defender stands up (7), steps in just as the attacker is about to try to recover (8), raises her leg before he has a chance to do anything (9), and executes a heel-stomp

kick to the attacker's face (10), making sure to follow through on the blow for maximum effectiveness (11), and puts an end to the struggle (12).

Defense Against Two-Handed Choke

The attacker grabs the defender in an attempt to choke off her breathing (1-2). She responds by dropping the point of her knee onto the bridge of the attacker's leading foot, bringing all her weight down to damage the small bones beneath her knee (3). The defender then uses her head to strike against the underside of the assailant's arm as she rises and moves to the outside of the attacker's reach (4-6). A ramming knee strike (7) then stuns the attacker's leg to

2

3

6

7

continued on next page

prevent him from readily following the defender's escape (8). The defender then plants her foot behind the attacker's weakened leg (9) and uses clawing fingers to grab the attacker's hair and lower lip (10) for a throw onto his back (11-14).

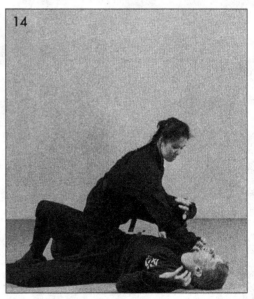

CHAPTER 23

When the true seeker of wisdom
> *hears of the mysterious powers of the shinobi warriors,*
> *he feels compelled to study them actively.*
When the ordinary man hears of those teachings,
> *he compares them with other disciplines.*
When the idiot hears of the teachings,
> *he smirks and laughs and shakes his head.*

THE FORCE OF INTENTION

Using esoteric sensitivity training, he learns to feel the intention of others

Many of the ancient legends concerning the historical ninja of feudal Japan are woven around tales of ninjutsu's incredible mystical powers that supposedly afforded the night warriors of Iga and Koga provinces vast capabilities far beyond the conventional fighters of the time. Various other martial arts, in addition to ninjutsu, are also said to employ mysterious qualities that seem to transcend the mundane limits of the physical realm. Tales of internal powers (*ki, chi*) and universal forces are indeed inspiring and fascinating to many martial artists today.

Unfortunately, for all too many martial artists, it is often true that the search for supernormal forces is actually a symptom of a seeker's refusal to accept his or her birth-given role in physical reality. If there were some "force" that could come down into our bodies to make us invulnerable, then we could effortlessly gain control over our world without having to do any work or make any investment in effort, it might be stated. The shortcut does sound tempting, and is alluring to many, but ultimately cannot exist independently of the physical.

If indeed there is any "mysterious force" that can be used by the common man or woman to enhance combat capabilities, its source will undoubtedly be found in the hard realities of the physical dimension. Only by first cultivating and working your way through a firm understanding of how your own body and its energies operate, relate with others, and create new realities can you ever hope to attain the keys to transcending the physical realm. As attractive as the seemingly cosmic methods may be, it is impossible to gain any control over the mental, let alone the spiritual, realms of power without first honestly coming to grips with all the aspects of our "physicalness." Unfortunately, this reality is often ignored or repressed in the methods of many martial, religious and intellectual systems.

There is indeed a realm of power that somehow lies accessible beyond the normal physical skills. This reality is often overlooked by a vast majority of contemporary martial artists who struggle on with the hopeless futility of relying on crude bone and muscle speed and strength despite the obvious warnings of advancing age. The point being emphasized here, however, is the fact that this supraphysical ability cannot be studied as a system of training in and of itself without first gaining competency in the physical techniques that make up the ninja's combat art. Just like you cannot get to work on the fifth story of a building without first constructing a foundation and the first four floors, diving into a study of spiritual power or ethereal forces without a firm foundation and internalized experience in physical training is merely putting off a cold reality that must eventually be faced.

Progressively Expanding Awareness

As an initial point of awareness when first exploring the possibility of there being something "beyond technique," one of the most difficult aspects of developing true skill in the ninja warrior arts is the ability to let go of personal individual focus when it is necessary to be more in touch with a broader range of influencing factors. The new student is primarily concerned with the performance of his or her own mechanical defensive movements and often finds it difficult to concentrate on, or even see, anything beyond immediate arm's reach. As years of training experiences accumulate, however, it becomes easier and easier for the student to relax his or her focus of attention and expand the awareness to take in more and more of the subtle factors that influence the potential outcome of any given conflict or confrontation.

The development of fighting skill in the ninja combat arts could be seen as a process of progressing through several distinct stages. Each stage is a level of ability that opens up even more possibilities for the student practitioner. These stages are in no way set with boundaries or degree licenses, nor are they easily definable with clearly marked points of transition. Instead, they can be seen to overlap considerably and in reality can be recognized only after several have been grown through to the point at which they can be looked back on.

First Stage

The first stage is best defined as one of concentration on your own physical capabilities. During this training period, strong emphasis is placed on learning the fundamental principles of the ninjutsu armed and unarmed combat methods with an eye toward gaining personal proficiency in the body skills that make up the *kihongata* (basic foundation) of the art. This stage is a time to focus on the way your body picks up, adapts and adapts to, and learns to perform all the mechanical aspects of getting a solid grounding in the art. Though effective self-protection is ever a concern of personal development in the ninja combat method, this first stage of training is a time to pay particular attention to how your body is operating and how much your body is capable of. There is less emphasis on being expected to generate specific results in relation to the varied moves an attacker could execute against you.

Second Stage

The second stage is best defined as one of concentration on your responsive relationship with an attacker and his advances against you. Once you have developed a reasonable level of skill in performing the mechanical fundamental movements of the art to the point at which you can deliver kicks, throws, strikes, cuts and so forth, with confidence in their effectiveness, you next begin to focus on applying those movement principles in response against an attacker. This stage is a time to focus on the distancing, spontaneous decision-making, and fitting in with an attacker's techniques that will make your techniques effective and ultimately superior. Proper response that facilitates effortless counter-technique is the goal of this stage of personal development in the ninja combat arts.

Third Stage

The third stage is best defined as one of concentration on your ability to control and direct the total energy of the conflict. Once you have developed familiarity with the mechanical pieces of the art and then have cultivated the skills of applying them scientifically against another's movements, it is time to focus on developing your ability to cause your assailant to have to do things in a manner that will prove to be to your benefit at his expense. Concepts of attacker and defender and assault and counter fade at this point. The fight somehow is no longer perceived as contending between two or more independent units but rather comes to be experienced as a single unit of give-and-take energy in continuous flow. You can at this point transcend the level of relating to an aggressor's movements with your own movements. As subject and object blend, you in essence become one with the energy of the fight.

Fourth Stage

The fourth stage is best defined as one of concentration on your ability to conceal yourself safely in the very center of the energy of the fight, thereby disappearing from the threat of danger by slipping into the middle of it. Difficult if not impossible to describe effectively through the written word, this stage of development allows you to transcend the conventional principles and strategies for dealing with combat situations. In this fourth stage, you enter a realm in which you can create the impression of certain kinds of energies, only to "break the rules" and defy seeming logic in order to overcome an assailant. The anti-principles of *kyojitsu tenkan ho* (the method of altering the perception of truth and falsehood) provide the insights necessary to take you to an ability level at which slowness can be seen to overcome speed, weakness can be seen to defeat strength, gentleness can be seen to crush force, and staying in the path of an attack can be seen to provide escape from vulnerability.

Void Realm

Those few rare individuals who continue their training quest long enough to go on beyond these four roughly categorized successive levels of personal development then enter into the vast range of freedom and effortless power experienced as the *ku no seikai* (realm devoid of specific recognizable manifestation). Mysterious and perplexing beyond description, and perhaps even terrifying to the uninitiated observer outside the tradition, this Void realm is not really a fifth stage as such but rather a complete leaving behind of so-called "stages" altogether. It is at this level that the warrior seems to become a wizard, capable of transcending and leaving behind the conventional limitations and appearances of the martial arts as most practitioners know them.

To the consternation of many Western-world students, there is no way to shortcut the process and go directly to the higher powers of the spiritual warrior. Exercises in ki power, flow sensitivities, chi storing and such without the benefit of first developing reliable skill in hands-on physical combat methods are as pointless as a company establishing a corporate marketing strategy without first deciding what type of product to produce.

There are, however, a variety of exercises that can provide a brief look at some of the budding refinements of higher skill once the physical fundamentals begin to be internalized. Though these energy awareness exercises in no way replace or supersede the need for diligent and disciplined training in the authentic and proven physical methods of the warrior arts, they can provide an idea of the type of awareness to which the maturation of physical skill could eventually lead.

EXERCISE ONE
Blending With Opponent's Efforts

To develop a sense of the energy involved in tuning into and blending with an adversary's moving attempts to gain control over the fight, students can practice a form of preset clash spontaneity in which one given technique is executed successfully and then rerun in a manner that permits the original victim to reverse the outcome.

The initial techniques used in this type of training should be fairly simple and direct in order to give a firm sense of effectiveness. That way, it is easier to feel the natural direction in which the attack is leading in order to better grasp the concept of how to "ride" the attack as a means of overcoming it.

Technique Reversal

The attacker steps forward with a straight punch at the face or upraised hands of the defender. The defender counters by allowing his body to slip to the outside of the attacker's punching arm (1-2). Once removed from danger, the defender can then counter with a step-through lunging

punch to the attacker's upper ribs (3-5). In the advanced application of this technique, the side slip and counterpunch are blended together to remove the "one-two" timing and streamline the action into a single slip and counterpunch move.

Technique Reversal Turnaround

The attacker steps in like before, and the defender attempts the identical counter (1-2). This time, however, the initial attacker perceives the punch coming in and allows his body to fade to the outside of the punching arm (3). The attacker's free trailing hand also can subtly

redirect the counter at the same time, if necessary. As the attacker continues forward with the momentum of his initial punch, he transforms his straight-line movement into an angled elbow strike as a means of successfully going after the repositioned target (4-6).

EXERCISE TWO
Subtle Energies

As a means of gaining more experience in the subtle energies involved in an attack contention situation, the students can practice a form of slow-motion perception movement that can give the idea of what is meant by a fight being one unit of give-and-take energy, as opposed to two independent energy units bouncing off each other with no relationship whatsoever. The object of the exercise is to attain the feeling of single-unit action and not at all to compete with the training partner or in any way attempt to fool or throw him or her off.

To begin the exercise, take several minutes to properly warm up. In addition to standard basic energy-stimulating calisthenics such as push-ups and brisk running, special attention should be paid to the hands. Then, as you do the exercise, be sure to breathe deeply and regularly, being aware of increasing energy with each incoming breath and the release of inhibiting factors with each outgoing breath. Explore the energy between your hands.

The in-and-out breathing process and the building and releasing of the body's energy field follows a positive and negative charging cycle that is captured in the Asian concept of *in* and *yo* in which all extremes of polarity are seen to reverse themselves eventually. This exercise gives the advanced student a direct experience of the relative nature of attack and defense energies. Which is the attacker: the student pulling the other student's energy along or the student pushing away the other student's energy?

Warm-Up for
Energy Sensitivity Exercise

Begin by shaking out the arms and hands vigorously to increase the blood circulation and tactile awareness (1-5). After a few moments of shaking out, pull your hands up in front of your chest, palm to palm, without allowing them to touch (6-8). See how far apart you can pull them while still feeling the increased warmth between them.

continued on next page ▶

Slowly push and pull the hands together and apart, and then begin to rotate them slightly against each other in a circular manner (9-12). Notice the sensations of heat, proximity, electromagnetic attraction or repulsion, and any other outstanding sensations previously unnoticed. Try to feel an imaginary ball of this energy rolling between your palms.

Energy Sensitivity Exercise

Maintain your heightened electromagnetic energy awareness, and move into position in front of your training partner with your hands still in front of your chest. Bring your hands together to the point at which you can begin to feel the other person's energy. Explore this energy by checking how far apart your hands can be and still feel some connection. Gradually begin to move slowly, checking how advancing pressure can be felt to move your hand back and retreating pull

continued on next page

can be felt to move your hand forward. With your knees flexed comfortably, see whether the hand energy awareness alone can be felt to direct your movements as you very slowly allow yourself to flow with the subtle currents. In more advanced stages of this exercise, both training partners can close their eyes to add to the subtlety of the perception required (1-11).

6

9

EXERCISE THREE
Drifting Just Beyond Reach

As an extremely advanced method of training to handle long-range speed punches that cannot be knocked aside or countered, a system of "riding" the expanding energy of a punch can be practiced for proficiency. Rather than leap far to the side or attempt to reach up and down with blocking actions, the skillful fighter can drift in the direction of the force of the punch in a manner that permits the punching arm to travel unhindered at the target and yet always be just a shade short of impact with the target. This action is not a boxer's duck or weave but rather a complete body movement away from the damage of the punch (or kick). By remaining just close enough to be missed barely or even touched with nondamaging results, the superior fighter allows his or her adversary to think that his or her strike is effective and on target. This encourages the adversary to continue to commit himself or herself to a punch that is actually useless rather than withdraw or redirect because of the perception that the punch will not work as thrown.

The exercise should be performed with the minimum of speed in the beginning. Take the time to get to know the flexibility possible within the factors of distance, timing and relative speed. Only after sufficient training at extremely slow speeds should you even consider practicing at real fight tempo.

Riding the Expanding Energy of an Attempted Strike

In this example, the attacking training partner advances with a leading hand shot to the face of the defender, who drifts back as the punch approaches his face. The defender rides the expanding energy of the punch to remain as a target

throughout the action but just beyond the reach of the attacker's punch. The defender employs all his perceptive skills in judging his physical relationship to the approaching blow (1-5). The attacker then begins a cross-punch to the midsection (6), which the

continued on next page ▶

defender evades in the same manner (7-9). Next, the attacker follows up with another leading hand shot to the face, which is again evaded (10-12). Of course, any punch or kick combination could be used for training. With each punch,

the defending training partner fades back with knee and hip gliding action to keep the target right where the attacker will expect it to be and yet just the smallest distance out of range.

EXERCISE FOUR
The Proper Approach to Training

Whenever your engaging in any exchange of set techniques with a training partner, remember to allow several repetitions of the drill or fight scenario for "combat feeling intensity," along with routine distance and timing work. All too often, the work of developing the technical aspects of a given action can overshadow the realization that if you were to apply the technique in question in actual life-or-death combat, your own commitment to a winning outcome would constitute the major deciding factor in the results. Beware the danger of playing around with fighting techniques in so-called "sparring," in which a succession of flicking, pecking darts and stings are ventured out and back with a great deal of preliminary footwork, bouncing or unnecessarily close body positioning that continuously produces tension.

Use your imagination when training with a fellow practitioner. Certainly you want to enjoy your training session, but do not drift into the negative habit of relying on cleverness or complex technique strings alone. Concentrate on the feeling. How would you be handling yourself and the situation if every move could lead to your damage or death? Pay attention and be there in the imaginary fight 100 percent.

Though some conventional martial artists would perhaps argue the point, the truth is that five minutes of intense full-awareness technique exchanging is far preferable to 20 minutes of drawn-out sparring, if actual combat fighting ability is the desired goal. You can always run or do aerobic conditioning later. When it comes to self-defense training, do not make the deadly mistake of watering down your combat training for the sake of indulging yourself in "a good workout."

EXERCISE FIVE
Sensing the Power of Intention

It is sometimes possible for the experienced warrior to feel the power of directed intentions through the action of the senses operating on a more subtle level than normal. Though one cannot train for this ability alone without progressing through countless hours of eye-to-eye clash situations, it is sometimes possible for an advanced student to experience the feeling in the remote almost nonphysical sense through various training exercises.

Perceiving Intention

Several students, one a stalker and the rest receivers, position themselves so that the receivers are in a circle with their eyes closed and their backs turned in toward the stalker, who stands in the center position in the middle of the ring. The stalker chooses one of the receivers as the "victim" and concentrates intently on moving up behind him with an attack (1). The stalker takes as much times as desired (2). The waiting receivers relax and allow themselves to be aware of any impressions that come to them. Sounds, moving air and even heat at close range could be possible cues. The stalker approaches his victim (3) and brings his hands up and around the receiver's neck to simulate a strangle (4). If the receiver feels the stalker moving up behind, he can raise one hand to indicate the impression that the stalker is there (5). If the stalker is indeed about to pounce on that receiver, a touch of the stalker's hand on the receiver's upraised hand tells him that the impression was true (6). If the wrong receiver lifts a hand prompted by an incorrect hunch, there will be no stalker there to touch it, and therefore the receiver will know to lower the hand after a few moments of no feedback. The receiver who fails to notice the stalker and therefore gets caught becomes the new stalker for a new round of the game. It should be emphasized that for the training exercise to be effective, the stalker must concentrate intently on his objective, for indeed it is a concentration exercise. While moving as silently as possible, the stalker pours forth intention in an attempt to arouse the receiver's attention.

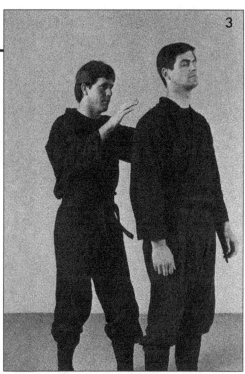

PART 5

Lore of the Shinobi Warrior

CHAPTER 24

In the words and actions
of the wise
there can arise
the appearance of contradiction.

Know confidently that the accumulation of
experience
tempered by
awareness
will eventually banish any of the confusion
that plays servant to
smallness of vision.

LESSONS BEHIND THE LESSONS

A personal reflection of progress in the art of the shadow warrior

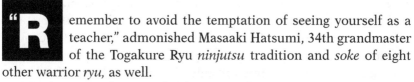

"**R**emember to avoid the temptation of seeing yourself as a teacher," admonished Masaaki Hatsumi, 34th grandmaster of the Togakure Ryu *ninjutsu* tradition and *soke* of eight other warrior *ryu,* as well.

My mentor and I were drinking Japanese green tea together on a rainy Sunday evening in August 1980. We sat on tatami (straw mats) at a low table in the grandmaster's home. His extensive collection of carved classical Japanese masks stared down from all four walls of the room as if to eavesdrop on our conversation. Having completed the first major portion of my apprenticeship under the personal direction of Hatsumi, I was to leave the ninja school in Japan and go out into the world on my own. Certainly, I would be permitted to come back to Japan to visit my teacher whenever I wanted, but the point he seemed to be making was that I needed time on my own, away from the comfort and security of being a student in the home of the grandmaster of ninjutsu. By being cut off from my teacher for a while, I would have the opportunity to experience challenges and pressures in the unpredictable world outside the safety of the *dojo.*

As always, the grandmaster's lesson seemed perplexingly contradictory to me. In September 1978, I had earned the title of *shidoshi,* ("teacher of the warrior ways of enlightenment"). My diploma was a license permitting me to establish my own training hall, and it had been handwritten by the grandmaster himself. Now I was being sent away from the school with the title of teacher, along with the admonition to avoid seeing myself as a teacher.

In my years as Hatsumi's personal student, I had learned not to question paradox. Indeed, the appearance of contradiction often seemed to be an integral part of most lessons. I knew the man well enough to know that finding the answer to that question was part of my assignment out in the world beyond Japan. I would figure it out later.

"Be wary whenever you reach the point where you feel that you have finally gotten down to the bottom line as to the essence of the warrior arts," the grandmaster continued. "To reach the bottom line is the same thing as being dead."

This would be our last night together as master and student before I left to take up the warrior path alone for the next several years. I already felt twinges of nostalgia for the future's past that was yet the present moment. I knew that this night and its significance would be looked back on as a milestone in my life. I acknowledged the fact that from this night forward, I would never be able to return to the comfort of knowing that as an apprentice, my teacher was always right around the corner in case I ran into difficulty. It was a frightening and yet at the same time exciting moment.

I was hoping to gain some last-minute perspectives on how to find that bottom line while out in the world so far away from my teacher and seniors at the dojo. Being warned that finding the bottom line was akin to death was the last thing I wanted to hear at that point. Though the testing journey had yet to actually begin, I suddenly felt myself grow very weary.

I so wanted to do a good job of representing my teacher's art in the United States. This would be the first exposure that Western-world martial artists would have to the legendary art of Japan's ninja invisible warriors. It would be up to me, and me alone, to establish the identity of Masaaki Hatsumi's ninja warrior legacy in North America. The job I did would perhaps determine whether I would be permitted to return some day in the future to explore higher levels of warrior power under his guidance.

"Ultimately, you must not allow yourself to be consumed by striving for strength as opposed to weakness, hardness as opposed to softness, or speed as opposed to slowness in the warrior arts. The only way to attain total invincibility is to let go of concern with the limitations of the body and allow yourself to become one with the *ku no seikai* [Void realm] that will permit you complete freedom of adapting." The grandmaster brushed the Japanese characters in black ink on a sheet of rice paper, and he told me to display the admonition in any dojo that I was to establish in my home country.

Again, I was confronted by internal conflict and confusion. In America, where speed and power were considered the only standard criteria for determining martial prowess, how was I to prove my art? There were no solo *kata* patterns I could perform. My methods would not fit the limitations of the contest ring. The visceral sensitivity to the energy of the fight would be impossible to portray graphically on the movie screen. Full-bore damaging combat with a ruthless aggressor in an actual war or crime was out of the question. It was going to be very difficult making an impression on the martial artists of my native country without spectacular displays of the speed and power that the grandmaster considered a hindrance to warrior development.

As I walked along the rain-slicked side streets of Noda City that night in 1980, I knew that I was on the threshold of a great adventure. Returning to my native land to offer a martial art that no one else there had ever experienced would be a fascinating test of my own ability to make things happen. How would this art be received in the land of group kata to rock music, American flag karate suits with red rubber boxing gloves, and the post-Bruce Lee era modernist disdain for relying on the combat training methods that had been handed down by Asian warrior masters for generations? What if no one else in the States was interested in my combat and enlightenment art at all? What if the sports arts really were the wave of the future in the West and I was to be received as some sort of bizarre anachronism with my insistence on combat application realism and personal responsibility for the prevention of danger? The prospect of my future was at the same time exciting and terrifying.

As it turned out, I arrived in the United States just in time to witness

the birth of what would later be referred to as the "ninja boom" of the 1980s. As the months quickly flew by, the art of ninjutsu was propelled forward to become the most talked about and controversial force to hit the martial arts community since the emergence of the Bruce Lee phenomenon. Many moviemakers, book and magazine publishers, mail-order merchants and television producers grabbed up the fascinating allure of the ninja to promote their projects and run up their profits.

With all the publicity generated by my story as the first American ever taught the art of ninjutsu in Japan by the grandmaster, I was no longer concerned with how to go about getting people to notice my art. That stage seemed well behind me. I had to be concerned with how to prevent the commercial forces from completely taking over my art and transforming it into a monster that even the grandmaster could no longer recognize.

I began to concentrate on the task of educating the martial arts community about what the true art of the ninja was, commercialism and sensationalism aside. Through books and magazine articles, I worked to inform the public that ninjutsu was *not* solely an art of assassination and employment of dark powers, as seemed to be the prevailing stereo-type, but was instead an approach to the prevention of danger based on harmony with the natural environment, scientific analysis of intel-ligence, and an intuitive attunement with the energy of events coming into manifestation around us. The true historical ninja operated out of love and responsibility for his family and not for mere money or the thrill of murderous violence as is so often intimated in less knowledge-able authors' books on the subject.

Rather than attempt to settle in one place with training-hall respon-sibilities that would restrict my mobility and my freedom to explore and learn, I first established the Shadows of Iga Festival as an annual event in Ohio and then set out on a tour of seminars all around the North American continent. Newly found friends who came to adopt the *nin-po* lifestyle as their own went on to organize groups of enthusiasts in their home areas, and I began to build a small network of students despite my refusal to sit down and concentrate on creating a tightly controlled organization.

My own personal goal was still the same one that had taken me across the Pacific to Japan on that daring gamble in the first place those many years ago. I wanted knowledge and skill, all the knowledge and skill that was possible to gain, that would lead me to eventual mastery of the warrior arts of combat and enlightenment. I traveled throughout North America, Europe, the Himalayas and Asia looking for martial artists, military and espionage professionals, and combat veterans with whom I could compare my art and skills. Sometimes the knowledge comparisons took the form of demonstrations and reflections on others' past experience stories. Sometimes the comparisons took the more pointed form of actual bloody confrontations in which I was required to deal with hostile individuals who wanted to put my claims to the test.

Slowly and subtly, without even realizing it at first, I began to come to an understanding of my teacher's parting admonitions. In confrontations and skill tests against younger, faster and stronger opponents, I was forced to muster up some quality beyond speed and strength and even technique itself in order to come out on top. I began to become more and more aware of experiencing what I would have to describe as something along the lines of supraphysical energy fields and forces that extended beyond mere strategy and technique application. On some occasions, it was as if I could tell where the attacker was headed before he even set into motion. As an experiment, I began to purposely decrease my own speed and then worked at easing up on the bone and muscle tension behind my techniques. I was shocked to find that I actually had an easier time fitting in with my attacker's dynamics and could more deftly use the momentum of my body rather than the motion of my limbs alone to down training partners who flew at me full speed.

It was something about the dynamics of the clash being experienced as a single unit of energy, as opposed to the separate energies of two independent contenders, which seemed to allow me to feel the attackers' intentions.

It became a somewhat humorously embarrassing regular occurrence at seminars. A spontaneous technique would just happen based on the unexpected sudden motions of an attacker. When the students would inevitably request to see the technique again, I was often unable to recreate the identical movements a second time. I would attempt to explain that the energy directing the flow was different the second time and that the attacker moved with slightly different dynamics or altered momentum and tension, so the initial technique was not appropriate the second time and would not "let itself happen" naturally. Because of the difference in energy details the second time around, I had to do something different in order to down the attacker. For many martial artists trained to believe in systems of rigid form classification and cataloging of techniques, my own retreat into realms of unexplainable formless "energies" must have been the height of frustration.

Though I could perceive my own skills improving as I gathered experience away from my teacher, I was curious as to the reason for my growing inability to verbally express and teach those skills to others in a scientific manner. I slowly began to wonder whether my difficulty in teaching might perhaps be the first step toward experiencing the beginning stages of familiarity with the "Void realm" that my teacher had emphasized as lying beyond the mechanics of speed and power and technique.

The more I continued to explore the interlocking disciplines of technique, energy sensitivity, mental flexibility and channeled intention, whether in exercises involving unarmed combat, weapon work, stalking and evasion scenarios or even nonmartial, real-life challenges, the more I began to understand the grandmaster's words of warning concerning "getting to the bottom line" as to the essence of the warrior arts. The more carefully and scientifically one can describe and explain the process of prevailing in a murderous attack situation, the more subtle yet crucial elements one is forced to leave out for the sake of a clear description. Therefore, the clearer one is as to what the truth is, the more likely it is that he is further away from the whole truth in its ultimate form.

It is a great lesson in the warrior arts to realize that the more tenaciously you cling to the comfort of any given theory, the more firmly prevented you are from exploring other possibilities and therefore growing in your knowledge. As grandmaster Hatsumi had warned, getting down to that bottom-line conviction that we know all there is to know is the same thing as being dead. In the sense that to experience no more growth is akin to being dead, the warning is valid. In the grimmer realities of the martial arts, the man who has willfully stopped his growth by proclaiming himself a master faces the all too real prospect of defeat at the hands of a warrior who has discovered the power that is available to one who will never settle for yesterday's lessons. By dwelling in the realms of unclarity, one is forced to seek ever onward for the elusive truth that always waits one step beyond the next lesson that life brings.

As I continued my own personal quest for exploration of growth in personal power through the warrior tradition of ninjutsu, a distinct and decidedly distasteful public image of the art seemed to grow up around me. Curiously, this public image, fostered by many movies, television, novels, and increasing numbers of ninjutsu textbooks and magazine articles written by people with no experience in the authentic art whatsoever, began to deviate more and more from the actual history and purpose of the art I had brought back with me on my return from Japan. I increased my efforts to turn the image back toward one more in keeping with the authentic history behind the art.

Ironically, directing my attention toward salvaging the reputation of the art that was so dear to me brought me face to face with an understanding of the grandmaster's initial admonition. As I reluctantly evolved into the position of spokesman for the art of ninjutsu, I began to encounter growing resistance to my message. While many martial artists claimed to have found great inspiration in the art I was introducing, others felt threatened and moved to confront my progress through the media.

Predictably, I would not be America's "only ninja" for long. Within one year of my return to the United States and the subsequent publicity it generated, there appeared growing numbers of martial arts teachers suddenly attempting to convince the public that they too were masters of the ninja arts. The allure of the ninja image was just too strong for these people to resist, it seems. The world was soon subjected to all the highly dubious claims of those who clamored to jump on the ninja bandwagon in the wake of the publicity given to my work in the Togakure Ryu.

This sudden emergence of those people hoping to capitalize on the excitement and publicity surrounding this newly introduced art is not necessarily bad. It did, however, cloud the issue as to just what true ninjutsu is. Many of these self-styled ninjutsu authorities wrote their own books and articles emphasizing savage and brutal training, flaunting hidden murder weapons, and reflecting the anti-social viewpoints characteristic of those people who have allowed themselves to degenerate into neurotic realms of self-pity and feelings of victimization at the hands of society. Soon, newspapers began to carry accounts of criminals and lunatics carrying out robberies and murders while clad in mail-order ninja suits. Unlicensed ninja schools began popping up in all cities across the country, luring the young and impressionable into their morbid influence.

Hundreds of letters per week poured into my office from people around the world who wanted to know the truth behind all the stories and claims that they had read. Gradually, as the months turned into years, I began to realize that policing the image of the treasured art my teacher had given me was growing into a task that was beyond my limits. Interestingly enough, there was also a certain segment of the world that seemed to want the art to be all those twisted or morbid things it was not. I slowly came to realize that ultimately it could not be my responsibility to educate all people about what the true art of ninjutsu encompasses. The beauty and power of the ninja tradition had been misunderstood for centuries by all but those who personally lived the art, so where was the urgent need now to change the course of history?

Had I finally broken through to what Masaaki Hatsumi meant that night those years ago when he admonished me to avoid the temptation of considering myself a teacher? Being the one to educate all the others is an unending job. Ultimately, the art of the *shinobi* invisible warrior tradition is an extremely personal and demanding one, not meant to be easy to understand or convenient to package for the mass-market consumer. The student enters a path with no end and sets out on a journey of discovery. The subtle irony is that the one who would prematurely label himself a teacher must by necessity *cease his journey* and begin to look backward for the sake of others who would be warriors. Thus ends the development of his own martial skills.

My own path of discovery now looks somewhat different than I had once imagined the future to be. Over the years, thousands of others have joined me on this adventure that is the lore of the shinobi warrior, and now those students are carrying the message of joy in movement and power of directed intention to other new participants around the world. Happily, there is no longer any need for a Stephen Hayes to single-handedly champion the ninja's combat art of enlightenment now that there are so many authentic practitioners who have taken up the challenge of making this warrior enlightenment system operate in the world. I have after my years of work been freed to resume the path of the warrior quest, once more rededicated to the discovery of expanded knowledge in all forms.

That was, after all, the lesson my teacher seemed to challenge me to uncover when he sent me out into the world on my own all those years ago. How interesting it is that the ultimate secrets are always right there in front of us, if only we have collected enough experience and cultivated enough insight to see them.

CHAPTER 25

Kyojitsu ten kan
   Truth in the guise of falsehood
   falsehood disguised as truth.
The ninja's powers of illusion
   rely on the mind's insistence that
   what we wish to see
   indeed takes the form of
   that which we seem to see.

MYTHS OF NINJUTSU

Sorting fact from fiction

Many false notions and erroneous impressions have grown up around the legendary shadow warriors known as the ninja. Many of these misconceptions have roots in fact but have developed as falsehoods over the centuries of secrecy that have surrounded the art. Many of the incorrect ideas have grown out of a lack of discrimination between truth and falsehood on the part of moviemakers and book publishers. Also, some of the negative myths are the direct work of those outside the tradition who believed they had reason to fear the authentic ninja legacy.

The following popular impressions embody several of the most common fallacies and misconceptions. Following each inaccurate statement is a clarification of fact that better describes the truth behind the legends.

• Ninjutsu is the dark side of the martial arts, the clandestine techniques of stealth, intelligence gathering and assassination.

The art of ninjutsu was born of a unique set of cultural, political, religious and economic forces that played themselves out a thousand years ago in Japanese history. History's authentic ninja were forced into existence by the shifting fortunes of feudal Japanese political and military conflicts.

Contrary to common misconception, the ninja were not unsophisticated and superstitious low-class peasants. The ninja were the descendants of powerful noble warriors who, through the inevitable workings of fate, happened to be allied in support of powerful warlords who ultimately did not succeed in the collection of battles that made up the war for supremacy. With the defeat of their side's cause, these noble warriors were forced into lives of exile, dwelling in the mountain stretches of wilderness to the south of the Heian-kyo (now Kyoto) capital. These original ancestors of the ninja were then barred forever from the professions of state administration, trade, military command and public service to which at one time they had successfully devoted their energies.

As exiles concerned with the rugged demands of survival in a harsh natural environment and a deadly political climate, the ninja families of south central Japan were forced to alter their tactics and strategies to better suit their precarious status. In truth, no one wanted to be a ninja; such status was a burden inflicted by fate. The ninja were the "underdogs," the oppressed hounded by a well-financed and mechanically ruthless government intent on stamping out any and all possible threats to its supremacy and control. Thus, subtle and shadowed means grew to take the place of the bold and forceful ways used by those people holding power. Because the ninja families' numbers were so much smaller than those of the ruling powers that worked to eradicate them, intelligence gathering became a vastly more important task than troop drilling. With the very survival of the family at stake, the ninja warriors of Iga were required to devise a whole new approach to warfare, and the motivation behind that approach has been misunderstood for centuries.

• The historical ninja of feudal Japan would serve any master who offered the right amount of cash.

Because the historical ninja of five centuries ago in Japan served his own family and community above all else, he was highly unlikely to swear allegiance to any one military ruler. The military ally who found it convenient to link forces with the ninja family one day could just as easily change his needs and priorities the next day and turn his forces against his former ally. Such was the conduct of military government aggression that characterized the Sengoku Jidai (Warring States Period) of Japanese history. Therefore, the ninja was only as loyal as suited his family's needs.

The ninja fought to retain his rights to dwell unhindered in the mountains that enshrined the ashes of his father's grandfather. His cultural and political opposite, the samurai, more often fought for other reasons. Territorial governorships and the right to appropriate heavy taxes from the local inhabitants were often the political rewards for siding with a military dictator who eventually conquered all rivals. Therefore, the samurai often found himself maintaining order in a region far from his ancestral home.

Unhindered by rigid codes of honor that could force other more conventional men into suicidal actions despite their own better judgment, the historical ninja was free to employ his common sense in order to accomplish needed objectives while reducing personal vulnerability. Naturally, from the culturally biased viewpoint of the samurai historians of the time, the ninja who would not pledge undying loyalties to one political dictator was seen as the lowest form of mercenary.

• *The black suit, hood and mask symbolize the essence and character of the art of ninjutsu.*

In truth, the historical ninja of feudal Japan probably never wore anything that looked at all like what we would call a "ninja suit" today. Ironically enough, the infamous ninja costume *(shinobi shozoku)* was most likely a product of the popular entertainment media of the 18th century in Japan. The Kabuki theater of the time relied on crews of black-clad scene changers and prop handlers. They were ignored as "invisible" by theatergoers who through necessity played along with the game in order to enjoy the dramatic illusions onstage (just like we in the Western world have learned to ignore as "invisible" the strings that control marionette puppet actions). Eventually, as the Kabuki plays began to include ninja characters in the storylines, some creative individual came up with the idea to use the "invisible" prop handlers' black costume as a visual trick to suggest the invisibility of the ninja character to the audience. Up until that time, the ninja in plays and art were usually depicted as being clothed in conventional warrior dress of the period.

In the historical ninjutsu reference work *Shoninki*, written in the 1600s, the traditional ninja operational costume colors are listed as subdued greens and browns, dark persimmons (black or gray-toned oranges), rusts, navy blues and black. These colors were commonly worn by the people of the times and therefore were excellent choices for the ninja's concealment costumes. In darkness of night, pure black tends to stand out too much, actually being darker than shadows and thereby creating the effect of a black shape in the darkness. Dull orange, maroon or gray are colors that blend into the shadows much more effectively.

It is also highly likely that the historical ninja of feudal Japan rarely wore black masks and hoods as is so often indicated in the popular entertainment of Japan and the Western world. This costume affectation is also probably a cultural innovation spurred by the Kabuki plays of the peaceful ages under the rule of the Tokugawa shoguns.

There is nonetheless a proper method for tying on a breath-muffling mask, should such a tool be needed. Interestingly enough (or perhaps predictably enough), such a mask would be a far cry from the comical commercial toys being hustled to the public as Halloween costumes. In the backward commercial products, the head and face components are always reversed and worn inside out. The mask covers the face and then a cowl-like piece is tied on around the head. This silly backward setup has been seen in all the sensationalist ninja movies made in the United States. This arrangement will not work, of course, because the cowl will easily shift around in the wind, all that cloth will block sound from the ears, and the overhanging lip of fabric that frames the face will make an excellent handle for an adversary to grab when he or she needs to control the ninja.

Today, some practitioners of the ninja arts will occasionally appear in the stereotypical dress because it is expected. The illustrations in this series of books often feature such antique suits as a way of stimulating the imaginations of the readers. More often, however, authentic practitioners of ninjutsu today wear a simple black karate style *do-gi* (training suit) with the trouser legs tucked into the tops of a pair of split-toed *tabi* (footwear). For outdoor work in the woods or field, authentic practitioners have adapted Western-style black military or hunting garments for their training wear. Using the garb of the current time and culture is much more in keeping with the true spirit of the shinobi arts than is clinging to a museum stereotype.

• *The historical ninja wore a chain-mail shirt beneath his operational jacket because the mail was more flexible than the traditional samurai plate armor.*

NINJA

The common Japanese ninja comic book image portrays the night warrior with crosshatched lines at his wrists and throat, suggesting chain-link armor under the cloth top of the operational costume. In truth, the extremely heavy weight of the iron or steel links made the wearing of *kusarikatabira* (chain-mail armor) extremely rare. For espionage or sabotage guerrilla tactics, during which lightness and speed were needed, the weight of the armor was too high a price to pay for the remote possibilities that the protection provided by the armor would be needed. The ninja's chain-mail armor was more likely adopted only on rare occasions when the extreme weight of the armor was justifiable in terms of required protection dictated by close-combat danger on a battlefield or in a war zone.

• *With a quick toss of a smoke or concussion grenade, an ambushed ninja could create an opening for his escape.*

Historically, the ninja's flares, firearms, smoke bombs, rocket arrows and stun grenades incorporated a black-powder explosive base. Niter, sulfur and willow-wood charcoal were mixed in specific proportions with alcohol usually derived from *sake* (rice wine), kneaded together and dried. This historical black powder was incapable of being ignited through mere friction or shock, as is so often depicted in ninja movies. In reality, the black-powder mixture required a burning fuse for ignition, therefore also requiring some sort of mechanism for setting the fuse on fire in the first place. The state of the art of feudal Japanese pyrotechnics rules out the possibility of so many scenes that we are used to seeing in which an escaping ninja agent tosses out an unseen packet that suddenly detonates to the surprise of following enemies.

• *The traditional ninja wore his sword tied diagonally across his back, whereas the samurai carried his sword tucked in his sash at his side.*

The ninja with his sword tied to his back is a popular image but one highly unlikely in the light of history. When protruding up from behind, the sword would become a deadly hindrance to effective concealment, escape through tight spaces or climbs through rafters and tree limbs. Rolling on the ground as a part of concealed escapes and hand-to-hand combat tactics also would be ruled out by the stereotypical ninja sword across the back.

Typically, the ninja used his sword as a cutting tool, club, scouting probe in the darkness, climbing aid and as a carrier for blinding material. Therefore, the ninja most often carried his short sword in hand or tucked into his sash at his left side. From its position in the ninja's sash, the sword could be slipped around to the back or the front, or simply pulled out, to prevent it from becoming an obstacle. Indeed, certain ninja sword-combat techniques employ a body configuration with the drawn blade in the right hand and the empty scabbard in the left.

The ninja's *shinobigatana* (sword) did incorporate a very long *sageo* (scabbard cord), however, which might be used to tie the sword across the back for occasions like long-distance running or underwater progression. When carried across the back, the ninja sword was worn with the hilt above the shoulder blade to facilitate easier drawing, if needed.

• *The ninja's sword is short, straight-bladed and features a large square* **tsuba** *(hand guard).*

Another cultural stereotype, the image of the short and straight ninja sword with its huge square tsuba probably came from two likely sources. From one viewpoint, it might be argued that because the ninja were legally barred from owning swords, the swords that they did come up with were probably homemade slabs of iron or steel that were ground to a cutting edge on a fairly crude stone sharpener. Straight blades were probably easier to forge than the gently curving works of art turned out by the master sword makers commissioned by the powerful and moneyed samurai families. For the same reasons, a homemade utilitarian sword guard would most likely be little more than a flat, unadorned square of steel.

As a second possible source of origin, it could be mentioned that the *choku-to* (straight-bladed short sword) could have been a stereotypical depiction of the straight sword brandished by images of the wrathful Buddhist deity Fudo Myo-oh, often cited as a patron guardian of the ninja families who protected the *mikkyo* (esoteric Buddhist) temples southeast of the ancient capitals of Kyoto and Nara. The oversized tsuba also could be another exaggeration adopted from the Kabuki stage.

In truth, a gracefully curving blade is a much better cutting instrument in a fight than is a straight blade. It is interesting to note that the majority of the better ninja swords in the personal collection of grandmaster Masaaki Hatsumi have curved blades, small oval tsuba hand guards and scabbards several inches longer than the blades.

• *Today's elite military small-unit tactics are the modern Western version of ninjutsu.*

Though it has become popular to refer to groups such as the American Green Berets and British Special Air Service as "modern ninja," the label is nonetheless quite inappropriate for several reasons. The modern soldier, even a member of the so-called elite units, is restricted in his possibilities of action by national and international laws governing the waging of warfare. Certain actions and tactics are legally out of the question, even for the shadowy Delta Force operatives. Because the ninja families were viewed as outlaws by their oppressors from the beginning, nothing was considered as off-limits when it came down to protecting loved ones and homesteads. Also, the modern soldier takes his orders from superiors who in turn take their orders from other superiors. The elite soldier is therefore limited to acting as the weapon of his government and is discouraged from "interpreting" orders through the screen of his own political views and conscience.

The feudal ninja, on the other hand, had to combine three areas of expertise: He was required to be a physically adept combatant, a clever tactician and political operator, and his own philosopher and future forecaster. Perhaps the most significant difference between the ninja and the modern elite unit soldier, however, is the fact that the ninja only went into action because he was forced to as a means of securing his homeland. His only other choice was to surrender and submit to the wishes of his oppressors. Today's modern fighting man most often carries out his duties as a professional who is engaged in a chosen career. He is not forced to fight for survival; he selects his occupation from a wide range of possible choices.

• *Because all martial arts are similar, the outstanding feature of ninjutsu training is night-stealth exercises.*

As a system of studying for the cultivation of martial prowess, virtue and invincibility, the art of ninjutsu has no parallels today. Because of the societal roots of the ninja warrior tradition, there was never a "birth" or founding of the art of ninjutsu as there would have been for other more modern martial arts such as karate, judo or *aikido*. Unlike the popular sports systems that first come to mind when hearing the term "martial arts," the warrior tradition of ninjutsu reaches back over a millennium of Japanese history to roots in combat survival in a world that seemed to know only war. As that original warfare survival method, the art that later came to be referred to as ninjutsu encompassed virtually every type of fighting skill that could be imagined as necessary to handle a killer enemy. Bare hands, bows and arrows, swords, explosives, battle-axes, spying methods and castle fortifications were studied for their benefits. No possible vulnerability was left unacknowledged.

It was only within the past 150 years of Japanese history that the once pragmatic and all-encompassing combat arts were fractioned and separated into individual and seemingly unrelated disciplines. The martial artist can now study the art of grappling without having to consider blades or kicks. A person can study the art of drawing the sword without having to acknowledge arrows or arm locks. A person can study the art of striking without having to enter into techniques for shooting a rifle or diving to the ground from horseback. Such systems of martial exclusivity are contrary to the spirit of the original ninja combat method and therefore cannot form a basis, even in combination with other pieces of the warrior whole, for that which could possibly be taught as ninjutsu in name.

• The ninja of old was the ultimate warrior in all aspects: incredibly conditioned fighting machine, intelligence expert, wilderness survivalist, chemist, priest, doctor, explosives technician, etc.

Because the ninja families of feudal Japan were vastly outnumbered by their powerful enemies, they had to rely on far more than mere battlefield skills alone. Training covered the complete range of skills and tactics needed to survive in an incredibly hostile world. However, the truth is that no one person could actually master all those disciplines, each one of which alone would require a lifetime study for mastery.

One of the tactics employed by the ninja was the cultivation of illusion as a means of thwarting an enemy. Because the ninja was an unknown adversary, a man of no name and no identity, it was a simple matter to create the illusion that the consummate skills of several different warriors and craftsmen were the work of a single ninja. In actual application, the ninja family would assign a team of experts in varied fields to complete the job that was perceived by others as being handled by a lone agent. Further, if all ninja were seen to be capable of such extremely refined and broad-reaching skills, the enemy was even more discouraged in his labor of trying to defeat the ninja families.

• *Because of the ninja's ability to call on his training in the occult and supernatural, it is possible for him to defeat adversaries of greater speed, strength and fighting prowess.*

The ninja's working knowledge of natural laws was based on his exposure to the concepts of mystical knowledge that found their fuller expression in the practices of mikkyo esoteric doctrines, *shugendo* (mountain cultivation of power) and related mind/body/spirit disciplines. In its legitimate practice, mysticism is the study of natural laws in their fullest and embodies an approach to becoming the most fully developed human being possible.

In truth, the teachings of the ninja's mystical lore do not deal with anything "supernatural" at all. To the contrary, it is the intimate familiarization with the natural laws of the universe that make up the ninja's esoteric studies. This close-working familiarity with the principles of nature can, however, provide the mistaken impression that the ninja is somehow able to "bend" the laws and accomplish that which is beyond physical possibility.

Because of the ninja's heightened senses of awareness and years of developmental training, it is sometimes possible for the ninja to actually move slower than his faster adversary and still defeat him through the sensitivity that permits perfect timing. Likewise, it is also possible for the ninja to defeat an attacker who generates superior muscle power. With effective body placement and timing, the larger attacker in effect knocks himself out by running into the fist of the defending ninja.

The realms of psychological perspective are as well areas for application of the ninja's occult teaching skills. Through growing familiarization with the psychological states that result from facing conflict and confrontation, the ninja learns how to read the intentions of others. As with the physical training of ninjutsu, this mental training focuses on developing heightened awareness; it is not a matter of learning "supernatural" or "unnatural" skills.

• *There are no true ninja in existence today.*

This was written by a respected American scholar of the Japanese martial arts. It is so typical of a whole set of martial artists who would do anything possible to avoid acknowledging the power and significance of what it is we have to offer the world. Apparently what that writer meant was that there are no longer any feudal Japanese survivalist clans living clandestine lives on pain of death if exposed in the mountains of south central Japan. I would not argue with that. What I would argue with is the writer's inappropriately narrow definition of ninjutsu.

All things grow and change with the passage of the centuries. It is no longer necessary to use the ninja arts against the governing powers that rule Japan. Therefore, the philosophies and methods of the once underground counterforce are no longer illegal. People wearing blue long-tailed coats and white-powdered wigs freezing in tiny log cabins at Valley Forge were once recognized as the Army of the struggling colonies of America. Because U.S. infantrymen no longer wear such costumes in the 21st century, are we required to state that there is no true Army in existence today?

CHAPTER 26

The sculpting artist
> *endeavors to remove only just enough rock*
> *to free the desired image trapped within.*
The martial artist
> *likewise works to let go of all limitations*
> *that bar him from the freedom and power he seeks.*

TAIJUTSU UNARMED COMBAT

Movement as art

T he term "martial artist" is an interesting example of a commonly accepted usage of words that somehow does not accurately live up to the truth of the concept it attempts to express. Contrary to the common usage of the term "martial artist," as used to describe a person training in Asian combat disciplines, true martial artists do not become artists until they have perfected the usage of their tools and have gone on to the level of pure spontaneous creativity. Therefore, the use of the word "artist" is in the vast majority of cases applied far too prematurely.

People accumulate skills that lead to the ability to generate works of art; artistic abilities are not merely acquired as a product of taking a course of instruction. A musician first learns how to make sounds mechanically and how to read music so that he or she can explore all possibilities. Eventually, pure creativity in an improvisation session earns the musician the reputation of being a musical artist. A painter first learns to pencil in perspective and shade colors mechanically so that he or she can eventually create works of art. Once the painter has transcended the mechanics, he or she then can enter the realm of pure self-expression through the medium of the graphic image.

Martial arts are no different. We accumulate experiences in technique and split-second decision-making that eventually lead to a level of ability that can be described by others as artistic. We cannot simply acquire martial artistry by enrolling in a course of study at the local martial arts school.

In its ultimate form as a guide to a way of living, the warrior path to enlightenment is a process of cultivating capabilities based on personally experienced insights while at the same time letting go of negative limiting factors that hinder the openness and freedom that are required for advancement. Our martial art is our method of approaching this process of transformation. We work and study and progress in the direction of becoming artists. We do not presuppose ourselves to be already worthy of the title by the mere fact that we are dressed in a martial training suit.

Approaching the Embodiment of Art

One of the first major mistakes that must be eliminated when moving from the limiting realm of martial hobbyist to the level of accomplished martial artist is the insistence on momentarily freezing in place at the completion of each individual move in a string of combat actions and reactions. This deviation from the dynamics required to prevail in a real-life defensive encounter is often inappropriately labeled as "focus" in many of the modern (developed within the past 100 years) kick and punch martial systems. The tendency to break the flow of the fight into individual frozen sections of seemingly independent actions is perhaps understandable as a temporary gimmick to assist beginners with little experience to isolate and perfect specific movements that will later be blended back into a natural flow. When the teachers of those systems insist on performing their techniques with the regularly timed freeze-pauses inserted between moves, however, it is more clearly an indication of lack of depth in understanding moving energy in a condition of confrontation than it is a matter of being merely a "different style" than the flow-oriented training methods.

This unreal aberration in training for possible real-world street or field survival is a major problem in the martial arts world today, in that two powerful forces continue to reinforce and restate this point-to-point method of movement that has no parallel whatsoever in the world of nature. These two forces work to distract martial practitioners from the reality they claim to seek, in that the mistake in all its bizarrely affected unnaturalness is presented as being "above," and therefore preferable to, the natural flow of movements as they occur in unself-conscious beings in nature.

The first factor contributing to the myth of freeze-frame action as being desirable is the popular glamorization of this method in the martial arts movies. What the viewers do not realize, however, is that escapist adventure films regularly rely on the *exaggeration* of the natural to excite audiences. Therefore, the hero of the martial art film is taken out of the limiting reality of true-life street combat and given what the producers consider to be an edge or advantage that sets him apart from all the others. While the film's bad guys swing and lunge like lesser mortals, the hero carries himself magically through the carnage with a series of deft pose-strike freeze actions. Often, his face also reflects this bizarre "statue comes to life and then returns to statue" approach to movement in a movie fight.

There is a natural follow-up phenomenon to this first factor contributing to the illusion that point-to-point action is the preferred way to handle a fight. If the screen heroes of the world's junior martial hopefuls dramatically defeat all their adversaries with whip-and-freeze stop-action techniques, it is, of course, only natural for young martial competitors to emulate their heroes when in the sports ring. The powerful urge to imitate is difficult if not impossible for the less-than-confident to overcome. Because the majority of people studying the martial arts in the Western world seem to get involved at least tangentially with teachers who relate to the competitive sport scene, it is highly unlikely that there would be any great popular shift away from the odd point-to-point grimace and tension dynamics that have somehow wormed their way into our culture as the accepted way to do things in the martial arts. Ironically enough, in light of the facts behind why the martial arts were developed in the feudal ages of Japan, very few people today seem involved with or interested in pragmatic nonsport martial training methods. Therefore, the myth somehow lives on, growing stronger with every generation.

Also, there is a second factor contributing to the prevalence of the freeze-frame tension approach to what in reality can only be experienced as a dynamic flow of projecting and receiving exchanges. In ages past, the only exposure a student could get to the martial arts was direct contact with a master technician. Whether actively studying that fighter's art or merely watching a demonstration of the techniques, personal contact was the only exposure a person could have. Today, the majority of martial hopefuls find their first exposure to the martial arts through films, magazines or books. Many people even attempt to teach themselves the martial arts from books and magazines when they are not able to find access to a teacher who they respect. Because the printed medium is restricted to two-dimensional views and single-moment glimpses, it is difficult to experience anything having to do with timing on the printed page.

This chapter of this volume then must work to further illuminate the proper way to take the mechanics of this martial system and bring them to life in the context of a vibrant, spontaneous and fully self-expressing art form. This author must attempt the impossible by relating in static printed words and pictures the ultimate reality of freedom of choice in movement and the blending of cause with effect that makes up the actual experience of street and field combat survival.

In the *Tao Te Ching*, the timeless and legendary volume of Taoist lore attributed to the ancient Chinese sage Lao Tsu, it is said that "the Tao (universal process of the flow of all that is) that can be described is not the true Tao." Likewise, any ultimate observation or discussion of the universe becomes an awkward impossibility because that very discussion itself can only be but a part of the vastness of the universe being described; it is not possible to move outside the universal process to observe that universe. Therefore, to describe a physical sensation such as proper movement dynamics in ninja *taijutsu* through the printed media is as frustrating as trying to pin down the Tao or step outside the universe for an outsider's view.

Body Attitudes

There are, however, some natural places to begin a look at how to interpret and embody the ability to capture and become part of that natural flow that characterizes the ninja's approach to handling all opposition in life. Perhaps the most obvious place to begin is a look at the *kamae* (fighting attitudes) of the ninja's taijutsu combat method.

Someone once wrote that emotion could be thought of as "e-motion," or "energy in motion." That is a perfect way to describe the kamae fighting postures of taijutsu. Not poses, postures or stances as such, the kamae are better described as bodily manifestations of our emotional processes as they flow from one second to the next. Through the kamae, we enact in the exterior world those privately observed needs that come into being and well up in our own interior world.

Properly assumed under the pressure of self-protection combat, the kamae does not at all need to be remembered; it is a totally natural and spontaneous phenomenon. If I am feeling overwhelmed, I just naturally tend to want to draw my body back and away from the danger. In the ninja's taijutsu training, we call this action of pulling the body trunk away from the attack the *ichimonji no kamae*. If I believe that stopping an attack before it builds its momentum is the only way to handle the current situation, I just naturally tend to want to move in close to my adversary so I can take control of him. In our training hall, we call this action of sending the body trunk forward into building danger the *ju-monji no kamae*.

The kamae of the ninja fighting arts are in truth actions. They are movements and not static stances. The kamae should not be thought of as poses, although the words "pose" or "posture" are used occasionally in my books for the sake of convenience in describing verbally the actions experienced in the physical world. As actions, the kamae come into being as our thought processes spontaneously mold our bodies into the form needed from within, based on the growing perception of the demands of external reality. Therefore, the kamae need not be remembered once the training process has come into flower. The kamae just *happen* as they are needed and leave the body frame as they are no longer appropriate.

Because the kamae are summoned up as they are needed, it is not necessary to think ahead and assume the kamae as a pose before the action comes into being. New students often do not understand this concept and express their doubts and uncertainties with off-base questions such as, "What if I am attacked before I have time to get into my fighting stance?" The ninja does not need to be in any set stance or posture before the attack. The kamae is assumed as the attack from an adversary begins to unfold. Therefore, assuming the kamae is an actual part of the protective action itself.

In the following examples, the kamae are shown coming into manifestation as the action of the confrontation develops. Note that the kamae are not assumed as static postures or stances before the energy of the conflict erupts into fighting action.

BODY ATTITUDES MANIFESTED IN COMBAT

Ichimonji No Kamae (Defensive Posture)

The defender drops back away from the potential damage delivered by the aggressor's first attack

(1-3). As the second punch is thrown, the defender shifts again to allow the punch to miss its intended target (4-5).

continued on next page

The attacker grabs the defender's left wrist (6). The ichimonji no kamae is assumed as the defender then takes control of his attacker's actions (6A). Using an armbar

to the attacker's right arm, the defender goes on to use the aggressor's own motions against him, twisting the attacker's left arm under his own right arm and bringing him down (7-11).

Doko No Kamae
(Responsive Posture)

The defender moves alongside the aggressor's attack, slips

past the punch (1-5) and assumes a doko no kamae (5A).

continued on next page ►

6

7

The defender punches the aggressor's moving arm as it reaches out to where the target used to be. The defender then applies a musha-dori (arm-scoop elbow lock) to

8

capture the attacker's left arm and lead him into submission (6-11). Note the defender's use of body motion to lead the adversary into positions of unbalance.

Jumonji No Kamae (Offensive Posture)

In this example of a possible fight scenario, the defender responds to his attacker's advance with a committed forward action (1-2). Angling his advance so as to avoid the attacker's leading hand punch (3), the defender counter-punches into the adversary's arm from the forward-moving

jumonji no kamae (3A). A left-leading arm slam, a right-cross punch (4), and then a left-leading hand punch are driven into the attacker's arm to move him into a position from which it is difficult for him to continue forward (5). The defender then executes an upward-hooking leap kick

continued on next page ▶

7

8

to fold the attacker (6) and a leaping-downward stomp kick

9

10

to the knee to down his larger adversary (7-12).

11

12

Hoko No Kamae
(Evasive Posture)

From close range, the aggressor moves in with a short strong hook punch to the defender's head (1-2). Rather than attempt to stop his stronger assailant, the defender instead shifts evasively to the inside of the attacker's punch (3). While he moves, the defender assumes the

hoko no kamae and executes a right forearm slam to the attacker's head (3A). The defender simultaneously pins the attacker's left fist against the attacker's chest with his right forearm. The defender immediately shifts back to his left to avoid a possible left follow-up punch from the attacker (4-5).

continued on next page

5

6

He maintains forearm pressure on the attacker's face the entire time. Continuing on around the attacker, the defender

advances with his right leg to form a tripping fulcrum (6) over which he throws his adversary to the ground (7-9).

Hicho No Kamae
(Single-Leg Posture)

The defender intercepts the aggressor's front kick with a stamping heel kick of his own

(1-3). The attacker continues with a wrist grab (4-5) and a

continued on next page ▶

second kick (6-7). The defender shifts out of the way of the second kick while applying a rising knee strike to the underside of the attacker's extended leg. From the hicho no kamae (7A), the defender

steps in the direction of the momentum of the attacker's kick, trapping his leg and arm with the same move (8). From his unbalanced position, the attacker is easily forced to the ground (9-11).

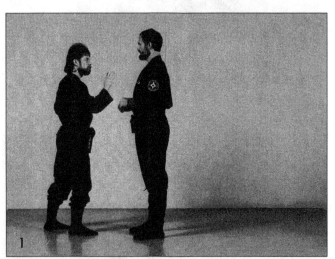

Hira No Kamae
(Receiving Posture)
Example One

The defender's sleeve is grabbed by an attacker (1-2). Rather than attempt to deal with the entangled arm, the defender instead uses the momentum of his turning body

to propel his left forearm into the right side of the attacker's head (3-4). The defender continues to turn, stepping forward with his left foot (5) into a hira no kamae (5A),

continued on next page ➤

which flings the attacker to the ground (6-7). Continuing to permit the attacker to maintain his grip on his sleeve, the defender positions himself

so that his right knee props up the attacker's right arm while his left knee exerts painful downward pressure (8-10).

637

Hira No Kamae
(Receiving Posture)

Example Two

In this example, two aggressors confront the single defender (1). One attacker grabs the defender's wrist to hold him in place for a punch (2). The defender responds by shifting to his right suddenly (3) and using his bodyweight in motion to carry his trapped

arm into the face of the second attacker (4). Assuming
the hira no kamae as he
moves (4A), the defender is
able to use his body motion to
unbalance the two attackers
against one another and throw
them to the ground (5-6).

Seiza
(Grounded Posture)

The defender is grabbed from behind (1). He leans forward (2) and then snaps his head back to strike the attacker in the face with a stunning blow (3). The defender then kicks forward (4-5), swinging both legs upward to

continued on next page ▶

build momentum (6) for a downward leg swing that brings the defender to the ground on his knees (7-8). From the stability of this seiza (8A), the defender captures the attacker's forward staggering motion and propels him over on his back (9-10).

Dakentaijutsu Striking Skills

"A punch is a punch," it has been said. At an ultimate level, that is of course true. Getting to the point at which your body demonstrates that truth as a natural and unconscious way of moving, however, does take some work.

Like many people, you may have begun your martial arts training with a basic ability to ball up your hand, tighten your shoulder and hurl your fist with accuracy toward a target. The more you examine this basic self-developed skill, however, the more small flaws you might uncover. Thus begins the training phase in which a punch is studied for the details that will make it a more effective tool. Many martial artists are a bit dismayed to find that their punching skills actually deteriorate a bit during this phase because of the temporary heavy emphasis placed on intellectually monitoring the small subtle actions that make up the response and delivery of that process that we label a "punch." Eventually, the new realizations discovered become internalized, and the punch once again returns to its original unself-conscious position in your arsenal of usable self-protection tools.

As a scientific way of going about learning to punch effectively, you first need to understand a few structural principles. Then you have to work at developing the physical skills that properly embody those principles. In other words, first you have to understand how to do it, then you have to develop the ability to actually put what you know into action. Real development can only come once you have had a chance to integrate an intellectual understanding of the "tricks" that allow the mechanics to work on a purely physical level.

Standard punching dynamics fundamentals can be broken down for examination into a series of three ranges, three angles of impact, three height levels and three methods of delivery dynamics.

The three ranges include targets for which you must extend your reach, targets within natural easy reach and targets so close as to cause you to shorten your natural reach.

The three angles of impact include inward hooking, direct forward piercing and outward swatting.

The three heights include targets that require you to reach above your shoulder, relatively level with your shoulder and below your shoulder—high, middle and low levels (*jodan, chudan* and *gedan* in Japanese).

The three methods of delivery mechanics include punching with your leading hand, punching with your rear hand (the cross punch), and punching with what begins as your rear hand and becomes your leading hand as you lunge forward with a step during the punch.

From this collection of possibilities, 81 different combinations of heights, distancing, dynamics and angling can be put together from this most basic grouping of 12 components. Many students could feel that the thought of consistently drilling 81 different strikes with right and left hands is more than a bit intimidating or even discouraging, however. Therefore, temporarily concentrating on being aware of these 12 basic working components is an excellent place to begin your intellectual study of the mechanics of punching, which you will then take on to personalization through repetition of punching drills.

The following examples demonstrate possible *fudoken* (fore-fist) punches embodying combinations from the list of 12 fundamental components.

THREE RANGES OF REACH

The following three technique series illustrate the three ranges of reach. Each of the three actions employs a similar straight right-cross punch for purposes of illustration.

Long Range

In this first series, the defender executes a middle-level,

long-range, rear-hand cross, straight piercing punch (1-4).

Middle Range

In this second series, the defender executes a lower-

level, middle-range, rear-hand cross, straight piercing punch (1-4).

Close Range

In this third series, the defender executes a lower-level, close-range, rear-hand cross, straight piercing punch (1-3).

2

3

651

THREE ANGLES OF IMPACT

The following three series illustrate the three angles of impact. Each of the three actions employs a similar middle-range, leading-hand, upper-level punch for purposes of illustration.

Inward Hooking

In the first series, the defender executes an upper-level, middle-range, leading hand inward, hooking punch into his adversary's moving right arm (1-4).

Outward Swatting

In the second series, the defender executes an upper-level, middle-range, leading

hand outward, swatting punch against his adversary's right-hand speed jab (1-4).

Direct Forward Piercing

In the third series, the defender demonstrates an upper-level, middle-range, leading hand

direct forward, piercing punch into the adversary's right-hand speed jab (1-4).

THREE HEIGHT LEVELS

Shoulder height is used as the standard of judgment. Targets more or less level with the shoulder are considered middle-level targets. Below shoulder height are the lower-level targets, and above shoulder height are the high-level targets.

Middle Level

This series shows a combination of two middle-level, long-range, forward-piercing punches. The first of the two punches, a left-leading hand

strike, is directed at the adversary's upraised left guard arm (1-3). After the impact of the initial punch (4), the adversary attempts to counterattack

continued on next page ▶

with a right punch (5-6). The adversary's punch is jammed, however, by means of a quickly executed right-cross punch into the adversary's moving right forearm (7-8). Note the defender's reliance on body shifting to place himself safely in a position to avoid possible counterpunches. The body moving through space on flexing knees also serves to generate additional power for the punches.

Lower Level

This series embodies a principle similar to that demonstrated in the previous example. In this case, however, the defender executes a lower-level, inward-hooking, left-leading

punch to the adversary's left-cross punch attack (1-3). The defender then follows up with a right shoulder-level mid-range straight punch to the head (4-5).

High Level

This series of actions demonstrates a high level of long-range, rear-to-front lunging inward hooking punch. The defender moves from a left

forward posture to a right forward posture while delivering
a quick right-hand hook punch
to the adversary's upraised
right guard arm (1-4).

THREE METHODS OF DELIVERY DYNAMICS

Here, instead of the punch, the kick is used as an example not only to illustrate the three methods of delivery but also to remind the reader that these delivery dynamics apply to punching and kicking.

Lead

The defender is attacked by an adversary who comes forward with an intended kick (1-2). The defender applies a sokuyaku kick with his lead leg to the assailant's lower leg to effectively stop his aggressive technique (3). The defender's lead leg remains in the lead as he steps down (4).

Cross

Here, the defender again applies a bottom-of-the-foot stamp kick to the adversary's midsection. In this case, however, what begins as the rear

leg is retained in a rear position, resulting in a cross-body kick similar in principle to the cross punch (1-5).

Cross and Forward Step

In this application of the heel kick, the defender pulls his knee high (1-4) and sends the sole of his foot into the adversary's midsection to knock

him backward. What was the defender's rear leg becomes his leading leg in the course of this technique (5-6).

Natural Striking Tools

The ninja warrior's *nin-po taijutsu dakenjutsu* (striking methods) employ a fundamental arsenal of natural body weapons known as the *juroppoken* (16 body-striking tools). As a place to begin your training, whether for *koppojutsu* (bone attack methods) or *koshijutsu* (muscle and organ attack methods), the basic tools can be listed as follows:

Kikakuken Zutsuki: Head butt smash

Taiken Katatsuki: Right and left shoulder slam

Shukiken: Right and left elbow smash

Fudoken: Right and left clenched-fist strike

Taiken Dembutsuki: Right and left hip slam

Sokkiken: Right and left knee strike

Sokuyaku: Right and left heel strike

Sokugyaku: Right and left toe-drive kick

Shizenken: Total-body weapon variations. In addition to the more common weapons associated with unarmed combat, there is also the option of using any part of the body if it serves the overall purpose. Shizenken include an infinite collection of strikes and hits from all parts of the body. Shin strikes, shoulder shoves, hip slams and bites are possibilities of self-defense tools from the ninja's shizenken classification.

With 81 different types of single hits (based on combinations of the 12 components) to practice from left and right sides as applied with each of the taijutsu juroppoken, the student of the *kihon* (fundamentals) has 1,296 basic strikes to practice just to get started. Beyond that, there come a lot of drills to personalize and internalize the striking skills.

STRIKING TOOLS

Kikakuken Zutsuki (Head-Butt Smash)

The defender, though held in place by his adversary (1), still has the freedom to apply a zutsuki to the face (2). Note that the defender uses crouching knees, rather than a torso-hunching action, to position and deliver the strike.

Taiken Katatsuki
(Shoulder Slam)

The shoulder is an underrated weapon in many scientific combat teaching systems. Here, the defender uses his left shoulder to strike and deflect the attacker's right-leading hand punch. The defender then quickly shifts on his feet to drive his right shoulder into the attacker's face as the attacker attempts a left follow-up punch (1-2).

Shukiken
(Elbow Smash)

To defend himself against an incoming roundhouse kick, the defender shifts inside the radius of the circular kick (1) and allows the kicker's momentum to supply the power for a shukiken to the face (2-3).

2

3

677

1

Fudoken
(Clenched-Fist Strike)

Proper body positioning allows the defender to respond aggressively to the attacker's front kick without the neces-

2

sity of blocking first (1). A fudoken punch stops the attacker's forward momentum (2-4).

Taiken Dembutsuki
(Hip Slam)

Even the hip can be used as an effective punching weapon. Here, the defender drops his weight onto the assailant's forward leg, using his hip to straighten (1-2) and then damage the attacker's trapped knee (3).

681

Sokkiken
(Knee Strike)

The sokkiken is applied against an immobilized elbow joint to free the defender from an attacker's grab. Note that the defender uses his entire body to apply the strike rather than merely popping his knee into place and back (1-2).

Sokuyaku
(Heel Strike)

When grabbed from behind, the defender uses an upward-hooking sokuyaku to the adversary's groin. The defender first leans slightly forward to unbalance his attacker (1) before shifting into his single-legged kicking position (2-3).

Sokugyaku
(Toe-Drive Kick)

The defender uses sokugyaku to reduce the fighting capabilities of his adversary (1-4). Note the flexed knee and

solid footing of the defender's ground leg. This allows the kicking leg to deliver maximum power to its target.

CHAPTER 27

You are indeed worth defending.
There are those whose love you share
> *those whose days brighten with your presence*
> *those who count on you.*
Just how much
> *are you willing to do*
> *in order to assure*
> *that the twisted actions of the perverse*
> *do not destroy the joy*
> *in the hearts of those you love?*

JISSEN NO HO

Self-defense fighting

Before beginning my training in the Japanese tradition of ninjutsu, I studied with a martial arts instructor who advocated that his art was only 10 percent physical and fully 90 percent mental when it came to street self-defense. By this statement, that instructor meant to imply that all the technique in the world would still be found to be lacking if the martial artist was unable to summon up and engage the proper frame of mind and fighting spirit when it came time to face a murderous attacker.

This grim reality is indeed even more appropriate to acknowledge in this age of "enforced peace" in which we all live. Just where do we go to get our lessons in cultivating this all-important "90 percent" that hovers above training in mechanical technique itself? How are students of the fighting arts to know whether their teachers and lessons are valid and are taking them progressively toward the twin goals of confidence and safety that so often inspire citizens of the modern world to seek out the study of the arts of self-protection?

It is common for instructors of the formalized martial sports and recreation systems so popular in the world today to assume that because they are skilled in their system's set way of performing basic movements, kata, steps, strikes and throws, they are automatically qualified to discuss and give expert instruction in self-defense and street-combat survival. This often completely false assumption is made despite the fact that the majority of popular martial arts available in the world today were not founded on the premise of self-protection combat. Most of today's martial arts were established either as sports or spiritual development systems; their founders did not intend for them to be used as methods for street fighting. In truth, the majority of martial systems popularly offered today are nowhere near being related to the cold and often horrible realities of self-protection combat.

It could be argued that there is only one truly reliable way to become a master of the technique of fighting other people. Facetiously of course, I offer the following suggestions as to how to become good at fighting.

First of all, find a place where you are sure to encounter people who fit the following categories:

- They all feel deprived of many of the benefits that life has presented others (financially, culturally, racially, politically, etc.) and resent those others as actually being less deserving than they themselves, even though those others live more satisfying lives.

- They all experience inner annoyance and lack of fulfillment as a result of agitated internal electrochemical imbalances (inability to attain a sufficient level of satiation for sexual demands or proper nutritional balance).

- They all blur any possible realization of personal social and community responsibilities by inculcating reduced powers of discretion, discernment and rational thought through the intentional abuse of intoxicating substances.

In other words, the first major step in this procedure of learning how to be a tough fighter is to find a low-class pickup bar.

The second step is to enter the bar and shove some of the patrons around, either verbally or physically.

The third step is to experience the action of the fight.

The fourth step is to check out of the hospital and wait for the next weekend so that you can repeat the process all over again.

Continue to follow these four steps until you have gained sufficient experience to enable you to eliminate the necessity of going through the fourth step every time.

Perhaps the ultimate in efficient and effective methods for developing the skill of defeating other people in fights is to arrange to be born into a family that dwells in the heart of a violent and deprived community and that lacks the collective education to understand the mechanics of how fear, cruelty, violence, disease and ignorance perpetuate themselves from one generation to the next. After growing up hungry, abused and frustrated, by the time you reach young adulthood, you will undoubtedly be a good fighter if you survive the training of your youth.

What of training for those people who were not born in the inhumane realms of hatred, aggression, abusive greed, intolerance and ignorance? How are those people who were born in realms of peace, fulfillment, joy and enlightened growth to go about cultivating the combat self-protection skills necessary for survival when forced to enter the darker, less-elevated strata of human society?

Here are some practical suggestions for cultivating fighting spirit without going so far as to poison your positive outlook on life in general:

- *Be honest about your feelings.* Recognize and acknowledge those emotions that could save you in a confrontation as they appear in your consciousness. Do not back down from rightful anger in the face of danger just because you were culturally patterned to be a "good little child" 30 years ago. Muggers, thieves and rapists often count on their potential victims to be "good and moral citizens," unwilling to resort to the same kind of brutal and unsocial violence that the criminal chooses to direct at them.

- *Be aware.* Do not allow yourself to travel through life as if encased in a narrow envelope of fog. Actively expand the scope of your senses. Whenever you catch yourself drifting or pulling in your awareness when you are out in a public place, firmly remind yourself that that is not what you are training to do and return your conscious perception out to your surroundings once again. Remember that this will take time and work, so do not let yourself get discouraged if past bad habits are tough to shake off.

- *Listen to your hunches.* Do not venture into situations that you think somehow have a high percentage of probability of turning into dangerous confrontations. If you are not sure of yourself in a certain situation, why take a chance unnecessarily? Find a safer, more reliable way to get done what you must do.

- *Be creative.* Do not think that conventional fistfighting must always be the answer when confronted by a hostile assailant. Sometimes it is possible to confuse your attacker so that he does not see you as the victim, sometimes you can disappear from the dangerous situation and sometimes you can set up an inescapable trap from which your assailant cannot get at you.

- *Know your own powers and limitations.* Long before you find yourself in a physical confrontation, take the time to explore the various things you can and cannot do. With knowledgeable friends or a qualified martial arts instructor, try out your basic strikes and kicks, body shifts and dodges, and grabs and throws. Find out what you are best at doing and hone those skills into useable form. Find out what you are weakest at doing and either train diligently to build up those skills or be especially careful to avoid situations in which those weak points will have to be faced.

- *Plan ahead.* Practice with realistic drills just exactly what you will say, think and do in the case of an actual attack. Do not waste your time trying to develop fancy exotic technique skills like you see in the movies. Do not confuse tactics for winning martial arts contests with life-protecting combat skills; street fights rarely ever resemble sports contests. Stick to realistic and reliable basic moves that have a lesser chance of going wrong. Use your meditation sessions to rehearse mentally just what you will do in those scenarios most likely to happen in your own life. Have your strategy planned out so that you are not forced to think everything through in a time of extreme pressure and danger.

- *Be appropriate.* Honestly acknowledge just what the purpose of self-defense is all about. Keep in mind that your goal is to get home in a safe and healthy manner. Do not get fooled or pressured into thinking that you are obligated in any way to handle the confrontation in a set way. In a life-threatening self-defense situation, you are not at all obliged to win a fighting contest, convert a criminal mind to morally enlightened behavior, prove how special you are, clean up the streets for other potential victims, embody ideal macho movie-hero behavior or do anything at all beyond not being killed or maimed. If you can acknowledge this in a sincere and from-the-heart manner, you can create a lot more room for potential actions other than a toe-to-toe hook and jab fistfight. You can see that running, trickery, "dirty" tactics, "unfair" fighting techniques or anything at all that comes to mind or hand is a valid means for getting home in a safe and healthy condition.

- *Be realistic.* Do not kid yourself about just how far you would be willing to go in a self-defense confrontation. It is easy to talk tough about all you will do if assaulted and yet quite another situation when the events suddenly bring a human being against you as an attacker. Will you really be able to go through with all the violent actions that you can so easily describe in theory? If your response to any discussion of self-protection is, "I'll just rely on my trusty .45," are you truly willing to draw and fire no matter what the attack, and are you really willing to stand up and take the legal consequences resulting from such action?

- *Keep in touch with local events.* Check newspapers, listen to the radio, watch TV news and keep on the alert for information concerning local trends in personal attacks in your community or in areas that you may be traveling to visit. Take appropriate cautions and plan ahead so that you are not caught off-guard by something that you could have known about ahead of time.

- *Use everything at hand!* A self-defense situation is nothing at all like a sports competition. An attacker will easily use your hesitation to resort to "unfair" tactics as an aid to accomplishing his lowly intentions. Therefore, cultivate a mindset of doing whatever it takes to guarantee your safety.

SELF-DEFENSE EXAMPLES

Self-Defense
Example One

In this scenario, an assailant confronts the defender with a clothing-grab choke (1). The defender responds with a palm-heel strike to the attacker's face (2), which sets up the momentum for a rear hip throw (3-6). Note that the defender uses walking steps, not jerking motions or upper-body strength alone, to unbalance the adversary and complete the throw.

Self-Defense
Example Two

It is important to use body momentum to confuse an attacker's sense of balance and control in a fight. Here, an attacker grabs the defender's wrist in an attempt to hold him in place (1) for a punch or kick (2). The defender quickly shifts back and then forward while rolling and straightening his captured arm to reverse the control back against the grabber (3). Once wedged into an armbar hold, the assailant is held in place by the defender's action of grabbing the fabric of his trouser leg with his left barring hand (4-7).

Self-Defense
Example Three

The defender is grabbed by both arms (1). He responds by moving toward his attacker (2) and around to the side (3-4). The sudden move causes the attacker to hold on to the defender's arms even tighter in a desperate attempt to retain control. By relying on body placement, the defender ends up in a position to guide the attacker's strength against itself, driving the attacker's face down and into the defender's knee (5-7).

Self-Defense Example Four

As much as possible, train to use whatever is thrown at you as an assist rather than a hindrance. In this scenario, the assailant suddenly turns a pointing finger into a head grab, taking the defender by

surprise (1-2). The defender uses the attacker's movement to his advantage, however, ducking under and emerging along the outside of the aggressor's grabbing left arm, using it as a shield (3-4).

continued on next page

The defender then rises with a palm-heel strike and eye jab (5), and he continues through

with an immediate knee-lock sweep takedown to throw the attacker to the ground (6-8).

1

Self-Defense
Example Five

In this case, the defender is grabbed by an attacker as he attempts to defuse the assailant's anger (1). In the process, the defender's hand is grabbed (2) and his fingers bent backward (2A). Rather than resist the surprise attack with tension moves, the defender goes with the force

2A

2

of the assault and allows his body position to accommodate the attacker's intentions. By stepping forward with his free side (3), the defender alters his angle to remove the attacker's leverage advantage and take control of the attacker's body (3A). From the attacker's position of unbalance,

continued on next page ▶

it is then a natural process to further pull him over (4-5) and off his feet. A swinging kick

into the straightened elbow
of the aggressor finishes the
fight (6-9).

Self-Defense
Example Six

Of course, the "handshake trap" is one of the most common of aggressive body-capture techniques. Here, an attacker grabs the defender's hand and applies a crushing grip (1-2). The defender guides the attacker's arm out and away, momentarily reducing the aggressor's leverage (3). The defender then immediately shifts forward with a zutsuki head-butt strike (4), making no effort to extract his trapped hand, and jams the assailant's elbow into his lower abdomen (5). Crouching on his knees, the defender then trips the attacker onto his back. He is subdued with an armbar control and a descending knee to the head (6-7).

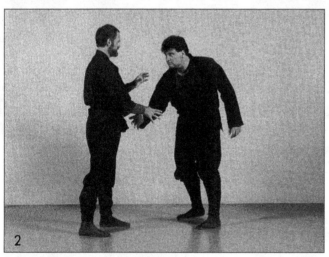

Self-Defense
Example Seven

The assailant's grab temporarily overpowers the defender (1-3). The defender

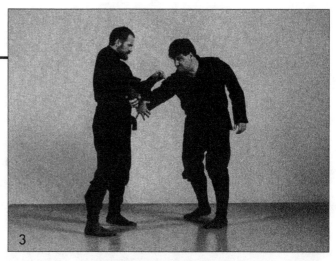

uses a strike to the face as a distraction (4-5) to allow him to shift his body position

continued on next page ▶

slightly (6). As the attacker recovers and reapplies his force, he is surprised to find that the defender's body has moved backward (the key is to move with a subtle knee flex) and is no longer susceptible to the same dynamics as used previously (7). When the attacker applies his pull-

ing force, he unwittingly pulls himself forward into an arm trap (8). He supplies the power to unbalance his own body all by himself. The defender then uses his own bodyweight in a straight drop downward (9-11) to damage the assailant's wrist (11A).

Self-Defense
Example Eight

The defender is surprised by an attacker who suddenly produces a knife and charges (1). The defender assumes a covering position (2) and then captures the assailant's at-

tacking motion with his hand and leg (3). A looping swing kick bars the aggressor's arm and drives him face-first into the ground (4).

Self-Defense
Example Nine

An aggressor grabs the leg of a defender on the ground (1). The defender relies on the attacker's strong left-hand grip and circles his foot over and to

2 A

2

the outside of the attacker's arm (2-3 and insets). Wedging his foot beneath the attacker's arm (4), the defender uses the tense resistance in the

continued on next page

attacker's body as a tool for his defeat (5). He traps the attacker's left leg to prevent him from recovering his balance as

he (6-7) pulls him down by his trapped arm (8).

Self-Defense Example Ten

A technique similar to that in Example Nine can be used

to counter a grab from the assailant's right arm (1-6).

continued on next page

The defender makes a big sweeping loop with his trapped leg and then applies a tripping

action with his left leg once the attacker begins to lose his balance to bring him down (7-12).

Self-Defense
Example Eleven

The assailant attacks the downed defender with an ankle-wrenching foot twist (1-2). The defender goes with the force and allows his body to flip over with the attacker's

exertion (3). As he rolls over to accommodate the pain, the defender entwines his free leg around the support leg of the unsuspecting attacker (4-5).

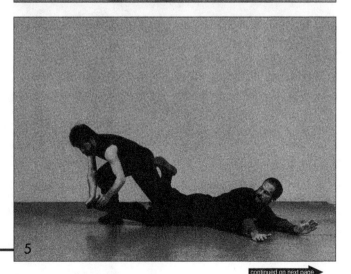

continued on next page ➤

As the defender continues to roll, the attacker is levered

off-balance and thrown to the ground (6-10).

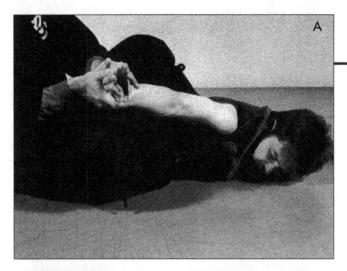

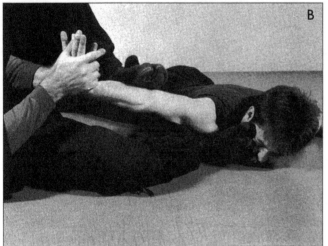

ADDITIONAL GROUND CONTROL METHODS

Stretching Armbars

These stretching armbars (A-C) rely on leg extension to work the trapped limb into a position of control.

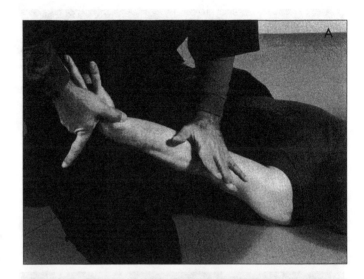

Straightened Levered Armbars

You may use either (A) the flattened palm or (B) the sole of the foot to apply pressure.

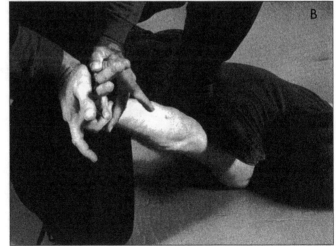

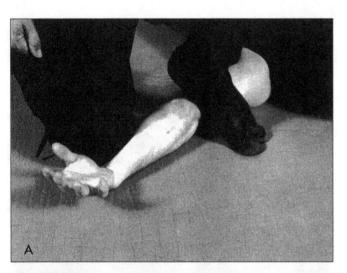

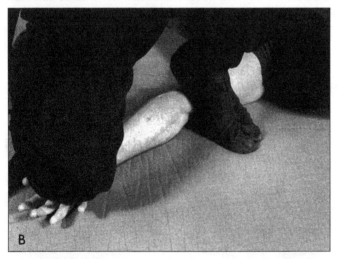

Crushing Armbar

Employ the ground beneath the assailant's body as a tool for control (A-B).

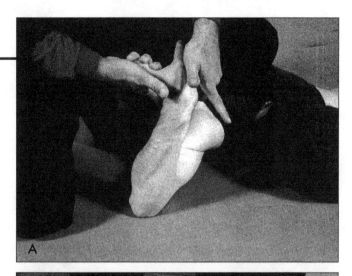

Limb Twists and Shears

These are applied against an immoveable limb using the ground as a base (A-C).

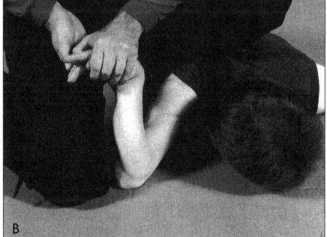

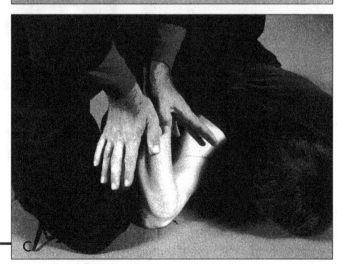

PART 6

Secret Scrolls of the Warrior Sage

CHAPTER 28

This moment
here and now before you!
Why do you falter?
Here is the answer
you have sought for a lifetime.
If only you could remember
asking the question.

OMEN FROM TOGAKURE

The Togakure Mountain goddess grants a sign to encourage bringing a treasure of Japan to the Western world

My *ninjutsu* teacher in Japan, Masaaki Hatsumi, told me that after learning and polishing one's technique in the *dojo* for a number of years, the traditional "next step" in a warrior's development is a time of *musha shugyo*, a period of leaving the training hall and going out into the world to test and experience the significance of all the lessons learned. In his own life, my teacher trained regularly with his teacher, Toshitsugu Takamatsu, for a period of 15 years, stretching from the mid-1950s to the early 1970s. For the next 15 years, he worked to explore and test the lessons he had been taught by his warrior mentor. By the mid-1980s, then in his early 50s, Hatsumi *sensei* had attained a 30-year maturity that would allow him to emerge in the world as a teacher with something to teach. Ironically, when looking back over the decades, the point at which my teacher became a public figure just happened to be in the middle of the 1980s "ninja boom" in the world of martial arts magazines and movies. That phenomenon, coupled with the first five volumes in this series of books, brought him international attention.

After 10 years of martial arts study in America, I moved to Japan in the mid-1970s and began training with my ninjutsu teacher. He was then at the beginning of his period without a teacher, which he now describes as his "second 15 years." At that time in my mid-20s, I of course had no concept that my teacher was going through a musha shugyo process for the attainment of matured warrior expertise. I simply accepted Hatsumi sensei for what his title described—the 34th-generation grandmaster of the Togakure Ryu ninja tradition. As a man in my 20s, Hatsumi in his 40s seemed like the mature and accomplished grandmaster that I had sought. I had no idea what was truly going on in his mind and spirit as he was setting out on the challenge of his second 15 years as a warrior on his own. By the late 1980s, I was on my way to completing my first 15 years of learning under the direct tutelage of my ninja martial arts teacher.

In the 1960s and early 1970s, I had studied and taught karate, but I moved to Japan in the late 1970s to start over as a fresh new student of a vastly different martial way. For the first years of my training, I took the train to the little Noda City dojo from my various places of employment in Tokyo. By the early 1980s, my Japanese visa expired, and I returned to my homeland with my new bride, Rumiko. My wife and I continued to visit my teacher in Japan every spring and fall for a month or two of training, and I took groups of my American and European students with me so they could have the opportunity to train with my teacher in his dojo. I also invited Hatsumi sensei to America several times to appear at the annual Shadows of Iga Festival I hosted. For many months of the year, I was physically and spiritually removed from any shelter my teacher's dojo and reputation could have afforded me, but I nonetheless continued to strive to learn as much as I could from my teacher in Japan.

Throughout the 1980s, I traveled all over America and Europe, presenting seminars and workshops as a way of meeting fellow martial artists and warriors. As a means of learning, I took the role of what appeared to be a teacher of others. I purposely avoided operating my own martial arts school from a set location and with a set time of operation so I could have the freedom to be where my lessons were to be learned. Through regular encounters on the seminar circuit in the 1980s, I was constantly challenged and forced to explore and test my skills and knowledge, and I had to face over and over again the question of just how close I was to being worthy of the title *tatsujin*—a fully actualized human being operating powerfully on the edge of life.

In the late 1980s, the conclusion of my first 15 years of study loomed near, and I was unsure how to view the 15 years ahead. According to Hatsumi sensei, it would be a time away from my teacher, a time for testing my skill and knowledge, a time for facing challenges, a time to come face to face with any doubts or uncertainties. Like my teacher before me, my next 15 years were to be spent in warrior errantry out in the world, away from the reassurance of my teacher's dojo, testing my right to be called a master of my trade.

In the fall of 1988, I brought a group of students to Japan for training. As part of the trip, we made a pilgrimage to Togakure Mountain, the homeland of Daisuke Togakure, who had inspired in the late 1100s the ninja tradition I studied. The return to Mount Togakure was something I had been looking forward to, and being there with several of my closest friends was a heartwarming experience. After several days of training with Hatsumi sensei in his Noda City dojo, we made our way north, from Chiba Prefecture to the Joshinetsu Plateau and the little mountain village north of Nagano that had been the founder's home more than 800 years ago.

One evening after dinner in our rustic lodgings, several friends accompanied me to Togakure's Chu-sha (middle shrine) that sat tucked away among towering cedar trees high above the center of the small community. We stopped at the large stone water basin to ritually wash and purify our hands and lips. It was fall and the water temperature was pleasant, and in the darkness, we climbed the steps leading to the weathered wooden structure that was the shrine. We chatted about what we had experienced so far on the trip and about our plans for the next day's climb up Mount Togakure to the high and remote Oku-sha (innermost shrine).

At the top of the steps stretched a wide flat courtyard that was the approach to the Chu-sha. It was night, so the building itself was of course closed and locked and silent. A few overhead lamps cast an eerie dim light on the courtyard, and we quietly made our way to the shrine's wooden steps. Now all were quiet, and each person was lost in his or her own private thoughts about the significance of where we were at that very moment. I thought of my first visit to the Togakure shrine in 1982, halfway through my first 15 years of training in the ninja arts. Rumiko had been carrying our unborn first daughter, and the visit had seemed a magical, spiritual homecoming of sorts. I had, at the time, thought about the second half of my first 15 years of study and wondered what was in store for me. I mused over the far-off second set of 15 years. Where would I be, what would I know, and what would the world be like by the time I passed my 30-year mark in the far-off year 2006, when our unborn first child would be a 24-year-old woman?

Though the Chu-sha's doors had been closed since sunset, our small group nonetheless formed in a row on the *rokka* veranda, along the front of the building, for a salute to the spirit of Mount Togakure honored within the walls before us. In traditional Japanese fashion, we bowed twice, pressed our hands together palm to palm, gave two sharp claps and then bowed once again.

Everyone in the group was silent in thought, and no one seemed inclined to leave. To break the spell and facilitate a return to the inn (and the deep tub of steaming bathwater that awaited), I commented that I had recently seen a photo in *National Geographic* of the Chu-sha in the middle of winter, blanketed in a layer of snow so deep that it required the priests to dig tunnels to get in and out. "I would love to see that, but Rumiko is a southern girl from Kyushu, and she doesn't like that kind of cold," I mentioned, "so it doesn't look like I will ever be here in the winter to see the Chu-sha in the snow. But I would love to see that, even though in reality I probably never will."

The next morning, we awoke for our trek the rest of the way up Mount Togakure. Oddly, the windows in our rooms were opaque, and only dim, white light came in where there should have been a beautiful view of mountain peaks in early fall foliage. Thinking that the window shutters must be closed, I slid the window open and was startled to have a wall of snow tumble into the room. Now visible, the scenery outside was covered in white, and snow continued to descend in a heavy fall. The freakish storm was beyond belief at that time of year.

We had planned to make the climb in our black martial arts training suits, and of course nobody had any kind of snow gear, so we layered what clothing we had under our jackets and headed up the now snow-clogged mountain trail leading to the Oku-sha. The trip up was difficult for all, with our feet slipping on the rocks buried under the snow, but definitely memorable.

At the top of the mountain, the Oku-sha is a cave-like shrine with a few outbuildings for the priests' offices and dwellings. Several in the group received new black-belt ranks in a ceremonial awarding from the chief priest, and we all made an offering in request of successful progress in our martial arts training.

On the snow-covered terrace outside the shrine, a member of the group teased me about my previous evening's comment concerning my wish to see the Togakure shrine in the snow: "Looks like the Togakure *kami* [spirits] were listening to you." I laughed good-naturedly and shook my head in mock astonishment. The Japanese tour guide we had hired overheard the comment and asked me what it meant. I explained the previous evening's conversation, and the guide, an oddly spiritual young woman for 20th-century Japan, became visibly disturbed.

She admonished me in blunt terms: "You should not play around with such things. This is not funny. If you made such a request, and apparently it was granted, there must be some connection with you that the Togakure Mountain goddess feels. This was her present to you. When we return to the village, you must go to the Chu-sha and thank her and apologize for being so frivolous."

Chided, I did not know what to say, so I thanked the guide and promised to do exactly as she had told me. This was indeed her country, and she seemed to believe strongly in what to me seemed to be a superstitious interpretation of a coincidence, but I did not argue the point. *"Hai!* I will do that," I assured her.

We had a day of martial arts ahead of us after the descent from the mountain, and all the snow would definitely be a problem for the outdoor training we had planned. I turned to a few of my friends and commented that if I really did have a connection to the spirit of the mountain, I wish she would warm things up so we could get in some training. We all smiled weakly, not really sure anymore where superstition blended into actual cause and effect.

Incredibly, by the time we had descended the upper reaches of the mountain, the sun had appeared and melted all the snow. We were back to normal autumn weather, and not a trace of white was seen anywhere. Even more discomforting, by the time we had finished lunch and were walking to the ninja training camp, it had become so hot that we had stripped off our jackets and were perspiring in T-shirts. With the radical change of weather—it was summer in the fall, whereas it had been winter just hours before—I had become extremely uneasy.

I asked the guide, Keiko, to tell me more about the spirit of the mountain. She explained that in Japan, the earth and especially certain mountains were thought to have a strongly feminine nature. She told me that Togakure Mountain was the domain of a powerful female nature spirit that was sometimes referred to as a goddess and sometimes even as a witch or demoness. If she likes you, she will do your bidding. If she does not like you, she will cause your death. "And she is extremely jealous," Keiko added. "That is why only men are permitted to be her priests on the mountain and why women need to ask special permission just to be here."

Awkwardly, I told the guide about the offhand comment I made in front of the deepest shrine about wanting warmer weather. Her eyes grew large and she stared at me silently for a moment as I toweled off perspiration with a handkerchief.

I received a furious scolding and was ordered—not requested—to go to the shrine a third time and apologize and give thanks for the goddess' gift. "Obviously, she is listening to you and wants to please you, and here you are playing with all this," Keiko said. "You must seriously thank her and ask of her a real request so that she will know that you acknowledge her connection." She continued with even more extreme comments about my supposed connection with the goddess, and she made such dire warnings about making the goddess (or demoness) angry by not showing her proper respect for her affection that I would be embarrassed to relate the specific details.

That night, a hand-picked group of student friends accompanied me back to the Chu-sha. Wordlessly, we climbed the long stone staircase to the front of the shrine. Willfully leaving behind any sense of nervousness or embarrassment concerning what other Westerners might brand superstition, I struggled to pick a real request that would be worthy of the goddess. I approached the front of the darkened shrine. I had never been more serious in my life.

We performed the traditional, respectful greeting of bowing and clapping and then continued to stand there, palms pressed together in silence. My friends waited to hear what I would request, but I still had no idea what to ask as my third and truly meaningful petition. Moments passed and thoughts tumbled through my mind. I was frozen with uncertainty. I really did want to ask something of great significance, and now I thought that I could no longer brush aside all the talk of goddess-demons that was so foreign to my Western mind.

As I mentally groped for direction, I wondered what the goddess herself would want me to ask of her. Wisps of thought slowly transformed into the touch of emotional perception. Seemingly out of nowhere, a persistently recurring awareness of my first 15 years of ninja training drawing to a close kept moving through my mind. Where was I after this first 15 years? What had I accomplished, if anything? On the threshold of a second 15 years that would be musha shugyo on my own, mirroring in my life that point at which my own teacher no longer had a teacher on which to rely, where should I go? What should I take on? Is this even real? Am I really qualified to represent the Togakure ninja lineage, or is all this merely an exercise in my own self-importance or self-aggrandizement? Am I just making up this sense of significance out of ego or hope or arrogance?

As my training extended through the 1980s, my teacher gently but firmly suggested that I "lighten up" in my public insistence on the highest of warrior ideals. *"Majimesugiru,"* he would chide me during night walks through the streets of his small Japanese town when I flew in from America to visit him. "You are too serious, too sincere. You are building up a situation where you have too much to lose, and that will make you too visible and tempting a target for enemies who resent your success."

More than a few times, he urged me to provide an easier course for new students who wanted to feel like they were a part of our ninja phenomenon. "You are way too demanding," he insisted. "You should make room for even the weaker ones. They can be of value, too. Knowing how to allow each one of them to serve is the true way of the ninja. Everyone has a possible value, even the ones who will never be any good as martial artists or fighters." I would always nod in agreement, acknowledging intellectually his counsel but, in truth, resisting it emotionally deep down in my heart. I was confused about what my teacher was really suggesting.

He was right, in that the early 1980s had been heady years of sky-rocketing acclaim as I traveled and taught and wrote of my discoveries. Nobody could pick up a martial arts magazine in the 1980s without reading something about me and my Togakure Ryu ninja training. After my first books had been published, Hatsumi sensei had been catapulted from obscurity as a *seikotsu* (bone therapist) to international acclaim as a martial arts grandmaster. Whereas once only a dozen students trained in his dojo, he now taught seminars for hundreds at a time. The dojo of my friends in Japan were packed with foreigners eager to learn what I had moved to Japan to study as a lone pioneer once upon a time so many years ago. All that attention, warned the grandmaster, could only result in increasing challenges from tough young bucks with nothing to lose and everything to gain by taking me down.

It was also true that once my books appeared, I had not remained the sole American practitioner for long. Others desired the same adventure I had found, and they soon began to trickle and then pour into Japan. Of course, by then ninja training in Noda City was no longer even remotely an adventure, with many of my Japanese friends opening dojo to cater to the new foreign customers and Hatsumi sensei now teaching huge seminars around the world. And as is likely to be the case with other martial arts, not every new student was a model of proper motivation and elevated spirit. Truth be told, some of the people pouring into Japan seemed haunted by fears of personal inadequacy. I had inadvertently spawned a subgroup of people who enviously resented my work and who misperceived my example as not an inspiration but rather an obstacle to their achieving the recognition they so craved. And when insecure people who perceive themselves as being inadequate bump into the truth that what they want may be beyond their capabilities, they often choose to disparage the one who has already earned what they desire. Instead of using their senior's accomplishments as a model of what they too could achieve, they furiously conspire to pull him down.

Entering middle age and admittedly still perhaps overly idealistic, I continued to cling to my original notion of the martial arts as a thing of nobility, inspiration and impossibly high ideals for which to strive. I had attracted many friends who joined me in my search for these ideals, and they encouraged me to take an even more resolute stand regarding what the martial arts should be. Did this contradict what the grandmaster was trying to get me to do?

Now, standing in silence before the Chu-sha on Mount Togakure, my palms pressed together, I knew the request I needed to make of the mountain goddess. I took a deep breath and set my resolve. In my mind, more than anything else at that moment, I wished for some indication that my Western teaching adaptation (what I had to say about training in as authentic a manner as possible for the most demanding and realistic of protection scenarios), which was based on what I had studied and tested in the world so far, was a valid statement and not just some wishful or egotistical styling of myself as a would-be teacher.

So I asked the Togakure Mountain goddess that night to grant me a sign that what I had to say was a right and fitting and helpful modern extension of the ancient Togakure ninja legacy that I had come to Japan to learn. I requested a reassuring omen that what I am teaching in the West is a legitimate extension born of inspiration and authentic interpretation of the Togakure martial arts and not some aberration born of haste and hubris.

I spent the rest of the trip examining every possible coincidence for a hint of an omen. Nothing even remotely prophetic came my way. After waiting for 81 days with no hint of any possible portent, and after returning to America, I felt a bit sheepish about my seemingly irrational faith in Japanese folk reverence for mountain goddesses. Risking operating from an undetected sense of self-importance, I made the decision to wait no longer. I quietly resolved to go ahead with a commitment to offer what would be the world's most comprehensive system of *nin-po* warrior cultivation, in the spirit of that which I had experienced in the Hatsumi dojo before the new public acclaim.

I set to work on writing English translations of all the formal training *kata* and arranged the material like it would appear in my belt grading system based on a vision of the best possible educational approach for Westerners. After three days and nights of work, the entire documentation process had been completed.

I wrestled with what to call my interpretation. When Hatsumi sensei had completed his first 15 years and set up his own dojo, he created the name Bujinkan, or "Hall of Warrior Divine Spirit." I was too self-conscious to use a name of such high import *(bujin* is a reversal of the two kanji characters for the name Jinmu, Japan's legendary first emperor). When I asked him what I should call my school, he unhesitatingly replied with a simple, "Call it Hayes Dojo."

I balked at using my own name, unsure of my right to claim that what "Hayes says" was of proper inspiration. After much deliberation, I settled on the name Kasumi-An for our newly chartered training system and my home training center. *Kasumi* is Japanese for "haze"—when vision is obscured by unclear air and the imagination is so tempted to fill in the missing details of what the mind believes to be certain. The word "kasumi" was often found in reference to historical Japanese ninja traditions as a code for creating illusory perceptions in the minds of enemies, and coincidentally, the English word "haze" was a phonetic match of my own family name.

In Japanese, the *an* is a place of retreat and renewal, often a rustic dwelling associated with a temple or shrine, a hermitage where warriors or spiritual seekers might spend time in reflection and regeneration before returning to the challenges of a life serving and protecting others. The Kasumi-An (Haze Hermitage) designation was a deliberately humble name for the training and ideals that would be the base of my own service in the world. I was still mildly disappointed over the lack of a hoped-for omen indicating the rightness of my decision to forge ahead with the Kasumi-An plan. Nonetheless, I stoked my courage and considered the issue finished—despite the absence of an affirmative omen that had been asked of the Togakure Mountain goddess.

On the afternoon of Friday, January 6, 1989, as I completed my curriculum organization work, Rumiko hosted a group of her Japanese friends for a New Year's luncheon at our home. They went into our home dojo to salute the *kamidana* (shrine) we had there, which was traditional for Japanese people observing the first week of the new year. Deep in thought, I barely noticed them leave and was only mildly aware of the television they had left on when they walked out to the dojo. A satellite broadcast of Japanese television was playing a historical drama, when a sudden newscast interrupted the program. My wife and her Japanese friends just happened to be in the dojo in front of our private *kamiza* (shrine) at the moment when, in a respectfully hushed and formal voice, the newscaster announced that Japan's Emperor Hirohito had slid into the last few moments of his earthly life before leaving the 124th-generation imperial legacy to his son, Akihito.

Japan's long-living wartime emperor had died, and the new emperor would take the Chrysanthemum Throne in an age of international cooperation and peace. Was the birth of a new era in Japan—a Japan that now shouldered a greatly expanded custodianship for the world community at large—a suitable omen for chartering an extension of a once solely Japanese secret warrior lineage? Not even half convinced, I seriously questioned calling such a dramatic international event the awaited encouraging omen in my small personal life.

Hours later, the news from Japan announced that the Japanese Imperial Household Agency's astrologers and diviners had determined a proper and fitting name for the reign of the new Emperor Akihito. The reign of the now-deceased Emperor Hirohito had been called the Showa era, with Showa translated as "Coexisting in Peace and Prosperity." The reign of the new Emperor Akihito, it had been determined, would be called "Universal Peace," and that new era had begun just hours ago. I sat frozen in intimidated silence when I heard the name of the new era, the new beginning that occurred at the moment I found myself struggling for verification of my right to teach my interpretation of the Japanese tradition of creating peace when others sought violence. Was the goddess of Togakure Mountain laughing so very far away?

The name of the new era was Heisei, and those familiar with Japanese pronunciation will tell you that Heisei does indeed sound an awful lot like "Hayes say."

CHAPTER 29

Ninja skills in which we train
would best be known as
the art of winning.
We will know that we have won
when we have attained what we needed
and the world is a better place
as a result of it.

NINJA BODYGUARDS
FOR ASIAN ROYALTY

The Dalai Lama's ninja bodyguard
shares lessons for protecting brightness

I t was not my original intention to end up as a bodyguard for the Dalai Lama, divine king to more than 6 million Tibetan people, spiritual inspiration to millions around the world and Nobel Peace Prize laureate. Life just somehow brought me to that role as one of the steps on my own personal path of the warrior. What I had always dreamed of being was a ninja.

When I first began my 1970s apprenticeship in Japan in the home of the Togakure Ryu ninjutsu grandmaster, I believed I was fulfilling a childhood destiny. At that time, I had been training in karate for 10 years. I even ran my own martial arts school. However, I was beginning to feel more and more closed in by the limits of the system I was practicing. I had never thought of myself as a sportsman, and yet my involvement in the martial arts world kept pushing me closer to a career as a competitor or coach. I did not want that at all. In a final desperate lunge for the depths of the martial truth I had been seeking since my youth, I left America and moved to rural Japan, where I hoped to be accepted as a student of the ancient legacy of Japan's ninja night warriors.

In the days of ancient feudal Japan, the ninja families of the Iga and Koga regions were legendary for the craft of "invisible warfare." Relying on extensive underground networks of contacts and the specially developed physical skills of climbing, gaining undetected access to secured places and individual combat techniques, the ninja families played a major role behind the scenes in the shaping of feudal Japanese history and culture.

Of particular importance in the history of feudal Japan was the connection that existed between the ninja, the esoteric *vajrayana* Buddhist temples, and various groups of spiritual ascetics known as *yamabushi* (mountain seekers of power). The ninja often relied on interpretations of esoteric Buddhist models of the workings of universal natural laws as a means of successfully overcoming even the fiercest of adversaries. Even today, modern practitioners of the traditional combat methods of Iga and Koga refer to many of their training kata by names derived from cryptic Buddhist references. Perhaps most famous in the history of feudal Japan was the common enemy shared by the ninja families of Iga and the Tendai sect's Buddhist temples northeast of Kyoto on Mount Hiei; both were the targets of massive invasions by the cruel and powerful shogun Oda Nobunaga. Hundreds of years later, ironically enough, owing to massive Muslim invasions and purges throughout India and China over the centuries, the only two places on earth remote and unreachable enough for the vajrayana Buddhist teachings to survive eradication at the hands of the conquerors were Japan and Tibet.

"Leave room for magic," my ninjutsu teacher would tease me on occasion, when I would get myself too tied up in trying to control my future and champion the reputation of his martial art. And sure enough, magic happened. By the late 1980s, incredible coincidences in my adventure travels brought me to a totally unexpected personal relationship with the exiled spiritual leader Tenzin Gyatso, the Dalai Lama. Impossible to plan, such an outlandish development seemed like a storybook fantasy or unimaginable dream for a former karate student just hoping to learn how to punch a little faster and harder as a green belt in the basement of his Midwestern American college gymnasium in the 1960s.

Within a few years of first meeting him, I was traveling in the 1990s with His Holiness the Dalai Lama as his personal security escort during the Tibetan leader's North American public appearances. My duties included coordinating local and state law-enforcement personnel assigned to the Dalai Lama's visit and interfacing between local law enforcement and His Holiness' corps of Tibetan security agents, some of whom spoke little or no English. It was also my duty to walk at the Dalai Lama's left side and maintain a last line of defense in case the outer rings of police security were ever breached.

By providing protection to this world figure, I had the opportunity to exercise the most authentic quality of warriorship and to put myself to the ultimate test. My skills, awareness, ability to make fast and accurate decisions under enormous pressure, and insights into the attacker mindset were no longer abstract practice or self-development training for my own sake. I found myself required to set aside self-regard in the work of providing safety for another human being, a most worthy being and blessing presence beloved by millions.

The Dalai Lama now lives in exile as a guest of the government of India. He travels the world promoting spiritual intelligence demonstrated as compassion, and he speaks out on the political plight of the Tibetan people forced to live under Chinese occupation since 1950. As an exiled leader, he is vilified by the Communist Chinese government as a counterrevolutionary influence. Because of pressure from the Chinese government, supported by much of the Western business community seeking lucrative trade opportunities in China, Tibet is not recognized as a separate state and the Dalai Lama is not recognized by the United States as a head of state, which would qualify him for Secret Service protection during U.S. visits. For years, the Dalai Lama's government in exile had to rely on private sources of protection for its leader during his trips outside of India. By the end of the 1990s, the U.S. government extended Department of State Dignitary Security Services protection to the Dalai Lama whenever he was in U.S. territory. I was able to retire to a position of assisting with liaison duties by coordinating with the Dalai Lama's family, the Tibetan administration and the State Department agents assigned to provide higher-level protection.

I first met His Holiness during a Himalayan trip in 1986. This was just a few months before the civil uprisings in Lhasa, the capital of Tibet, which were quelled by Chinese police with lethal force. Tibetan protesters were beaten, imprisoned and killed to restore control by the government. Perhaps having knowledge that things were building to an intolerable state, the Dalai Lama had apparently wanted to speak with

me about the conditions I had witnessed during my trek through Tibet and over the Himalayas. I subsequently had several personal meetings with His Holiness over the next three years after that first encounter.

The most appropriate physical security specialist for a public figure such as the Dalai Lama is one who appears to blend in to the entourage most of the time and yet can stand out when it seems necessary. The highly benevolent nature of the Dalai Lama's message of awareness and compassion made it totally inappropriate to have him surrounded by tough or cruel-looking guards. For this reason, an agent trained in the martial art of Japan's ninja seemed perfect, and I had to work to embody the ideal of projecting my presence as a subtle "iron hand in a velvet glove." Perhaps in the case of certain entertainment world celebrities, there might be some point to hiring a team of huge, beefy heavies in mirrored sunglasses. One must really wonder, however, whether such overstated muscle is more an attention grabber for career-advancing publicity than an honest attempt at legitimate security.

Despite the Dalai Lama's personal demeanor of humility, spirituality and compassionate concern for all, he was nonetheless the exiled temporal ruler of Tibet and still functions as the primary symbol of hope for the independence of the Tibetan people. This makes him an extremely embarrassing annoyance to the Chinese government, which invaded and occupied Tibet in the early 1950s under the justification of "liberating" it. He is also a high-profile spokesman for the rationality and validity of the Buddhist path of life. This makes him a possible target for religious-fundamentalist extremists who oppose what they see as a threat to their cultural control from proponents of "new age" views. For these reasons, plus the fact that he is an international dignitary who draws thousands of admirers to each of his appearances, strictly managed security for his safety is mandatory.

The Japanese word "samurai" is derived from the Japanese word *saburau,* which means "to serve." When I examined this most important definition, I came to understand that the noble warrior is not one who causes wars but one who serves the highest of ideals when the specter of violence threatens. As a server of the peace, I focused on maintaining a foundation for that peace rather than being concerned with self-satisfying glory as a champion.

The job of a security agent is to provide the means for as smooth, convenient and productive a day for the principal as possible. First on the list of responsibilities is the protection agent's ability to make everything seamless and convenient for the one being served. This means being aware of everything—arranging for elevator doors to open at just the right moment, knowing what is ahead on the schedule and when to make sudden changes, and anticipating the protectee's personal needs before they are even requested. If I do my job well, I am preventing danger rather than having to fight it when it arises unexpectedly.

In many cases, it is helpful for the security agent to have a personal network of acquaintances who can assist in getting past restrictions that would hinder ordinary people in their daily activities. In this respect, the ancient legacy of Japan's historical ninja networks provides a very appropriate model for us today. It was crucial to the ninja family's survival to lay the groundwork to facilitate the defeat of an enemy long before actual warfare broke out. This establishment of a reliable undercover intelligence-gathering network was known as *to-iri no jutsu* (the art of entering from a remote vantage point). In the Japanese language, *to* can refer to remoteness in timing and distance, indicating wise preparation for future danger. Ninjutsu to-iri no jutsu tactics acted as the guidelines for sending ninja agents into a potential enemy's region before war broke out. Once in place, the ninja were able to set up their network and establish the means for eventually weakening and overcoming the enemy from within.

Beyond all this preparation for the prevention of danger is the arena of actual physical protection that most people would associate with the work of a bodyguard. As a personal physical security agent in the service of the Dalai Lama, my role was to provide three fundamental types of protection:

1. Protection From Physical Danger

First, and perhaps most obvious, is physical bodily protection. I walked alongside the Dalai Lama, always within an arm's reach. Put bluntly, my job was to keep anyone wishing to harm the Dalai Lama from gaining access to him. It is especially important for martial artists to note that the job was not to *fight and defeat an enemy* but to prevent that person from harming the man I had made a commitment to protect. If a dangerous person managed to get close enough to the Dalai Lama, my team's responsibility was to get His Holiness out of harm's way and get the assailant restrained and out of the picture as quickly and unobtrusively as possible. Often, this meant intercepting the intruder in such a way as to cause him to have to fight against losing control of his momentum and balance. I wanted to prevent him from being able to focus on fighting me as an identifiable adversary. I did not have the time, space or desire to engage a possible killer in some sort of boxing or wrestling contest to see who the tougher guy was or who had the best technique; my tactics were to unbalance and disarm the invader in such a way as to render him incapable of continuing an attack.

Because I was protecting a world figure known for his views on compassion as a means of encouraging world peace, most often this meant using techniques that were neither flashy nor dramatic. We were definitely not talking about the kinds of flamboyant things audiences cheer for in martial arts movies, and more often than not, such scenarios did not involve finishing or "winning" the fight. I was flanked by badge-carrying, armed local and federal agents who were authorized to arrest and detain anyone I threw their way as an attacker attempting to harm the Dalai Lama. I intercepted anyone who managed to get by them and restrained the attacker for the agents, who would then make the actual arrest.

The second-to-last thing I wanted was to get into some sort of visibly violent clash in which an agent of the Tibetan king and Buddhist holy man was seen pounding and kicking a screaming person into unconsciousness. Of course, the absolute last thing we wanted was to see the Dalai Lama harmed, so it must be said that nothing was ever really ruled out.

2. Protection From Personal Embarrassment

Second, and perhaps not so obvious, was my role in preventing the Dalai Lama from having to endure awkward or embarrassing situations. These could include a zealous fan who bursts onto the stage during a presentation, a pushy interviewer who oversteps the boundaries of propriety, or unknown men or women who pretend to have special relationships with the Dalai Lama as a means of slipping past the security net. Most of these situations required split-second judgment calls on my part. It was necessary to use my sensitivity to the potential for danger as the sole basis for deciding whether to admit a person to the room or physically make him or her leave the area. It was also often part of my responsibility to check the Dalai Lama's rooms before his return to his residence, in case any person or object was hidden away that could cause an embarrassing scene.

It was crucial to be able to move someone against his or her will without causing undue damage or attracting undue attention. This required using very subtle techniques—again, nothing at all like you would see in a martial arts movie about bodyguards. Our ninja martial art contains several methods of getting an attacker off-balance and thereby robbing him of his ability to deliver damage. My team was very sensitive to the fact that it would be most compromising to the Dalai Lama's message of compassion to have his personal security agent hitting or wrenching some person out of the scene. It would be even worse if it turned out that the person had the right to be there.

3. Emergency Medical Assistance

Third, my job was to be prepared for any emergency medical situations that might come up and to have trained medical technicians at hand, ready to jump into action. This meant being able to make quick decisions vis-à-vis unexpected symptoms, like fainting, falling or choking—or in cases of drastic injury caused by the likes of auto or plane wrecks or gunfire, actually moving the principal.

Other instructors of the ninja martial arts worked with our Dalai Lama protection detail, as well. Though I provided protective services out of personal dedication and admiration for the Dalai Lama, some of my students are still full-time professionals in the world of dignitary protection.

Every detail, no matter how small, matters, and each decision can be the difference in the outcome of your role as protector. Long days and short nights are the rule. Being able to clearly anticipate a potential problem and avoid it is the key to a successful protective detail. The minute we hesitate, it is too late. Over and over, I was required to find subtle means of accomplishing my goals. The techniques I used most often were a smile, a firm tone and, on rare occasions, a forceful, physical action. Sometimes it was nothing more than moving into just the right position. Creating a situation in which people go in the direction I need them to go—with smiles on their faces and no real awareness that I was the one who sent them there—is the height of ninjutsu, as well as the end goal in the security field.

CHAPTER 30

Use patience, receptivity, and unshakable spirit
*   to overcome the enemy's raw brash strength.*
Push forward your arms
*   and allow him to fall helplessly onto your weapon.*
How coldly simple.

CLASSICAL STRUCTURE OF THE WARRIOR'S LEARNING PHASES

How the warriors of old Japan moved phase by phase from novice to master

The now familiar Japanese invention of using colored belts as markers of skill and experience is more than 100 years old. Historically, what are referred to as Japanese classical martial arts often used a system of three to five or more scrolls of knowledge to indicate a student's level of development in the warrior tradition. There were no distinctive belt or clothing colors to distinguish different levels of learning. Though there might be variations or even completely different lists of categories for skill levels, a generally similar educational structure can be detected in a large number of traditional Japanese martial arts. Interestingly, similar systems are also found in non-martial Japanese arts, such as flower arranging and musical instrument performance.

EDUCATIONAL LEVELS
Shoden

Hundreds of years ago, new students entering the martial arts training hall first concentrated on learning the *kihon* fundamentals of basic techniques and principles of the martial art being studied. This body of knowledge included foundational skills, such as basic footwork and body posturing, body-movement dynamics, perhaps some ground hitting or tumbling escape skills, body-conditioning exercises, grips for barehanded or weapons techniques, and defense and counter-techniques.

Rarely acknowledged with any sort of diploma or symbol of graduation, completion of kihon study more often than not led directly to studying the *shoden* (initial teachings) of the art. In many martial education systems—whether studied by samurai or ninja in the Warring States Period of Japanese history or by civilian commoners in the later part of the Edo era in the late 1700s through the mid-1800s—shoden focused on a limited set of *waza* techniques, *kotsu* principles, *keiko* conditioning exercises, and kata demonstrating how a fight might be won by skilled practitioners of the martial art being studied.

The list of kata fight scenarios in the martial arts making up the historical ninja warrior traditions of Japan ranged in number from as few as eight up to usually 12 to 16; rarely, some historical systems taught as many as 18 or 20 shoden kata. As an educational system, the idea was to focus in the beginning on those attacks most likely to occur in the students' lives and on the most basic, reliable techniques and skills for countering those attacks. Upon gaining sufficient mastery of those skills, a student might be awarded a shoden scroll sealed with the master instructor's name, listing the techniques learned (as a form of skill verification or endorsement), acknowledging that it was time to move on to the next level of learning. In modern martial art belt-ranking systems, a shoden scroll diploma might be compared to a first- or second-degree black belt.

In the ninja *taijutsu* unarmed combat that I studied in Japan with my teacher in the 1970s, there were nine specific *ryu-ha* (traditional lineages of technique), each with its own unique educational structure and terminology. The Koto Ryu of *koppojutsu* (associated with the Momochi family's Iga ninja unarmed combat) used the term "shoden" to cover the phase of initial years and techniques of training. In a different use of terminology, the Gyokko Ryu of *koshijutsu*, covering the fundamental hand-to-hand skills taught to Togakure Ryu ninja, used the term *jo-ryaku*, indicating "highest collection," "uppermost" or "closest to the surface" body of knowledge, in place of the shoden designation.

The scrolls rarely contained any textbook mechanics or details of how to do the techniques and were often iconic at best. A list of names of techniques or principles might be brushed onto the paper, along with a list of current and previous headmasters of the school, and then sealed with the red-orange *hanko* signature block imprint of the issuing authority in order to serve as a form of graduation authorization in the martial art dojo.

Chuden

In many martial arts, the second level of learning might be a *chuden* set of "middle teachings." In some schools, like the Takagi Yoshin Ryu, a classification like *shoden ura* is used, meaning "behind the initial teachings"—a deeper or further interpretation of the *shoden omote* foundational teachings. The chuden's techniques and principles in many of the root traditions of the ninja arts are not necessarily harder or more complicated to perform, but they are continuations of the skills and knowledge needed for the kinds of attacks not included in the initial-level training. If shoden training concentrates on how to use the kihon fundamental skills in combat, chuden training places heavier emphasis on the importance of those tactics. In modern martial art belt-ranking systems, a chuden advanced practitioner might be compared to a third- or fourth-degree black belt; such a comparison of antique and modern rating systems is, of course, troublesome, in that there is no real standardization as to exactly what a typical third-degree black belt should be able to do or demonstrate in today's martial arts schools.

Okuden

After chuden training and the awarding of its respective scroll, a very limited number of graduates go on to *okuden* (innermost teachings). In some martial traditions, okuden training involves a substantial leap in terms of depth of knowledge or degree of difficulty. Some okuden lessons might even emphasize essential principles of strategy more so than fine details of mechanical technique.

In some cases, okuden skills might be deceptively simple in description but incredibly difficult in application. I remember being taught a Koto Ryu koppojutsu okuden exercise in which my technique was simply to walk up to an adversary and hit him in the throat. When the teacher demonstrated it for me, it was difficult to imagine that the simple act of walking up to a person in a normal gait—just walking, not bobbing or weaving like a fighter—and using a hand edge to the throat was a highly advanced skill. When I began to practice the technique, though, I quickly found out why this was considered such a difficult challenge, in that I had to invade the enemy's space without giving off any telltale signals that would warn him to bring his guard up. Even the slightest mental or physical tension or the smallest pause or adjustment to the approach timing owing to emotional or tactical hesitancy would be blatant giveaways to the target person observing. Try it, and you will see how difficult such a technique is.

In modern combat sports, the parallel to the okuden would be the highest level of coaching a successful champion might seek out in order to put him in that rarified league beyond the ordinary competitor, winning international titles or gold medals at the Olympics. To use a military comparison, okuden training would be akin to war college, where the study of past battles in different cultural or technological ages educates future generals in strategic thinking. In the modern martial art belt-ranking system, an okuden master might be compared to a fifth- or sixth-degree black belt.

Hiden

Hiden (secret teachings) training is restricted to only the top few warriors who might be candidates for the role of future grandmaster to take over and direct into a new generation the ryu-ha lineage tradition. To compare this level with the modern belt-degree system, those few warriors with access to the deepest secrets would likely be seventh- or eighth-degree black belts.

Compare this categorization of the levels of education in ancient warrior training with contemporary military training models of today. What we would call modern "military basic training" would cover fundamental combat weapons skills, fitness cultivation, dress and deportment, working within a chain of command, and understanding mission and operational parameters. From basic training (shoden), the warrior would go on to specialized schools to develop higher levels of operational proficiency and knowledge, akin to chuden training in the old Japanese warrior schools. Beyond that would be an okuden-type leap into different depths of training, either as an officer going to war college or an enlisted person going to combat or specialization courses. The very few at the highest levels of their military careers have their own rarefied schools for training to be a top general or admiral or air commander, teaching the secrets behind the secrets, as did ancient hiden-level training.

SHU-HA-RI: LEARNING CLASSIFICATIONS

Beneath the specific categorization of a warrior school's standard exercises in a series of scroll diplomas lies another, less-rigid system of interpreting progress toward mastery. *Shu-ha-ri* is a set of terms the Japanese use to describe the overall progression of martial arts training, as well as the lifelong relationship the student might maintain with his instructor. The shu-ha-ri progression as a concept for cataloging a student's progress is so natural that it is often observed by martial artists even without knowing the expression itself.

The three shu-ha-ri kanji describe the cycles of training for a martial arts student in a set of three specific phases of personal advancement. The application of shu-ha-ri is not only confined to the study of martial arts but also can serve as a model for any sort of learning. Shu-ha-ri can be seen as a map that lays out in three stages the potential progress of an individual in learning a traditional skill, be it music, calligraphy, pottery making or traditional martial arts. Like many Japanese cultural concepts, shu-ha-ri covers a lot in a short phrase.

Shu: Learn by Imitating

The first stage is known as *shu*, which also can be pronounced *mamoru*, and is translated as "to protect, defend, guard, obey, keep, observe." The characteristics of this particular stage are best thought of as being protected or defended by the teacher and the teaching, obeying the orders of the teacher and teaching, and carefully observing the teacher and teaching. The term describes the relationship between a martial arts student and teacher in the student's early stages, which can be compared to the relationship of a parent and a young child. The student will imitate and absorb all the teacher imparts and be eager to learn and willing to accept all correction and constructive observation. The teacher guards the student in the sense of watching out for his interests and encouraging his progress, much like a parent guards a child through the first years of growth.

Shu implies persistence in a single martial system. In the shu stage, the student works to copy the techniques as taught, without modification and without attempting to interpret the rationale of the techniques.

Technically, this stage is characterized by the learning and embodiment of the fundamentals through repetition, exactly as presented, without the burden of opinion or judgment. Shu stresses basics in an uncompromising fashion, so all students perform techniques in an identical fashion, even though their personalities, body structures, ages and abilities may differ. By following a single route to the goal, a lasting technical foundation is built on which a deeper understanding of the art can be based. Training in other schools too soon is frowned on because possibly conflicting techniques will confuse progress toward a sound theoretical or practical capability.

Shu is an important basic habituation period, physically and mentally, during which all the necessary conditions are carefully established

for advanced study. Physically, this is the time to first learn fighting postures, how to move, how to maintain a center of gravity, how to balance the use of hands and footwork, and how to condition the parts of the body—the joints, muscles and bones. Mentally, the student learns how to focus and concentrate on a particular part of the body and how to generate internal energy and direct its flow. The student also learns the basic attitudes of successful martial arts training—confidence, openness to new possibilities, trust and respect for his teachers, endurance and courage.

The most important thing in the shu phase is to find a good instructor and visit him as often as possible. Then, throughout your practice, you must continually and honestly compare your own actions against your mentor's example. Each time you visit your instructor, examine your movements and compare them with those of your instructor and the more advanced students. Refine your actions step by step. Slowly internalize the basics. The keys to advancement are careful observation and self-examination based on the instruction received.

The instructor is like a walking textbook in this stage. He appears and gives just enough knowledge and instruction, always exactly what is needed and no more or no less, and then disappears back into the dojo office. Watch carefully, and listen to everything your instructor has to say. Do not assume that corrections given to others do not apply to you or will not apply to you later. Learn from every single experience in the dojo. Examine your own motions for the problems the instructor points out and work to eradicate any flaws you find.

Ha: Learn by Exploring

The second stage of the shu-ha-ri process is referred to as *ha*, which can be translated as "to break, detach, tear up, rip, open or burst." In the ha stage, the student breaks free from the rigid observations of memorizing technique details to some extent. The student must now consider the meaning and purpose of everything that has been learned and come to a deeper understanding of the art than pure repetitive practice can allow. At this stage, each technique is thoroughly absorbed into muscle memory, so the student is prepared to explore the principles behind the techniques.

Ha is a time to break free in two ways. In terms of technique, the student will break free from the fundamentals and begin to apply the principles acquired in a new, freer and more imaginative way. The student's individuality will begin to emerge in the way he performs techniques. At a deeper level, the student will also break free of the need for rigid instruction from the teacher and will begin to question and discover more through personal experience. At the ha stage, the relationship between the student and teacher is similar to that of a parent and teenager, in which guidance and inspiration replace the insistence on imitation and the following of rules without question. At this stage, the one who teaches and the one who receives the teaching now simultaneously work toward the development of individualism.

Ha-level training develops the sense of self-affirmation and self-reliance, which is based on letting go of the first stage of complete reliance on the teacher. A new horizon appears. A totally different perception is needed to grasp the meaning of what is happening at this time. The ha stage demands careful preparation by teacher and student. The strength of the teaching and deep insight and recognition of the potential of the student by the teacher, as well as the ceaseless and earnest study carried out by the student in response to the teaching, are essential. This is not a superficial self-assertion or pose of individualism because its strength comes from having been through the flame of self-denial.

Ha is the stage in which the student must rearrange or adapt what the teacher has taught. This allows new elements to be brought into the study as prompters for growth. These changes are based on the true recognition of self together with surrounding conditions, such as temperament, personality, style, age, sex, weight, height and body strength.

This is the stage in which, spiritually or mentally, it is necessary to have a high mind of inquiry and self-reflection. More than anything else, it is necessary to develop a true and unshakable understanding of oneself as an individual. In other words, a clear vision of one's own potential and the best possible way to stimulate it is developed. This might require setting aside what is already an asset or strength in one's art. In this stage, gaining insight often means losing or abandoning rigid beliefs, and this plays an important part in the process. After years of practice, the flashes of insight bring about a deeper perception of the style. It is indeed a difficult task to carry out, and this is often a confusing and scary time for the student. This is when most people get stuck and cease to grow. It is a matter of insight and perception and courage in relation to the true recognition of self. Another, very significant part of this stage is moving from the complete passivity of the memorizer to active responsibility for one's own training.

Ha can be a frustrating time in training. A moment of perceived insight may be all wrong. It is difficult to tell whether a particular interpretation of the basics is inspiration or error. The teacher must be able to allow the student to come to a few false conclusions on the way to learning deeper truth. You cannot just give someone insight. The deeper meanings of the kata may remain hidden for a long time. While beginners may appreciate the precision or the practicality of what they have been taught, they are not likely to understand the fuller depth hidden in the details. That kind of learning can take several more years.

Ha is also a dangerous time in training. Shu-ha-ri developed as an educational tool for learning the martial arts in an age when the only test was actual combat. Under those conditions, too much exploration or interpretation too soon would have been fatal because a failed test would leave the student maimed or dead. It is also true that ha is sometimes misinterpreted as "breaking with the teacher," although sometimes students are so convinced of the importance of their insights that they do leave their teachers too soon. The sense of power that comes with a teacher asking, "What do *you* think it means?" can be intoxicating. Especially in Western cultures, in which individualism is so highly esteemed, a student can, out of arrogance, ignorance or naiveté, think of himself as ready for independence far too soon in the process.

Ri: Learn by Creating

The final stage is known as *ri,* which can be translated as "to separate, leave, release, set free or detach." Ri is the stage of going beyond or transcending, when the student separates from the instructor, having absorbed all he can learn from him. In this stage, the student is no longer a student in the earlier sense but has become a matured practitioner. The practitioner must then think originally and develop original thoughts about the art and test them against the reality of his background knowledge and conclusions, as well as the demands of everyday life. In the ri stage, the art truly becomes the practitioner's own, and to a large extent his own creation.

Ri is a time of graduation, though it is by no means the end of study. The student and teacher may now have an even stronger bond than before, much like a grandparent might have with a son or daughter who is now a parent. The teacher and student become more like old friends sharing the path than a child obeying a parent. Although the student is fully independent, he treasures the wisdom and patient counsel of the teacher, and there is a richness to their relationship that continues through shared experiences. The student is learning and progressing more through self-discovery than by receiving instruction. He must rely on his own creative impulses, and the student's techniques will bear an imprint of his personality and character.

In this stage, one has achieved mastery of the art and probably has achieved recognition as a complete individual with independent standing in the art. In this stage, one must continue to acquire every important bit of technical skill, knowledge and experience with a dauntless sense of personal responsibility. Spiritually and mentally, one no longer depends or relies on external help or guidance. One depends on one's own continual urge to inquire.

It goes without saying that few people will study the martial arts for the time it takes to get to ri authentically. Some practice for years and may only succeed in attaining a high level of shu, brightened by glimpses of ha. Shu-ha-ri is not a clearly defined, linear progression, but their progression might be acknowledged in some martial arts schools with a diploma awarded by the teacher. The fundamentals remain constant, but the subtleties of their execution and application change as the student progresses to where his own personality begins to flavor the techniques.

The student and teacher are bound together by their close relationship and the knowledge, experience, culture and tradition shared between them. Ultimately, shu-ha-ri should result in the student surpassing the master, both in knowledge and skill. This is the only way the art can ever grow and improve as a whole. If the student never surpasses his master, the art will stagnate. If the student never achieves the master's ability, the art will deteriorate. But if the student can assimilate all that the master has to impart and then progress to even higher levels of advancement, the art will continue to improve and flourish.

CHAPTER 31

When attacked
* you confound and confuse*
* the assailant's conventional expectations.*
Then you capture his vulnerability
* as he struggles in frustration for dominance.*
The ninja wins through the art of invisibility,
* allowing the enemy to bring to completion*
* what your will requires.*

HISTORY'S LESSONS REACH TO THE FUTURE

Tactics, strategies and mechanics of the once-secret ninja martial arts for intelligence gatherers

The techniques that follow are some of the classical lessons and, in some cases, contemporary adaptations of the principles being taught in the kata fight scenario. The reader should bear in mind that these techniques illustrate the strategies taught in a few of the historical warrior traditions that the author studied in Japan, but the limitations of the two-dimensional page prevent the presentation of anything resembling the actual timing of the movements. Therefore, the string of numbered photos can incorrectly appear to be some sort of "one-beat-at-a-time," step-by-step set of movements, but in reality, the timing of a fight starts and slows, speeds and catches, and one moment's lockup flows into the next moment's escape—all of which are impossible to show on the printed page. It is also true that there is a lateral angling that is impossible to convey on the two-dimensional printed page. It may look to the reader like the defender is standing flat in front of an attacker while blocking and countering, while in truth there are complex sets of repositioning shifts and angling moves going on all the time that throw off the attacker's sense of what ought to happen next.

Shoden Kata (Initial Training Examples)

Koto Ryu Koppojutsu Shoden Kata

1. Ko-Yoku (Deny Aggressor's Attack)

Inside His Attack

Practice moving decisively into an aggressor's attack at just the right moment. Move too soon, and he can retract his commitment and intercept you (or, in a modern courtroom, you could be accused of starting the fight and be found guilty of assault). Move too late, and you will be fighting with a physically and spiritually weakened sense of balance. Penetrate his strike and respond as needed to take advantage when he reflexively strikes or grabs as a follow-up.

The adversary (right) throws a high right strike, a swing-slap, a reach-around grab or a hook punch (1). Have your training partner practice these various attacks authentically so a good defense becomes your natural response.

From a left seigan no kamae, slip inside his punch with a subtle shift in your footwork (2).

Strike defensively inside his right arm with your left (3).

Throw a right cross to his chest (4-5).

Follow with a right shuto (hand-edge strike) to his temple (6). Or, at minimum, use a right palm heel to his face.

continued on next page

If your adversary lurches forward to wrestle you, catch his right shoulder from beneath with your left arm and twist into the center of his body, driving a right shuto into the right side of his neck or head (7).

Continue turning and throw him forward with a ganseki-nage throw (8-10).

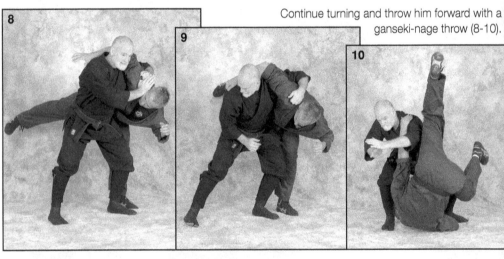

If the attacker (right) backs up after your initial defense, hook his right leg and hip with your right leg (11-13).

Take him down with an osoto-gake backward throw (14-15).

Ko-Yoku Ura-Kata
Adaptation One

When the aggressor (left) presses in heavily with tight hook punches or when he attempts to grab you, defend from inside (1-2).

As he attempts to grapple his way in, use your defending arm to shove his lowered attacking arm past your body (3).

Use both hands to pull his lowered arm past you from above (4).

Shift behind him and place your right knee behind his right knee (5).

Using his hips, pull him backward to the ground (6).

He lands in position for a finishing kick (7-8).

Ko-Yoku Ura-Kata
Adaptation Two

When the aggressor (right) is too close with tight hook punches or grabs, defend from inside (1-2).

As he attempts to grapple his way in, use your defending arm to shove his raised attacking arm above your head (3).

Use both hands to push his arm past you from below (4).

Shift behind him to smack down on his head, and kick his knee to pull him backward to the ground (5-7).

He lands in position for a finishing kick (8-9).

2. Yoku-To (Attack Throwback)

Outside His Attack

Practice making decisions under pressure. There may not be enough time to spot and recognize your opponent's technique, so you need a quick response that is capable of handling many possibilities. You will know what he is throwing at you only as the attack unfolds. With minimal information to indicate what is coming, you have to generate the maximum and best results with what you have. Use one standard move to deal with any number of variations.

The aggressor (right) reaches straight in with his right hand for a grab-pull, a shove or a straight punch (1). Have your training partner practice these various attacks authentically so you naturally respond with a good defense.

No matter what straight-in attack he throws, come in from the outside with your left palm to engage and lock up his right hand (2).

Swing a right boshiken thumb tip to the left corner of his jaw, and swing your right shin up and into his crotch (3). You also can use a knee to his right hip or a right boot toe to his ankle or lower leg.

Knock him back with a left shakoken palm to his chin while pulling your right leg all the way back and fully extending your left arm (4-6).

Be ready for whatever happens next. Prepare to kick him back down if he rises (7).

Yoku-To Ura-Kata
Adaptation One

When the aggressor (right) fires in with a leading straight punch or a grab, defend from outside with a smacking shove to the outside of his arm (1-2).

Use your free hand to strike his temple with an open-hand palm heel from outside (3).

Drive a knee into the side of his thigh or hip, causing him to lose his footing (4-5).

continued on next page ▶

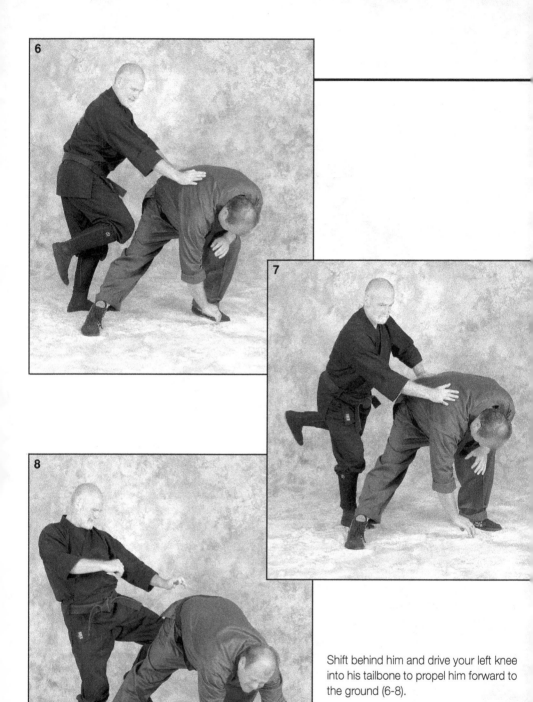

Shift behind him and drive your left knee into his tailbone to propel him forward to the ground (6-8).

Stomp down on his ankle to remove his ability to rise and continue to fight (9-10).

Stomp down on his thigh for a finishing kick (11).

Yoku-To Ura-Kata
Adaptation Two

When the aggressor (left) fires in with a leading straight punch or grab, block and counterstrike to his face in the same movement (1-2).

If he intercepts your right strike with a left palm-heel jam of his own, catch his left jamming-arm wrist with your original left deflecting hand (3-4).

Pull him close for a right punch or open-hand strike to the face (5).

continued on next page

Shove his right shoulder away with your right hand as you back away, and pull his captured left hand with your left hand (6-7).

Pull his left arm straight as you strike his face with a right shuto (8).

Bear down on his left triceps with your right forearm to drive him off-balance (9-10).

As you press with your right forearm, sweep your right leg back into the front of his left leg to take him to the ground (11).

Drop your right knee into the back of his extended left arm to pin him in a position of surrender (12).

Yoku-To Ura-Kata
Adaptation Three

When the aggressor (right) fires in with a leading straight punch or grab, block and counterstrike to his face in the same movement (1-3).

If he tries to continue with a left punch after his thwarted right strike, move inside his right, jamming him with a right elbow to his chest or face (4-5).

continued on next page

(Reverse Angle for Illustration) Keep the pressure on his retracting right arm as you move away from his left follow-up punch (6).

Use footwork—not wrestling strength—and take his hand over in a palm-out, thumb-down omote-gyaku wrist lock, pulling him off-balance (7).

Continue to guide, extend and twist his wrist and throw him to the ground or into a solid object like a wall or vehicle (8-10).

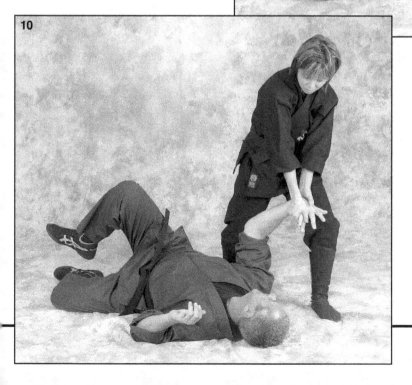

Gyokko Ryu Koshijutsu Jo-Ryaku No Maki

1. Dan-Shu (Bullet Hand)

Practice capturing an aggressor's attack as a means of creating your technique and achieving victory. Move with his attacks in the beginning, and fit into his pattern while taking advantage of the openings his movement creates. You then can attack his vulnerable points in the confusion that ensues as he reacts in surprise to the failure of his assault.

As you attempt to get to a safer position, the aggressor (left) grabs your right cuff with his left hand (1-2).

Pull back your right hand, wrapping and locking it counterclockwise over his left hand (3).

He punches at your face with his right fist (4).

Strike defensively with your left fist to the inside of his right arm (5-6).

continued on next page

Immediately rock forward on your left leg and, with a left shuto, strike his left temple (7-8).

Follow with a right heel stomp to his left knee, forcing him to the ground (9-11).

Lever his body forward with your right knee and create an armbar against his outstretched arm to dislocate his shoulder (12-13).

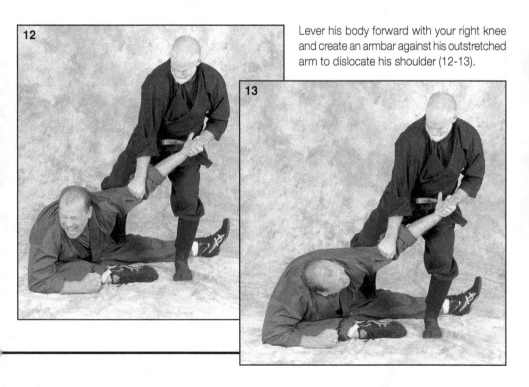

Dan-Shu Ura-Kata
Adaptation One

When your opponent (right) grabs your right wrist to hold you down or pull you off-balance, rotate your right hand under his grip and strike him in the face with your left hand (1-2).

Immediately circle away from his free right hand into position, where you can lock his left arm from behind (3-4).

Hug your trapped arm to his grabbing arm to pop your wrist out of his grip and lock his left wrist (5-6).

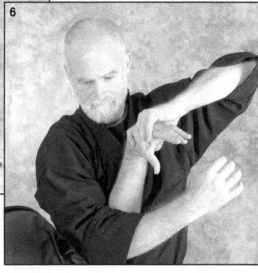

Dan-Shu Ura-Kata
Adaptation Two

As you attempt to get to a safer position, the aggressor (left) grabs your right wrist with his left hand to hold you down or pull you off-balance (1-2).

Extend your right arm and move into position behind his grabbing left arm, slipping your left palm between your arm and his to create a leveraged shove to pop your wrist out of his grip (3-5).

Secure his arm and strike his face several times with your right elbow (6-7).

Rock forward and lock his left shoulder with your right arm. You now can drive him to the ground or control him with a forward escort arrest (8-9).

Dan-Shu Ura-Kata
Adaptation Three

The aggressor (right) grabs your right arm with his left hand to hold you down or pull you off-balance (1).

Extend your right arm forward and advance into position behind his left arm, hitting him in the face, neck or collarbone as you move forward (2).

Pivot into him and strike his face while lifting his arm to lever him off-balance (3).

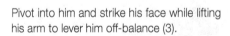

Shift forward and lock his left elbow and shoulder to throw him to the ground (4-6).

Dan-Shu Ura-Kata
Adaptation Four

In this variation, the aggressor (left) grabs your right arm with his left hand (thumb up) to pull you off-balance and into his strike (1).

Pull your right arm back and advance into position behind his left arm, hitting him in the face with your elbow as you move forward (2).

Slip your right elbow over his left arm and apply leverage to force him off-balance and down (3-4).

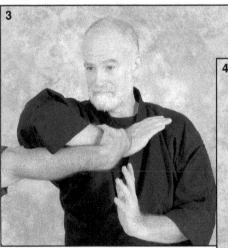

Peel his hand off your right wrist, and send your right elbow back to his face while bearing down to lock his left arm at the elbow and shoulder. You then can either lever him to the floor with the left shoulder lock or grab his free right hand with your right and twist his right wrist into a lock (5-7).

Dan-Shu Ura-Kata
Adaptation Five

The aggressor (right) grabs your left arm with his left hand to hold you down for a punch (1).

3 (REVERSE ANGLE)

As he punches, lift your trapped arm at an angle so his fist hits the tip of your elbow. The pain of the impact may make him recoil (2-4).

Stretch his left arm to the side to pull him off-balance and step into position behind his arm (5-7).

continued on next page

Rock your ribs forward to lock his left arm, and bring your right elbow back to his face to knock him backward (8).

Jam your knee into the back of his straightened elbow and apply pull-back pressure to lock or break his arm, and sling him forward onto his face (9-11).

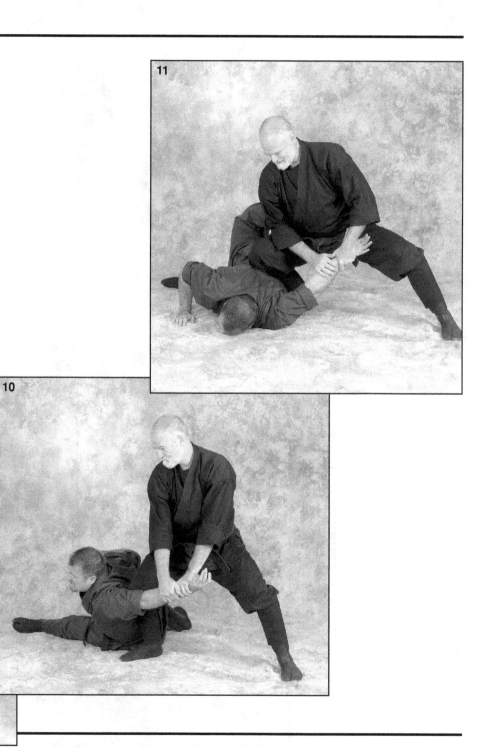

Dan-Shu Ura-Kata
Adaptation Six

The aggressor (left) grabs your left arm with his left hand (thumb up) to pull you into a punch or grappling clinch (1).

Drop your left arm clockwise to lock his gripping hand in an awkward upside-down position (2-3).

Grab his face with your free hand and move into position behind him, allowing him to hold onto your wrist (4-5).

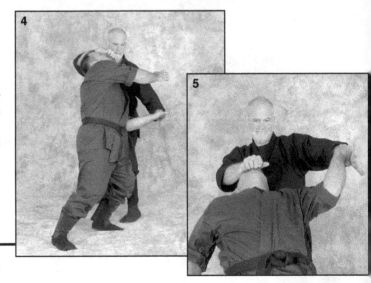

Continue to circle behind him and twist his gripping hand into a wrist lock (6-7).

Use his left arm to pull him backward and to the ground (8-9).

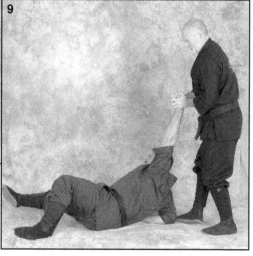

Dan-Shu Ura-Kata
Adaptation Seven

The aggressor (left) grabs your right arm with his left hand from behind and attempts to move you under his control (1-2).

Turn inward and lift your right arm in a circular swing to redirect his power, striking him in the face with the same momentum (3-4).

Continue rotating your arm to free yourself from his grip (5).

Continue your motion to grab his wrist and pull him into a strike (6-8).

continued on next page

Turn your strike into a jacket grab (9).

Drive your left heel into his knee to break his strength and balance (10).

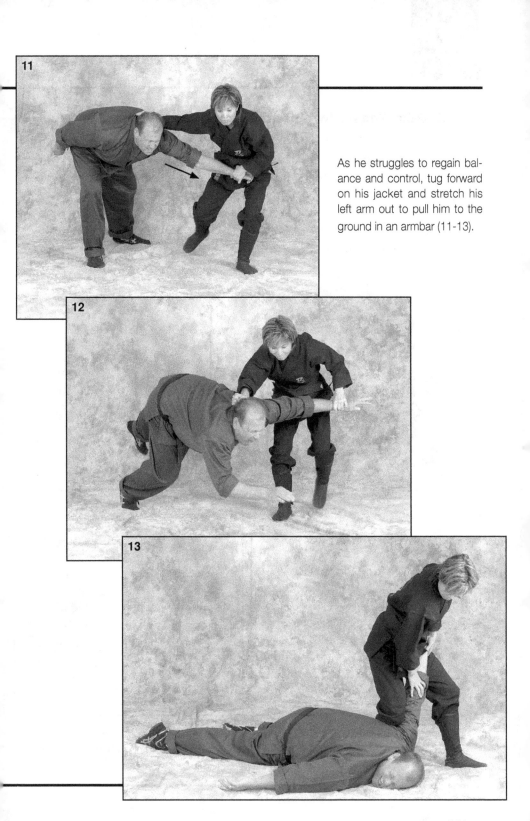

As he struggles to regain balance and control, tug forward on his jacket and stretch his left arm out to pull him to the ground in an armbar (11-13).

2. Saka-Nagare (Against the Flow)

Practice riding an aggressor's attacking momentum to create your technique and overcome his head start. Slip outside the reach of his attacks in the beginning, and ride the edge of his striking range while taking advantage of the openings his movement creates. As in the previous techniques, attack his vulnerable points in the confusion that ensues as he reacts in surprise to the failure of his assault.

You stand in a left-forward Gyokko Ryu ichimonji no kamae posture as the adversary (right) attacks with a high right punch. Slip to the outside of his arm and strike his punching arm with a right fudoken punch (1-4).

He continues with a right front kick to your midsection (5).

Shift left to the outside of his kick, allowing his foot to miss its target as you snag his right arm with your right hand (6).

If you need to, counter-kick to his right leg with a right swinging kick of your own (7).

continued on next page

As he spins back with a left uppercut to your midsection, drift to your left with a right lower-defensive strike inside his left forearm. Snag his right hand with your left (8-11).

Strike with a right urashuto (open-hand edge) to the right side of his neck (12-14).

continued on next page ▶

Lift his right hand with your left, and step to the left with an omotegyaku outward twist to his right wrist to throw him to the ground (15-17).

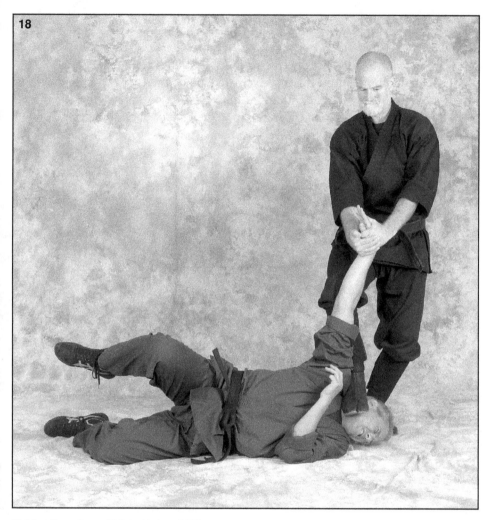

Finish with a stomp kick to his head (18).

Saka-Nagare

Adaptation

As with the historically classical form, practice riding an aggressor's attacking momentum to create your technique and overcome his head start. In this modern adaptation against a street boxer, stay outside the reach of his attacks in the beginning and then attack his vulnerable points in the confusion that ensues as he reacts in surprise to your evasion.

As the adversary (left) attacks with two quick left jabs, slip just out of range and strike his wrist with a quick right fudoken punch (1-4).

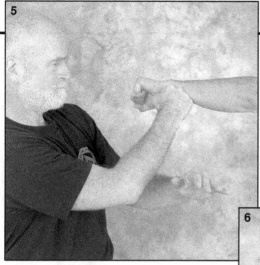

Hit his wrist from below and slap it to the side with your left hand to interrupt his flow (5-6).

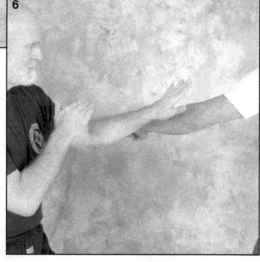

continued on next page ▶

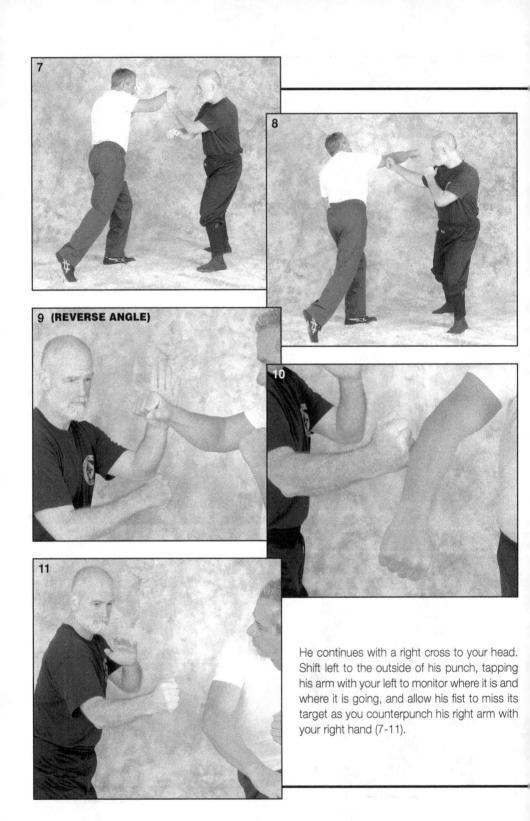

He continues with a right cross to your head. Shift left to the outside of his punch, tapping his arm with your left to monitor where it is and where it is going, and allow his fist to miss its target as you counterpunch his right arm with your right hand (7-11).

Deliver a right kick to his groin to drive his hips back (12-13).

If he is still in the fight and shoots in with an attempted midsection tackle, push his right arm with your left and strike with a right urashuto to the right side of his neck (14-15).

continued on next page

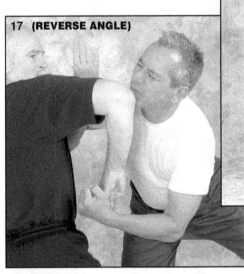

Straighten him up with a right elbow strike and a forearm lift to his face (16-17).

Drive his shoulders back with an elbow strike to the collarbone to weaken his balance (18).

Twist his right arm with your left, and step in beneath his right hip as he struggles to regain his balance (19).

Throw him to the ground on his left side (20-21).

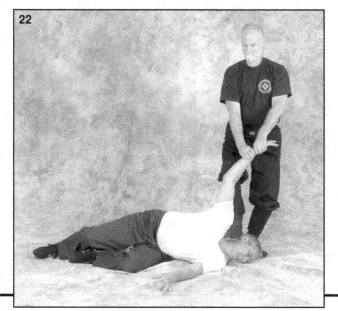

Finish with a stomp to his head (22).

Takagi Yoshin Ryu Jutaijutsu Shoden Omote Kata

1. Ran-Sho (Chaos Victory)

Practice evading the aggressor's attack. Slip outside the reach of his attacks in the beginning, and ride the edge of his striking range while taking advantage of the openings his movement creates. As always, attack his vulnerable points in the confusion that ensues as he reacts in surprise to your evasion.

As the adversary (left) attacks with a high right shove or grab, slip inside his attack and deflect it with your left arm, rotating it in a counterclockwise direction (1-3).

Rock back in with a right palm-heel strike to his throat or jaw (4).

Catch and twist his right wrist with your left hand as you shift to the left and pull him off-balance (5-6).

continued on next page ▶

Maintaining your right palm-heel pressure on his neck or jaw, shift your right heel behind his right leg and pull down on his right wrist to throw him to the ground (7-9).

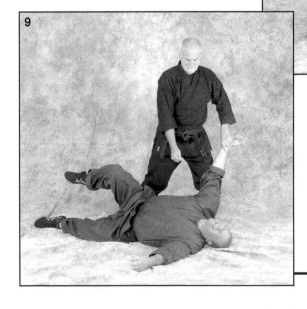

Stretch his arm forward and ram your knee into the back of his straightened elbow to incapacitate his right arm (10-11).

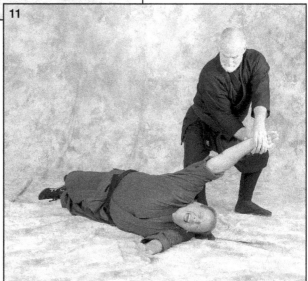

Ran-Sho
Adaptation

As before, the adversary (left) attacks with a high right shove or grab, and you slip inside his attack and deflect it with your left arm (1-2).

Rock back in with a crushing right claw-hand strike to his throat (3-4).

Push forward on his right arm with your left to move him off-balance, and duck beneath his right shoulder for a driving heel kick to the back of his right leg (5-6).

Continue your momentum to drive the back of his head into the floor (7-8).

2. Yui Gyaku

Practice capturing an aggressor's attacking moves from a position that negates his leverage. Slip outside or inside his attacks and capture his limbs to pull him off-balance. You then can use his loss of balance to throw him as he reacts in surprise to the failure of his conventional punch and kick assault.

As the adversary (right) attacks with a left jab, shove or grab, slip outside his attack and deflect his punching arm inward with your right hand (1-2).

The aggressor continues with an attempt to grab around your neck with his right hand. (This also could be a hook punch.) Shift back and knock his attack off-line with a rising left forearm inside his right arm (3-4).

Punch his throat or face with your right fist (5).

Grab his right shoulder with your right hand and his right wrist with your left hand, and step in with your right foot to knock him back and off-balance (6-7).

Swing your left leg behind you, and pull on his right wrist with your left hand while pushing his neck back with your right (8).

continued on next page

Sweep your right leg up inside his left leg, and pull him forward and off-balance (9).

Continue your twisting momentum to throw him to the ground on his back (10-11).

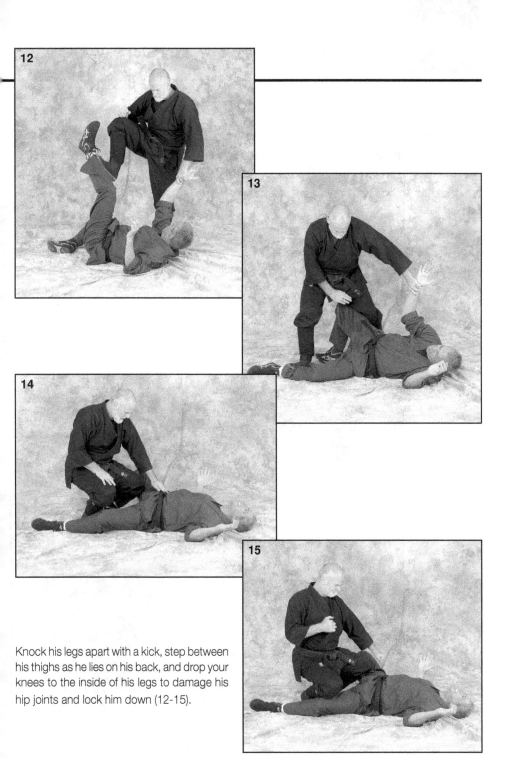

Knock his legs apart with a kick, step between his thighs as he lies on his back, and drop your knees to the inside of his legs to damage his hip joints and lock him down (12-15).

Yui Gyaku

Adaptation

The fight starts like it does in the previous technique, but you feel that the aggressor is too stable to knock over with an inside sweep kick.

Grab his right arm with your left hand, and deliver a right punch to his throat or face (1-2).

Slip your right hand under his right shoulder and grab his right wrist with your left hand, and drive your right shoulder into his right arm to knock him off-balance. Continue your twisting momentum to throw him on the ground (3-4).

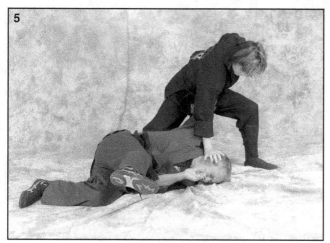

Use a right palm-heel strike to drive his head into the ground for a knockout (5).

Shinden Fudo Ryu Dakentaijutsu Shizen Shigoku No Kata (Natural Examples)

1. Ryo Te Gake (Two-Hand Hook)

Practice using the aggressor's tension as a way to take him off-balance and into a position of reduced power. Victims often respond in a predictable manner when hit with a surprise attack. Therefore, the aggressor often has a predictable expectation about what his victim's resistance will be. Counter in a way that defies expectation. (Do not fight back with conventional resistance.) That leaves him in a state of having to figure out why his actions are not working. He then must retreat back to stability and find a new approach for his continued onslaught. When he reacts in surprise to your unexpected positioning in the middle of his attack, you can take advantage of his disrupted balance and throw him.

The aggressor (right) attacks with a two-handed choke to the throat (1-2).

Lower your hips and step back with your left foot. Push up on the underside of his elbows (3).

The aggressor will most likely tighten his grip in an attempt to regain control. You should suddenly turn right and step in with your left foot and back with your right foot, pushing up on his right elbow and pulling down on his left (4).

continued on next page

Drop to your right knee, pull down on his left elbow and push up on his right elbow to flip him onto his back (5-7).

Grab his left wrist, drive your right forearm into the side of his neck and pressure him into the ground (8).

Position his left arm across your midsection, and use your legs and pelvis to jam his left shoulder into a lock to prevent escape or any possible follow-up move (9-10).

Ryo Te Gake
Adaptation

The aggressor (left) attacks with a two-handed choke to the throat (1-2).

Punch across his left arm and hit him in the face with a fist or palm-heel strike (3).

Continue the momentum of your strike and reach under his right arm while reaching over it with your left (4-5).

Push his right arm away and step around with your right foot. Wedge his arm into a lock from above and below (6-7).

continued on next page

Lift his captured right arm and step under, twisting his right wrist into a shearing lock (8-11).

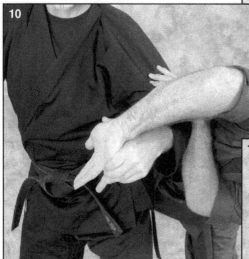

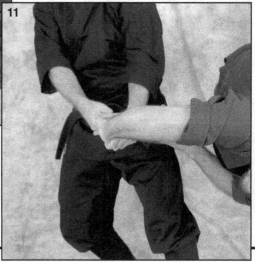

Step back with your right foot, and pull on his trapped right wrist to flip him onto his back (12-14).

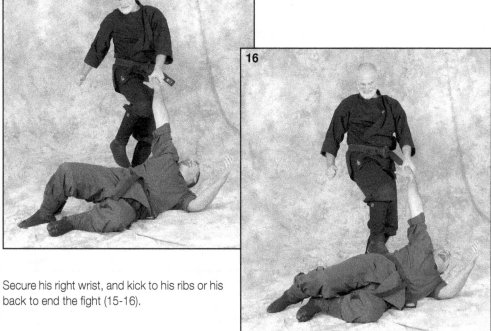

Secure his right wrist, and kick to his ribs or his back to end the fight (15-16).

2. Ro-To (Wolf Knockdown)

As the aggressor attacks with a left lapel grab and right punch, shift back with a left defensive strike inside his right arm (1-2).

Wedge his left wrist into your chest, and step out away from his center to pull his arm straight (3).

Rotate his left wrist into an inward-twisting wrist lock as you step around his straightened left arm, and deliver a driving right punch to his upper-left ribs (4-5).

continued on next page

Maintain the left-inward wrist twist, and swing back around to extend his arm and drop him to his chest (6-8).

Move forward against his wrist with your torso to lock his arm straight (9).

Position your body against his straightened arm to lock his shoulder and end the fight (10).

3. Fudo (Immovability)

As the aggressor attacks with a left lapel grab
and right punch, shift back with a left defensive
strike inside his right arm (1-2).

Rock back in on flexed knees,
and hit him with a palm-heel
slam to the face (3).

4

Dislodge his left grip with an inward wrist fold from beneath (4-5).

5 (REVERSE ANGLE)

continued on next page ▶

Maintain wrist-fold pressure. Grab his left shoulder with your left hand and back up into a safe position along his left side (6-7).

Step back in a counterclockwise turn with your left foot to sling him to the ground (8). If needed, drop to your left knee to generate sufficient momentum to throw him.

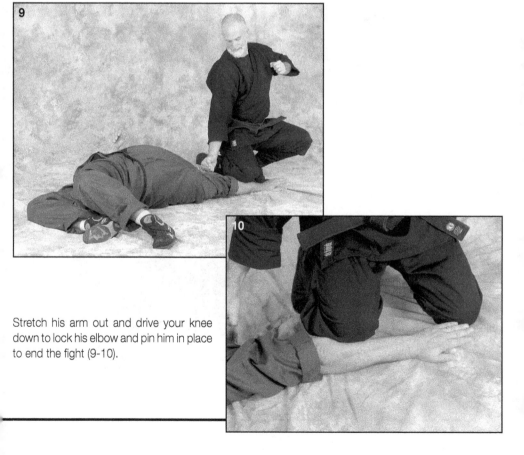

Stretch his arm out and drive your knee down to lock his elbow and pin him in place to end the fight (9-10).

4. U-Gari

Give way to the aggressor's throwing movement and turn it against him.

The adversary (right) grabs your lapel and sleeve in a shove-and-tussle wrestling attempt (1).

He pulls you in for a judo-style turning hip throw (2).

If he is successful in pulling you off-balance, grab his arms and pull him with you to decelerate your fall with a sideways body drop in front of his ankles (3-4).

Maintain your grip and use your bodyweight to pull him forward and off-balance onto his head or shoulder (5).

continued on next page

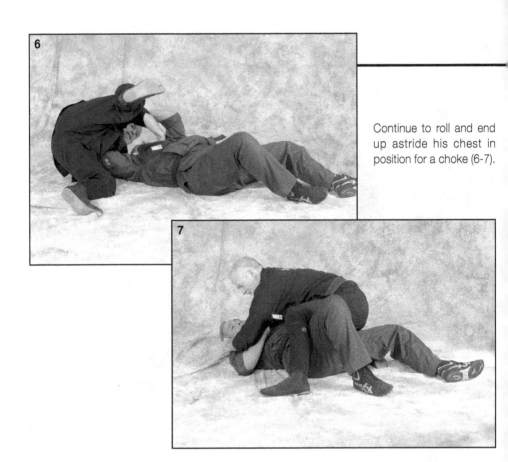

Continue to roll and end up astride his chest in position for a choke (6-7).

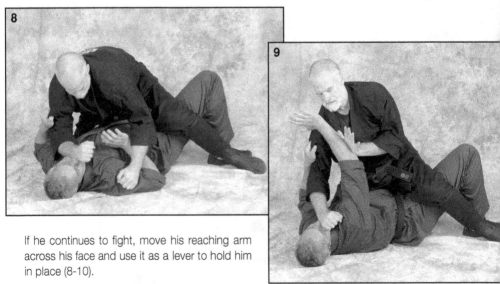

If he continues to fight, move his reaching arm across his face and use it as a lever to hold him in place (8-10).

If necessary, you can knock his head into the ground to end his will to fight (11).

U-Gari
Adaptation

The adversary (right) grabs your lapel and sleeve in a shove-and-tussle wrestling attempt (1).

He pulls you in tightly for a judo-style turning hip throw (2).

If he is successful in pushing in so deeply that you cannot regain your balance, grab his arms and pull him with you to decelerate your fall as you crouch backward with a sideways body drop behind his ankles (3-4).

Maintain your grip and use your bodyweight to pull him backward onto his seat or back (5).

continued on next page ▶

Continue to roll and end up astride his chest in position for a choke (6-8).

If he continues to fight, capture his arm across your chest and sit up, creating an armbar. Use that leverage to hold him in place, or damage his arm to end his will to fight (9-10).

To-Shin Do Bojutsu Kuji No Kata
(Long Staff "Nine Syllable" Forms)

In the mid-1300s, Yakushimaru Ryushin of Kumano used a broken spear as a 6-foot *bo* staff in a fierce fight with Northern Court rebels who had captured Emperor Godaigo. The rebels were unable to close in on him, so they pulled back and attacked with bows and arrows. Ryushin summoned fierce energy through *shinden kuji-kiri*, causing his enemies to retreat in confusion as a result of the explosive, righteous aura of the nine *kuji* patterns he drew in the air with his staff. Ryushin succeeded in rescuing Emperor Godaigo and moved him to the Zaodo on Mount Yoshino, which became a temporary Southern Court imperial palace. Afterward, Ryushin continued to develop his *bojutsu* knowledge and technique and created *kuji kyutsu kyuju kyuhon* (nine key winning strategies) as the roots of what would become the Kuki Shinden style of the bojutsu subset of *To-Shin Do* technique.

Kuki Shinden Ryu (Long Staff)
Kuji No Bo Dai Go Ho (Fifth Method)

Beat him down, take out his upper-control center and attack his foundation.

From a left-forward ten-chi-jin no kamae fighting posture, holding the bo in a spear grip, step forward with your right foot and reach toward the aggressor's head with the bo to attract his attention (1-3).

The goal is to make him have to respond—to move or get hit. This allows you to get in and strike with the next technique (4-6).

continued on next page ▶

Release your right hand and shift left with a clockwise rotation of the bo for a left yoko men uchi to the right side of the aggressor's head, re-gripping with the right hand at the bottom of the staff (7-8).

Note the lateral movement in relation to where the swordsman expects you to be (9-10).

Release your left hand and shift right with a counter-clockwise rotation of the bo for a right yoko men uchi to the left side of the aggressor's head (11-12).

As the aggressor attempts to parry, come around his sword and strike his head (13-15).

continued on next page ▶

Perform a left sune uchi ashi barai low-line hit to the aggressor's right shin (16-17).

Move just as he lifts his sword (18-19).

20

Perform a right sune uchi ashi barai to the aggressor's left shin (20-22).

21

22

continued on next page ▶

23

24

25

Use your footwork to move into the proper leverage position (23-25).

Pull back to a left-forward ten-chi-jin fighting posture (26-28).

Unarmed Contemporary Adaptation of Kuji No Bo Kata Five

From a left-forward ward-off posture, shift forward and reach or finger-jab toward the face of the adversary (left) to attract his attention and force him to lift his hands in defense (1-2).

Shift left and drop your right arm to avoid the aggressor's defensive counter, trap his right arm with your left hand and rotate your right hand edge up to the right side of his head (3-4).

Shift right and drop your right arm to avoid the aggressor's defensive counter, and rotate your left hand edge back up to the left side of his head (5-8).

continued on next page ▶

Deliver a left kick to his groin or lower abdomen (9-10).

Deliver a right knee to his midsection or head (11-13).

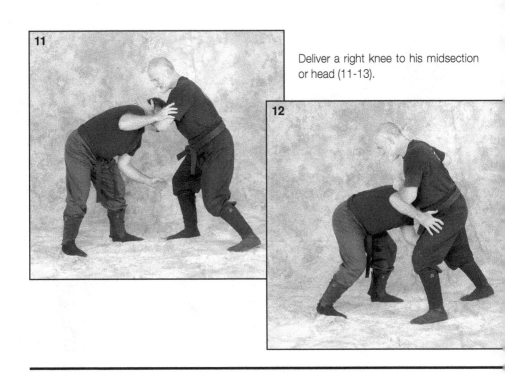

Push the adversary back and take control or escape (14-15).

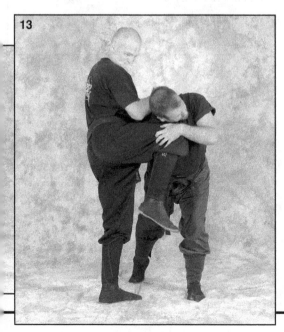

Chuden Kata (Middle Training Examples)

Takagi Yoshin Ryu Jutaijutsu Sabaki Kata (Body Movement Examples)

1. Oni-Kudaki (Demon Crush)

The attacker (left) steps forward with a high right grab or punch (1-2).

Counter with a left rising strike to the inside of his right arm while striking to the right side of his ribs with your right elbow (3).

Step forward with your right foot. Take the back of your left hand over the inside of his right wrist while swinging your right arm up behind his right elbow. Grasp your own extended left fingers (4-7).

continued on next page ▶

With an uplifting swing, step back with your left foot and pull up on his right shoulder to take him down with an inside shoulder lift (8-9).

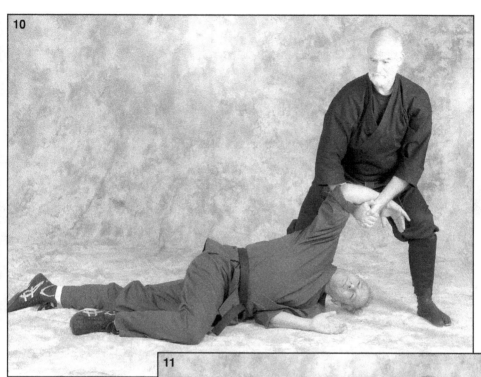

Pull up on his right wrist and jam down on his right shoulder to lock him into position on the ground (10-11).

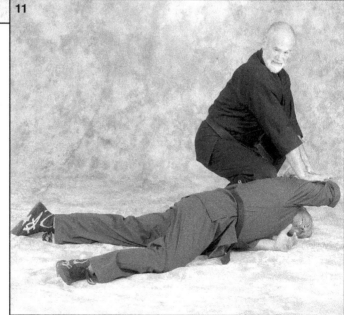

Oni-Kudaki
Unarmed Adaptation Against a Club Strike

The aggressor initiates a club attack (1).

You move inside the arc of his swing and counter with a left rising strike to the inside of his right arm as you strike his right ribs with your right elbow (2-3).

Step forward and take the back of your left hand over the inside of his right wrist while swinging your right arm up behind his right elbow. Grasp your own extended left fingers (4-6).

With an uplifting swing, step back with your left foot and pull up on his right shoulder to take him down with an inside shoulder lift (7-9).

Oni-Kudaki
Bent Arm Lock From the Ground

The adversary crouches and attempts a shoulder throw in response to your choke from behind (1).

As you roll forward over his shoulder, shove your hips as far under him as you can, reach up and pull his neck into a choke from below (2-3).

Continue your roll and pull him over your shoulder into a position beneath you (4-5).

Throw your right and then left leg forward. Secure his right wrist to block his attempt to roll you off him (6-8).

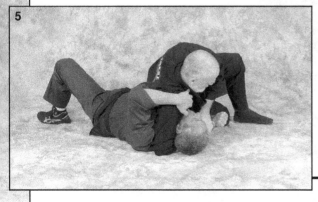

continued on next page

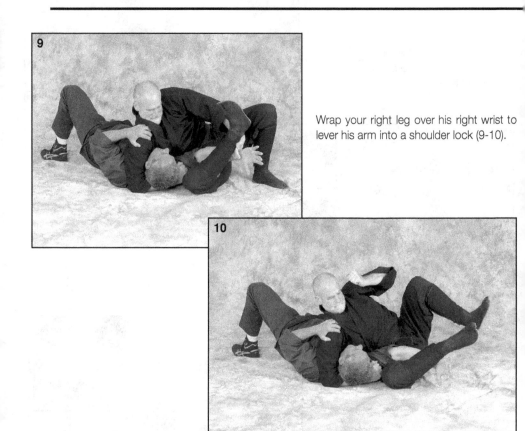

Wrap your right leg over his right wrist to lever his arm into a shoulder lock (9-10).

Strike his face to drive his head into the ground (11).

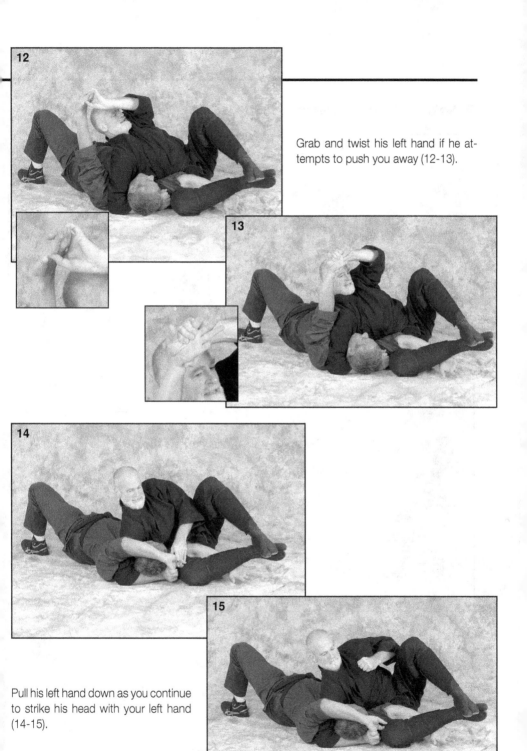

Grab and twist his left hand if he attempts to push you away (12-13).

Pull his left hand down as you continue to strike his head with your left hand (14-15).

2. Saka-Te Nage (Reversed Hand Throw)

In this modern adaptation of saka-te nage kata, you evade as the attacker cuts forward with inward and outward knife slashes (1-3).

In this advanced technique that requires a seasoned practitioner's skill, you must perfectly time an advance inside his next slash. Grab his right wrist with your left hand, and slam your right palm heel into his face to stun him (4).

Step in with your right foot, driving forward to keep up the pressure and push him off-balance (5).

Twist his right hand outward, and step in with a right grab to his underarm (6-7).

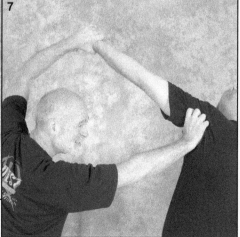

continued on next page ▶

Step behind his right foot to prevent him from stepping back (8).

Trap his right leg with your left and twist to your left to lever his right arm into a backward tripping takedown (9-11).

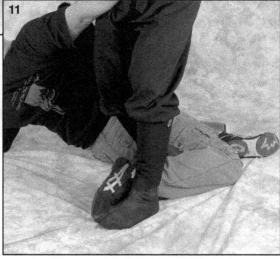

3. Oni Buse (Demon Crouch)

The attacker grabs your right wrist with his left hand and your throat or left lapel with his right hand (1-2).

Using your left fingernails, dig into the base of his right fingers, cutting into the skin, if necessary (3-5).

Lift his hand up and away (6).

continued on next page

If he maintains his grip on your right wrist, push down with your right knee for leverage to strip away his grip (7-9).

Suddenly step forward with your right foot and drive him back with elbow or fist strikes to his head (10-11).

Continue to control him with a wrist-twist lock to his right hand (12-13)

Koto Ryu Koppojutsu
1. Hi Cho

The adversary (right) walks toward you in an aggressive and hostile manner, intent on reaching out with a grab, shove or strike (1).

Surprise him by dropping low and executing a right fingertip and palm-heel claw to his face, driving his head back (2-4).

As he struggles to regain control, step back to capture his forward momentum and pull him forward to deliver a knee to his face or chest (5-7).

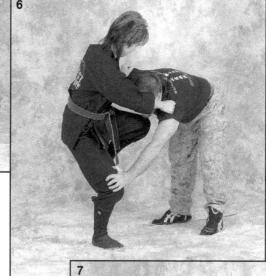

continued on next page

Step in toward his balance center and twist him forward to the ground with a leg-trip throw (8-11).

If necessary, kick his head to end the fight (12).

2. Hi Saku (Body Scissor and Takedown)

The adversary (top) takes you to the ground and crawls between your legs, preparing for a strike or choke (1).

Counterattack with strikes to his face to force him up and back (2).

Wrap your legs around his torso with a rib-crushing leg-scissor hold and shove him back with your hips (3).

He works his way to his feet in an attempt to escape the scissor hold (4-5).

Grab his ankles with both hands and pull up while driving his torso back with your legs and hips (6-8).

continued on next page

When he hits the ground, apply a leg lock to his calf to keep him from repositioning (9).

Knock him back with a heel stomp when he attempts to sit up and free himself (10-11).

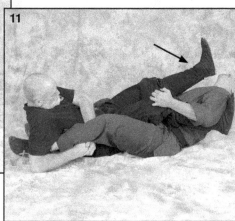

If he attempts to punch his way out of your hold, lean back and use your left leg to deflect his right arm from outside. Allow your left leg to wrap over his right arm in an elbow lock (12-14).

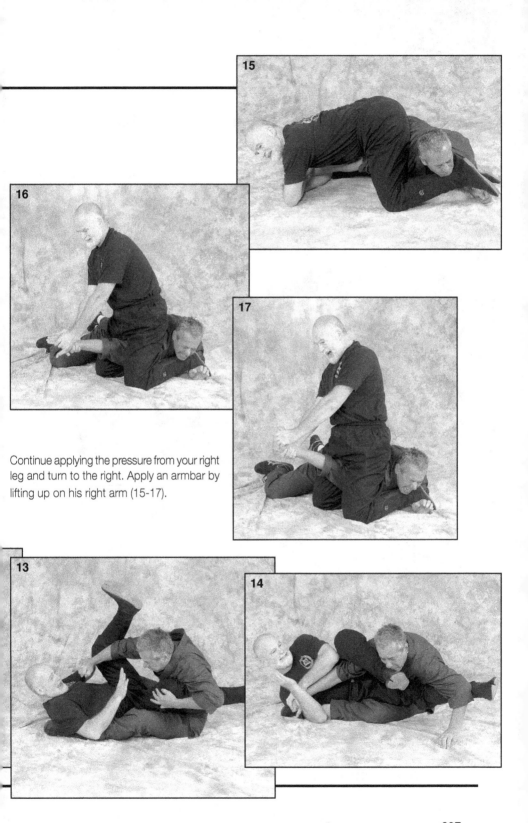

Continue applying the pressure from your right leg and turn to the right. Apply an armbar by lifting up on his right arm (15-17).

Gyokko Ryu Koshijutsu Chu-Ryaku No Maki
(Middle Scroll Collection of Essential Principles)

1. Sei-To (Mackerel Knockdown/ Move Like a Quick Fish)

The aggressor (left) attacks with a high right punch (1-2).

From a defensive posture, use a left defensive strike inside his right arm (3-4).

As he kicks with his right foot toward your midsection, apply a stopping kick to his leg (5-6).

As he punches to your midsection with his right fist, shift to the right while applying a left defensive strike to the inside of his right arm (7-8).

Rock forward on your left knee with a right fingertip strike to his eyes (9).

continued on next page

Grab his right wrist with your left hand and his right shoulder with your right hand, and pull him into a right kick to his right knee or thigh (10-11).

If he grabs your kicking leg, knee him in the face with it (12-13).

As he folds forward, pull him down onto his chest using leverage from a right shoulder-lifting lock (14-15).

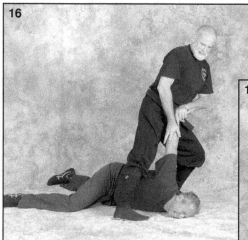

Step over his back with your left foot, and use your hips to bar his arm (16-17).

2. Ko-Rai (Tiger Takedown)

The aggressor slashes downward with a right single-hand short sword (1).

From a right ichimonji, shift to the left with your left foot and hit the outside of his descending right wrist with a right palm-heel slam (2).

Step forward with your left foot as you grab his right wrist with your right hand, and hit him with a left shuto to his right temple (3-4).

As he attempts to duck your strike and pull his captured right hand back, follow his momentum and slip under his arm with a left step and elbow strike to his ribs (5).

continued on next page

Continue to pass quickly in front of him, and end with your right side along his left while holding his right wrist in a twist lock and grabbing his left wrist with your left hand (6-7).

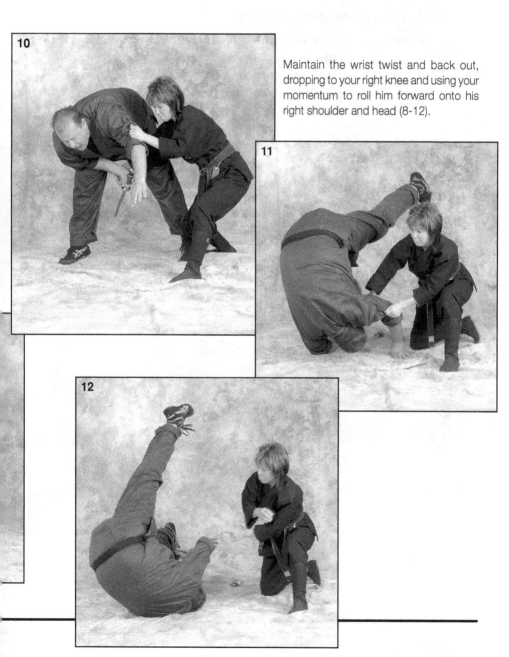

10

Maintain the wrist twist and back out, dropping to your right knee and using your momentum to roll him forward onto his right shoulder and head (8-12).

11

12

Okuden Kata (Inner-Secret Training Examples)

Koto Ryu Koppojutsu

1. San-To (Complementary Strike)

You can fly through space, riding the motion of the aggressor's throw, and strike at the vulnerable points his technique opens up for you. As a greater lesson, learn to watch for the *suki* (gaps) whenever the opposition moves against you. Where in the middle of his demonstration of strength is he actually weak?

The aggressor (right) attacks with an uchimata throw, sweeping inside your left thigh with his right leg in an attempt to throw you forward (1-3).

If it is too late to escape with a backward pull, tilt your right shoulder down and strike with a driving right hammerfist to the inside of his right knee (4-6).

As he staggers to gain his balance, pull away to straighten his grabbing arm and punch his right biceps with your right (7-9).

2. Jo-Setsu (Strike and Evade)

You can pre-empt an attack by causing your adversary to move in a predictable way and then strike vulnerable points he opens out of physiological reflex as he hastily struggles to come to grips with what is happening. As a greater lesson, learn to provoke the opposition's natural defensive habits and then capitalize on the responses that permit you to advance with the real finishing tactic. How can you trigger predictable defensive responses in a way that creates a position to take advantage of his ensuing vulnerabilities?

The adversary (left) walks toward you in an aggressive and hostile manner, intent on reaching out with a surprise grab, shove or strike, and you sense his intention (1).

Deliver a surprise right uppercut to his solar plexus (2-3).

As he hunches over as a result of your punch, move in front of his left leg, sliding your left leg behind your right, and pull away from the spot where he expects you to be (4).

Kick to the pit of his stomach with a right toe stab (5-6).

Chop down on his neck with a shuto to knock him out and end the fight (7-9).

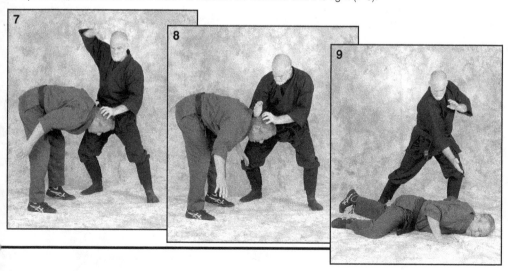

Jo-Setsu
Adaptation

The adversary (right) confronts you in an aggressive and hostile manner, and you sense his intention (1).

With a surprise move, deliver a right kick to his left shin (2-3).

As he crouches to pull his leg back from your kick, crouch and drive forward with your right shoulder to his face (4-5).

Kick to his groin with a right lifting shin (6-7).

As he pitches forward from your kick, crouch and drive forward with a right palm to his face, ending the fight (8-9).

3. So-Setsu (Seize and Throw)

You can pre-empt an attack by causing your adversary to react to pain and reflexively throw himself off-balance and into your control. As a greater lesson, learn to direct your intention in ways that move the opposition and leave him confused about how he got to where he ended up. How can you instigate reflex responses in a way that encourages an adversary to move into the vulnerable position you want him to be?

The adversary (left) confronts you in an aggressive and hostile manner, and you sense his intention to attack (1).

Jump forward with a head butt to his face, and grab the skin and muscles of his lower ribs (2).

Crouch and push him back as you twist your hands to drive your right thumb up and away from you and to pull your left thumb down and toward you (3).

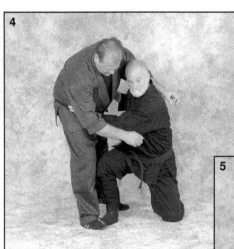

Pivot left, step back and kneel on your left knee. Use the combination of pain and your retreating momentum to throw him over his right shoulder and onto the ground (4-6).

continued on next page

Strike his face as you throw your leg over his torso to land astride him (7-8).

Follow with strikes to his head to end the fight (9-10).

Index of Techniques

D

E

Energy Awareness Exercises

F

Fighting Postures

Fighting Postures, Applications
Fight Scenarios

G

Grappling Method. *See* **Jutaijutsu**
Ground Control Methods

H

Hand Positions

M

R

Reach, Ranges in Striking

S

Self-Defense Examples
Shoden Kata

ORIGINAL *NINJA* SERIES CREDITS

Stephen K. Hayes' Ninja, Vol. 1: Spirit of the Shadow Warrior
Edited by Bill Griffeth
Graphic Design by Walter Rickell
Cover Art by Gregory Manchess

Stephen K. Hayes' Ninja, Vol. 2: Warrior Ways of Enlightenment
Edited by Bill Griffeth and Gregory Lee
Graphic Design by Karen Massad
Cover Art by Gregory Manchess

Stephen K. Hayes' Ninja, Vol. 3: Warrior Path of Togakure
Edited by Gregory Lee
Graphic Design by Karen Massad
Art Production by Mary Schepis
Cover Art by Gregory Manchess

Stephen K. Hayes' Ninja, Vol. 4: Legacy of the Night Warrior
Edited by Mike Lee
Graphic Design by Karen Massad
Front Cover Art by Gregory Manchess
Back Cover Photography by Rick Hustead

Stephen K. Hayes' Ninja, Vol. 5: Lore of the Shinobi Warrior
Edited by Mike Lee
Graphic Design by Sergio Onaga
Photography by Doug Churchill
Additional Photos by Stephen K. Hayes
Cover Art and Drawings by Gregory Manchess

Stephen K. Hayes' Ninja, Vol. 6: Secret Scrolls of the Warrior Sage
Edited by Raymond Horwitz, Jeannine Santiago and Jon Thibault
Photography by Rick Hustead
Graphic Design by John Bodine
Front Cover Art ©Gregory Manchess, 2007

CPSIA information can be obtained
at www.ICGtesting.com
Printed in the USA
LVHW032232190521
687904LV00005B/200